There Goes Gravity

THERE GOES GRAVITY

A Life in Rock and Roll

LISA ROBINSON

RIVERHEAD BOOKS

A member of Penguin Group (USA)

2014

RIVERHEAD BOOKS
Published by the Penguin Group
Penguin Group (USA) LLC
375 Hudson Street
New York, New York 10014

USA · Canada · UK · Ireland · Australia
New Zealand · India · South Africa · China

penguin.com
A Penguin Random House Company

Portions of this book appeared previously in *Vanity Fair* magazine.

Library of Congress Cataloging-in-Publication Data
Robinson, Lisa
There goes gravity : a life in rock and roll / Lisa Robinson.
p.   cm.
ISBN 978-1-59448-714-9
1. Robinson, Lisa (Music journalist)   2. Music journalists—United States—Biography.
3. Rock musicians.   4. Rock music—History and criticism.   I. Title.
ML429.R62A3   2013   2013037121
781.66092—dc23
[B]

Printed in the United States of America
1   3   5   7   9   10   8   6   4   2

Book design by Chris Welch

For Fran Lebowitz

PROLOGUE

My first job in the music business, in 1969, was filing for a few hours every afternoon for Richard Robinson. At that time, Richard was a syndicated newspaper columnist, had a syndicated radio show, and was the assistant to Neil Bogart, the president of Buddah Records. He also hosted the all-night "graveyard" shift at WNEW-FM radio in New York City. I was, for a short time, a substitute teacher in Harlem, teaching first grade. I heard Richard on the radio late at night and thought he had a great voice and great taste in music. Despite the fact that this was the beginning of so-called "free-form" radio and the disc jockeys were supposed to be able to play whatever records they chose, the truth was, they could not. Richard was fired—and then brought back—on three separate occasions. The first time was for playing "unfamiliar" music, which, at that time, meant black music—like Otis Redding and Tina Turner. The second time he was asked to leave was when he played Jimi Hendrix's "Star Spangled Banner"—deemed "unpatriotic" by the station's executives. The final blow was when he used the words "rock and roll." He was told in a letter he still has somewhere that "Surely your fertile mind can come up with a better phrase." When I saw him introduce a Janis Joplin concert at Hunter College, I thought he was great looking, tracked him down, and interviewed for a part-time job. Each day after teaching school, I'd change into jeans, fake lizard boots, a raccoon fur jacket I bought at a thrift shop, and go downtown to his office in the Graybar Building next door to Grand Central Station. I earned $25 a week to do his filing. Three months after we met, I quit my $300 a week teaching job and, despite my mother's warnings, went to work for Richard full time for $100 a week. Two months after that we were married, and remain so to this day.

At first, with all the free albums and concert tickets, it didn't feel like a job. It was a time when things just sort of . . . happened. There was no agenda. Nothing was planned. I had not taken any journalism classes. I had no plans to write. There were about five people in New York City who were writing about rock music then, and Richard was one of them. In 1969, he got tired of writing a weekly column for the British music weekly *Disc and Music Echo,* so he turned the column over to me. I didn't think I could do it, but he said if I could talk—which I certainly could—I could write. He opened the door, I walked right through it and never stopped.

For the first decade of my career, I certainly wouldn't have described it as a career. It was, as Keith Richards has said about so many things, a "lucky accident." In the 1970s, there were only a few rock publications aside from the fledgling *Rolling Stone,* and Richard and I wound up editing two of them: *Hit Parader* and, with Lenny Kaye, *Rock Scene.* Both Richard and I wrote for *Creem* magazine—he did an electronics column called "Rewire Yourself" and I wrote about the then unheard of topic of rock fashion and style. I called the column "Eleganza," after a clothing catalogue that appeared to cater to the pimp trade. My column in *Disc* eventually led, two years later, to a job writing the New York column for the more prestigious British music weekly the *New Musical Express.* Things were just so different then. One thing after another just sort of fell into place. By 1972, there were maybe twenty-five people in New York, Los Angeles, San Francisco and London who were writing about rock and roll. Some people took it very seriously. Some of us—who thought it was supposed to be about fun and sex and the thing that got us out of our parents' house and changed our lives—did not.

Being born and brought up in Manhattan automatically gave you the feeling that you were already at the center of the universe. I would never know how it felt to drive into Manhattan and see the skyline for the first time. I never felt that I had to get out of somewhere and come to New York City—I was already here. When I was a teenager, I listened to Symphony Sid's jazz radio show on a transistor radio under the covers in bed at night. This was my introduction to Miles Davis, Horace Silver, Ahmad Jamal. It opened up a sexy, sophisticated world. I heard the hip, British monologist Lord Buckley and memorized the Lenny Bruce records that were on Phil Spector's Philles Records label. I was way underage when I put on makeup and high heels and snuck out of my parents' apartment on the Upper West Side to go see Thelonious Monk at the Five Spot in Greenwich Village and Anita O'Day and Stan Getz at the Village Vanguard (I probably looked ridiculous, but I was allowed in). I went to see rock and roll shows starring Little Richard and Chuck Berry and Screamin' Jay Hawkins at the Brooklyn Fox. So, in 1973, by the time I met Led Zeppelin's Robert Plant, adorable as he was, and despite his band's superstar status, I thought he was a bit provincial. He was, after all, from some farm in the north of England. Even the Rolling Stones, with the worldly and urbane Mick Jagger, were from England, which is, let's face it, the size of Rhode Island. All those English boys had really bad teeth, were slightly ingenue, and were enamored of American black music—a subject I knew well. And while it's still hard to get people to believe this, not a one of them was as witty or smart as David Johansen of the New York Dolls, who came from Staten Island.

When I was very young, I went to Loews 83rd Street movie theater every Saturday afternoon. I loved movie musicals, I loved movie magazines, and I loved anyone who was considered even slightly rebellious. I had a Marlon Brando scrapbook and one for the Brooklyn Dodgers pitcher Don Newcombe. When I first saw Elvis Presley's black and white and pink and green self-titled album cover—the one the Clash would copy thirty years later—or saw those "Rock Around the Clock" movies at Loews—it was instant recognition. Either this hit you, or it didn't. And, all over the world, it hit a lot of us at the same time. Hard.

One

It was three in the morning on July 5, 1975, and I was just falling asleep when the phone rang in my Memphis hotel room. Mick Jagger was on the line, and he was slurring his words. "Listen," he said, "I'm with two girls and they've got a cute guy with them and I'm trying to get a girl for him because he's lonesome. He's not here right now, he's got his own room. I just thought you might be interested." I declined. "Well," he said, not skipping a beat, "who should we call? He's thirty years old and he's not bad looking. He's American and he just wants a little company. I've got the room list in front of me." He proceeded to run down the names of all the women on that 1975 summer tour, picked someone and suggested I call her—"girl-to-girl." I told him he should call. He said that would make him a hustler. We talked some more. He said they wouldn't have to fuck, they could just "rap" (his word, not mine). We hung up. I went back to sleep.

○ ○ ○

I will always remember 1973 as the year that Eugene from Cinandre ruined my summer because he cut my hair too short. That summer, I also met Mick Jagger for the first time. It was at Nassau Coliseum, at an Eric Clapton concert. I knew Richard Cole from traveling with Led Zeppelin—he was Eric's tour manager, and he placed me at the side of the stage. Mick was there too, and within minutes he sidled— there is no other word for it—over to me, and in a high, campy Monty Python–ish voice, said, *"Jimmy Page was wearing a pink satin jacket."* This was how I knew he had read things I wrote—either in the British weekly the *New Musical Express*, or my "Eleganza" column in *Creem* magazine. To him, I said that his shoes—sequined-covered Pappagallos or, more likely, Repettos—were tacky. Later that night, after Eric's show, Mick, Eric's manager Robert Stigwood, Richard Cole and I hung out at the Plaza Hotel's Oak Bar and gossipped for hours. Mostly about how Mick wouldn't share his costume ideas with David Bowie.

o o o

By 1975, I had traveled with, and written about, Led Zeppelin. The *New Musical Express* was read by all the English musicians and, more importantly, because their children were musicians, their parents. The bands, Zeppelin especially, wanted their families to know how big they were in America. I also spent many, many nights in the winter of 1974 at CBGB's with Patti Smith, the Ramones, and Television, writing about the scenes behind what was always incorrectly referred to as the New York punk rock scene. Having one foot in the bigtime Led Zeppelin camp and all the access and trust that had come with it, and the other foot in deep at CBGB's, is, I am certain, what made me different as a music journalist. Also, I wasn't a critic. I wrote gossippy columns and conducted interviews. This was somewhat of a rarity in the early 1970s when "rock journalism" was in its infancy and mostly populated by boys who had ambitions to become the next Norman Mailer.

In 1975, Mick Jagger was concerned; the English press had called the Stones—along with the Who and the Faces—a dinosaur band. The fact that the Stones had carted Lee Radziwill, Truman Capote and Andy Warhol around the country with them on their 1972 tour didn't help. That tour, which became known as the Stones' "jet set" tour, positioned the band—who just four or five years prior had been considered rebels—as aging rockers. *Then*. While he claimed otherwise, Mick was ever-mindful of the press and public opinion. He wanted to appear in touch. Jane Rose, now Keith Richards' longtime manager, was, at that time, working for the Stones' tour manager Peter Rudge. She recommended to Mick that I help him navigate the rock press. Mick was determined that the 1975 Tour of the Americas—which affectionately became known as TOTA—be different. He got Giorgio Sant'Angelo to design his costumes (and indeed, costumes they were). The Broadway stage and lighting designers Jules Fisher and Robin Wagner—who had done the production for David Bowie's "Diamond Dogs" tour—helped design the band's elaborate stage. And he stole the makeup artist Pierre Laroche away from David Bowie. In 1975, when punk was peaking, just *having* a makeup person on tour, unless you were Bowie or deeply involved with the fading glamrock scene, was telling.

o o o

In May 1975, the band pretended to spontaneously drive down six blocks of lower Fifth Avenue on a flatbed truck singing "Brown Sugar" and announced the tour. I had several meetings with Mick and Peter Rudge in Rudge's office at 110 West 57th Street. We agreed that I would come on board as a "special press liaison," which basically meant I would tell Mick who to talk to in the rock press, and try to pry photos out of tour photographer Annie Leibovitz to supply to the rock press. I was paid a fee, would travel with the band on their plane and stay in their hotels. "Conflict of interest" was not a concept in the rock press at that time. I could continue to file stories that summer in the *NME* and the various rock magazines I edited or contributed to (*Hit Parader, Creem, Rock Scene*). My editors at the *NME* were thrilled that I had this kind of access to the band.

Before the tour started, when I interviewed Mick, he said, "There really is no reason to have women on tour, unless they've got a job to do. The only other reason is to fuck. Otherwise they get bored; they just sit around and moan. It would be different if they did everything for you like answer the phones, make breakfast, look after your clothes and the packing, see if the car was ready—and fuck. Sort of a combination of what [logistics director] Alan Dunn does and a beautiful chick."

Shortly after my initial meetings with Mick and Peter, I went out to the Montauk, Long Island, compound owned by Andy Warhol and Paul Morrissey, where the Stones lived and rehearsed before the start of the tour. It was the middle of the afternoon, and Mick—ensconced in a cabin with Ava Cherry, a former Bowie paramour—was wearing a paisley silk bathrobe. In the main house, a cook named Lisa prepared breakfast. Up to this time, I'd been in various backstages, hotel suites and recording studios—with Zeppelin and other bands— but the only band house I'd ever seen was the Stooges' house in Ann Arbor, Michigan, in 1969. That place was a pigsty, with guitarist Ron Asheton's Nazi memorabilia prominently displayed on the walls. Another feature was the blood splatter on the walls—presumably from syringes. The Stones' Montauk house seemed spartan; big, but not luxurious. Scarves were thrown over lamps, guitars were strewn about, and *The Harder They Come* LP was on the turntable in the living room. Charlie Watts wandered into the kitchen, muttering how the cook was working for "this thankless lot." Bill Wyman came in, looking uptight. No one introduced us. He held 35 millimeter slides up to the light and asked Charlie for his opinion. In Ron Wood's bedroom, several striped suits from London's trendy shop Mr. Freedom were hanging in the closet, and a towel over his bathroom window proclaimed: "A little love can warm up a lonely place." The Stones might have been considered the greatest rock and roll band in the world, but the general ambience and disarray in this house resembled what I would discover in time was the norm for a group of guys on the road. There was that musty smell, a combination of patchouli or musk and cigarette smoke; half-filled glasses of alcohol, half-empty bottles of beer, dirty clothes. To this day, you can walk into any musician's hotel room or dressing room, or be in a van or a car or a limousine or a plane and there is still that smell. It was not unlike the smell of stale cigarettes and beer in a bar around closing time at four a.m.—when closing time was four a.m. and when you could smoke in a bar.

On that day in 1975, Ian Stewart (more about him later) hustled us all out of there—only an hour later than the original appointed time—into station wagons to get to the planes that would take us to the real rehearsals on the real stage in an airplane hangar on an Air Force base in Newburgh, New York. In the station wagon, Mick and Charlie made fun of journalists and me in particular: *"Jimmy Page was wearing a pink satin suit and he was with Lonnie Mack's wife. . . ."* And then: *"Do you still feel as if you are a member of the group as much as you felt this morning when you woke up? Or do you feel that your rebellion is not the same as when you formed the group last night?"* Mick, Ava and I flew up to Newburgh in a four-seater plane. Mick took over the controls for a few minutes. I asked him if he had a pilot's license. He laughed. I was then, as I am only slightly less now, terrified of flying. At Newburgh, I got a look at the band's lotus-petal stage for the first time. The big deal, and the reason it cost the rumored one million dollars, was that the "petals" opened to reveal the band. I shouldn't have been surprised that Freddie Sessler was there. Freddie, who looked a bit like Harpo Marx, had been introduced to me on a Zeppelin tour two years prior as "a pencil dealer with connections." Basically, he provided pharmaceutical cocaine to Zeppelin and the Stones, but he was really a friend of Keith's. We eventually developed a friendship because we both loved Keith, I didn't want any drugs from Freddie nor did I have any use for the underage girls he had hanging around, and he knew that the unspoken tradeoff for getting this sort of access was that I wasn't going to write a drug exposé. After the rehearsal, one of the promoters asked me if I wanted a ride back to New York City. I accepted, not realizing that the "ride" was a two-seater plane. So I, with my fear of flying, got into a two-seater plane with someone I barely knew. This was what it was like to be young. Stars were all around us in the sky and it was a beautiful sight. Later I was told that the guy who had flown the plane was a notorious drunk.

In one of our first meetings at Peter Rudge's office, discussing plans for the tour, Mick said to me, "These kids are all on downs, aren't they? They take some quaaludes and then some more downs and smoke pot, then they take heroin and cocaine and then some Ripple wine, right? Maybe we should take all that stuff and see what we would feel like and what would entertain us."

I had smoked enough pot in my life to know that all it did was make me want to eat a cake and go to sleep. Like every girl I knew in the 1960s, I took Dexamyls so I would be thin enough to wear Betsey Johnson and Rudi Gernreich minidresses and dance at discos like Arthur and Ondine all night. I'd take the gentle tranquilizer Miltown (sadly, no longer made) to fall asleep. I took mescaline once in the

'60s, looked in the mirror and my face turned into a cat. It was a horrendous experience; I was ill for twenty-four hours after the hallucinations wore off and never took it again. In 1970, I must have been unknowingly dosed at a press party with either very strong hash in a brownie or acid, because right afterwards I went to a movie theater to see a restored version of *Pinocchio* and I started screaming, "He's a real boy! He's a real boy!" Richard had to practically carry me out of the theater. I was the drug prude on the 1973 and 1975 Led Zeppelin tours and on the entire 1975 Rolling Stones summer tour. And with just about any other band that took drugs—which is just about any other band. I never indulged in any of the available free cocaine. Frankly, it wasn't even a temptation. To me, everyone sounded like a babbling idiot on cocaine. I talked enough as it was. This abstinence often allowed me to remain invisible while present. I could observe.

When the Stones' 1975 tour first began, Charlie Watts and Bill Wyman were suspicious about giving a journalist access to their inner circle. Keith Richards was completely oblivious to my presence. Newly added guitarist Ronnie Wood, who I'd previously interviewed with the Faces, was delighted to have someone around who paid any attention to him at all. The band took rooms on entire floors of hotels where only those in the official touring party were allowed to stay. Mick's alias in the hotels was Michael Benz. Keith's was Keith Bentley. Looking back now at the room lists from that tour, only four people are still with the Stones today: Mick, Keith, Woody, and Charlie. Dead are Ian Stewart, Billy Preston, Ron Wood's guitar tech Chuch Magee, and publicist Paul Wasserman. Except for Charlie, all of the band members have different wives. Peter Rudge has gone on to do other things. Annie Leibovitz is still Annie Leibovitz. The other tour photographer, Christopher Simon Sykes, a friend of Mick's by way of various Ormsby-Gores, emerged from the experience unscathed and is now a respected photographer and author. At the time, the tour seemed so big, so important, so major. Whatever tour you're on feels like it's the center of the universe—whether it's the Rolling Stones or a small band slogging across the country in a van to play clubs. In the case of the Stones or Zeppelin, there was a police escort. Without that escort, it's just a bunch of guys going somewhere. In retrospect, it was just a tour. And, compared to the big-business, corporate-sponsored, soulless tours of today, it was rather like the way Mick described his own 1964 performances to me, "ingenue."

By 1975, there had been other female rock journalists—Ellen Sander, Lillian Roxon, Gloria Stavers, Ellen Willis, Janet Maslin—but there were no other women journalists on that Stones tour. The rock world always was, and still is, predominantly a boys' club. Often, I was the only woman in the room and certainly the only one who wasn't sleeping with any of them. I wanted to keep everything professional, to get the stories. For me, the lure was always the music. But if you're not having sex with someone on a tour, or participating in the drugs, you really are on a different tour than everyone else. I took an occasional hit off a joint or from a water pipe in Keith Richards' rooms a couple of times. Or I'd take one of the prescription tranquilizers I carried to calm me down during flights. But over the course of the summer, Mick—who was always coming up to me backstage to ask if I had any extra Miltowns—depleted my supply.

Frankly, as far as I knew, the tour wasn't really all that wild. Maybe some of the more explosive stories that had come out of the Stones'

1972 tour were told by those enjoying their first taste of the sybaritic rock and roll road life. Perhaps I had seen this world two years earlier through the eyes of Led Zeppelin, who certainly were more flamboyant about their excesses. Years later, Keith and I discussed *Cocksucker Blues*, the Robert Frank–directed, unreleased, grainy black and white, X-rated "documentary" of the Stones' 1972 tour. It showed Keith shooting up in a hotel room and groupies engaging in sexual activities on the band's plane. "You have to really want to see it to see it," Keith said. "It's like watching the only copy of *The Birth of a Nation*. The legend is bigger than the actual movie."

In one of our interviews, talking about sex on the road, Mick said, "People have a lot of different ways of letting out their inhibitions. Like, they fuck a lot, or destroy rooms. One takes it out on a lot of people. I personally don't think that's the best way of doing it. Sex is quite important, sex does give you a lot of release. I get a lot of release of tension, just physically anyway, onstage. If I was just standing like Bill, I think I'd go mad."

In reviews, Bill Wyman was always described as having the demeanor of a friendly undertaker. He was smart, had a dry sense of humor, but it appeared to me that the rest of the band didn't really like him very much. Everyone thought he was a very good bass player. But he just didn't seem to . . . swing. (Imagine my surprise years later when I discovered just how much he did swing in the female department; he'd apparently been quite the ladies' man for years.) His then-wife Astrid and son Stephen accompanied Bill on the entire 1975 tour, and he was obsessed with making videotapes of old Laurel and Hardy movies. Onstage, he stood perfectly still. He didn't move a muscle except to chew gum and play bass. I'd often stand in the photographers' pit—down in front of the stage between the barricade that separated the stage from the audience—and make faces at Bill, trying to get him to crack a smile. Sometimes it worked; usually it didn't. But he was always fair game for a joke at his expense. One night we were all backstage and the band was about to go on. Bill was across the room, wearing a truly dreadful pair of shoes. I muttered to Mick, "He's not going on in those shoes, is he?" To which Mick promptly yelled across the room, "OH BILL, LISA WANTS TO KNOW IF YOU'RE GOING ON IN THOSE SHOES????"

o o o

On May 30, 1975, a bus was parked outside Peter Rudge's office on West 57th Street in New York City. It would take the TOTA touring party to Teterboro Airport in New Jersey, where the band's jet (affectionately called the "Starship") was waiting to take us to New Orleans and the start of the tour. Carly Simon, who was rumored to have had a fling with Mick, just happened to walk by the bus, wearing a striped dress and carrying a Henri Bendel's shopping bag. (A well-known music-business lawyer once told me, "If Carly could live in an apartment above Bloomingdale's, she would.") I scribbled on one of the pink Beverly Hills Hotel pads that I used for notes: "Three months. What did I get myself into?" And so, the tour began.

Keith arrived at Teterboro two hours late with Ron Wood. Then, we couldn't take off until Ronnie and the lawyers went over some papers. The Stones' plane was the same 707 I had traveled on with Zeppelin in 1973 and 1975. They had thought it was elegant. Mick took one look at the maroon shag carpeting, gilt-covered bar, vinyl sofas, black-fur-covered bed in the back bedroom and muttered to me, "It's so tacky."

In New Orleans we checked into the Royal Orleans Hotel—where I had first interviewed Led Zeppelin in 1973. After the dress rehearsal in Baton Rouge we went back to the hotel, and Mick wanted to read the article I was going to send to the *NME* about the start of the tour.

He came into Peter's office, sat down next to me on a sofa, and I handed him my typewritten pages. He started to read aloud in a campy, exaggerated falsetto, and after a few sentences, he just cracked up laughing. "You have a *much* harder job than I do, dear," he said. He never asked to read anything I wrote again.

It was eighty-four degrees in New Orleans, which, in 1975, was considered sweltering. The following afternoon, Mick was in the elevator, holding a copy of Alan Watts' *The Way of Zen*. He told me he had to wait too long for room service and was considering getting a hot plate to cook his own eggs. (Years later, soul singer Solomon Burke told me tales of how he always cooked his own food on hot plates in hotels. And Martha Reeves told me about how, when the Motown acts toured in the 1960s and had no money and slept on their bus, they used to cook eggs on the radiators in their tiny dressing rooms.) In the lobby of the hotel, Geraldo Rivera, who was there to interview Mick for his local New York City television show, signed autographs. Later, Atlantic Records president Ahmet Ertegun told me Geraldo was an asshole. I had become friends with Ahmet—the suave, cosmopolitan son of a Turkish diplomat—on Led Zeppelin tours. He, along with his extremely chic wife Mica, was a familiar presence on New York's music scene as well as a member of what was then called "the jet set." As a young man, Ahmet went to jazz clubs in Harlem and started Atlantic Records, where he worked with Ray Charles, Aretha Franklin, Solomon Burke, Wilson Pickett, and then, in quick succession, signed the bands that started coming from England: Cream, Led Zeppelin, the Rolling Stones and various others. Ahmet would go to any basement or to any penthouse—you just couldn't take him anywhere in between.

Journalists sat around in the lobby of the Royal Orleans Hotel discussing whether the Stones were still relevant while they waited to talk to Mick. That night, much to my dismay but to the delight of the crowd, Mick initiated his incredibly corny shtick of hitting the stage with the belt during "Midnight Rambler."

o o o

Although for the most part we stayed in really nice hotels, Mick made a big point of not wanting to stay in expensive hotels. "Why should I pay a hundred dollars for a suite?" he said to me. "It's a waste of money. We have a very large party, so obviously we get reduced rates. But the rates have to be lower than the Holiday Inn rates, and I think that's pretty wise, because what's the point of spending your money in these hotels? They're all the same, they're all bad. Except for maybe in two or three towns. It's the same with limousines—some bands may need that for their egos, but we don't—maybe because we've been through it. We've never been that oriented toward luxury. I mean I don't want to stay in flea-bitten rooms, but I don't need the best suite in the hotel. It just isn't worth it for me."

I love hotels. Put me in a Red Roof Inn on a highway outside of Pittsburgh after driving seventeen hours in a van with a "baby" (young, new) band, or the Beverly Wilshire in L.A. with the Rolling Stones, or the Royal Monceau in Paris with U2, and I'm happy. Obviously I'm happier in the Beverly Wilshire or the Royal Monceau, but the escape value is the same. There are no responsibilities. It's private, anonymous. In most cases, there's room service. And in the 1970s, when I went on tours with Led Zeppelin and the Rolling Stones and Patti Smith and the Clash and Aerosmith and the Who, it really was an escape from real life.

When you're on a big tour with a big band and you're there for a reason but are not one of the principals (a member of the band, or a manager), you need to feel your way. When a private plane is involved, you're not really sure who you should sit next to on the plane. If it's a day off, you don't always know if anyone has anything planned, or who you can hang out with or have dinner with that night. Or if there is anyone you can have dinner with that night. Or, if it's a show day, whether you're welcome in one part of the backstage and not another. Then there's always some waiting and wondering about what's happening after the show, if anything is happening after the show, and if you're invited to whatever is happening after the show. On tour with the Rolling Stones, there was always that unspoken but constant anticipation: would Mick show up, when would he show up, how long would he stay, who else would be there? At first, it was exciting just to be in the room. Then, after you got into the room, all those rooms were pretty much the same. Except for some Ahmet Ertegun–hosted parties or spontaneous hanging out in Keith's room. But often, whether it was a hotel ballroom in Minneapolis, or a nightclub in Chicago, we sat around at tables with the same people we saw every day on the plane or backstage at the shows. In New York or Los Angeles, celebrities showed up. But then, they always sat in a corner, often at a roped-off table, and talked to each other and Mick. We all drank, maybe had something to eat, and went back to our rooms around four a.m.

Laundry was always a big problem on the road. Unless you stayed in a hotel for a week, say, in L.A., Chicago or New York, you couldn't send your clothes to be dry-cleaned at the hotel. You weren't there long enough and "same day service" was always a risk. Plus, those of us who had to pay our own "incidentals" didn't want to waste money on laundry. If there was a washer/dryer in the hotel, you could do a wash there, but by the time you arrived at the end of a long night, or woke up late, or had a day off, laundry was the last thing on your mind. Still, there are numerous entries in my diaries from that

1975 summer tour with the Stones that simply read, "Laundry!" or "Unpack!"

If I stayed in a hotel for more than one night, I unpacked. It always made me feel more settled. I adopted the Keith Richards style of art direction and tossed scarves over the lamps. I asked the hotel maids for extra hangers and towels. The first thing I always did (and still do) when I entered a hotel room was to turn on the TV. It cut down on the loneliness. And it can get lonely. In 1975, there was no remote control, no cable, no CNN, no ESPN. So, you'd turn the dial to some game show, or soap opera, or, if you arrived in the middle of the night, an old black and white movie or even a test pattern—just to have something on. I'd take the Bible out of the drawer and put it under the bed or leave it outside the door. I wasn't against the Bible, I just resented—and still do—the fact that it was assumed that I would want one in a hotel room.

Except for the fancier hotels, in 1975, room service always left a lot to be desired. There were "Cheese Festivals"—slices of Kraft American cheese, provolone or the occasional Swiss, garnished with a strawberry or some sad-looking grapes. There was "hand-breaded shrimp." Tomato and egg wedges on a bed of iceberg lettuce. Except for two hotels that had twenty-four-hour room service on the 1975 tour, room service usually stopped at midnight—even at luxury hotels like the Beverly Wilshire in L.A. and the Ambassador East in Chicago—and often, at six p.m. Sometimes I would order something in the afternoon so I'd have it in the room when I returned, ravenous, after midnight. The concept of ordering fresh fruit—except for grapefruit before ten a.m. because it was considered a "breakfast item"—was totally alien to American hotels in 1975. Minibars filled with little bottles of liquor and wine were rare. In the hotels of Detroit, Kansas City, Milwaukee or Buffalo, before food became such a big deal in the U.S., before there ever was a cheese section in an American supermarket, food was often a problem. (Even in the 1990s, traveling with a "baby" band in a van, to come across a Denny's on a highway would be a treat, an Olive Garden a thrill. Many times, I stopped at a Kroger's supermarket and purchased French's mustard to spread on pita bread. That, choked down in a parking lot, often was my food for the day.) However, when you were with the Rolling Stones or Led Zeppelin, there were catered meals on the plane or backstage.

In Buffalo, an invitation to the Stones from Harvey Weinstein, who was then the local rock promoter with Harvey and Corky Productions, read: *"You are humbly invited to a buffet dinner, Sunday, June 15th at 7:30 p.m. in Buffalo Memorial Auditorium Party Room. The dinner has been specially prepared by Vincent, the head chef of Mulligan's Private club, for your enjoyment. We know what it is like to be on a hectic tour, and we hope you can find a few minutes to unwind and relax under our care. The menu: Spinach Salad, Homemade French bread, Seafood Platter—including Clams Casino, Shrimps, Oysters, etc— Lobster, Veal Oscar—the specialty of the house. Dessert—a Mulligan's Mud Pie (a Buffalo favorite) and fresh strawberries. Vincent will be on hand for your dining pleasure."*

This sort of backstage spread was put on only for a band of the stature of the Rolling Stones, which meant it was only done for the Rolling Stones. Then again, it might have been billed to the band, which could have been the reason that Led Zeppelin never indulged in this sort of backstage culinary excess. When Mick was involved, good wine was involved. (Mick and I once had lunch in a hotel restaurant in Chicago while a teenage girl hysterically screamed to him from outside the window. Eventually, she was taken away by security guards, but Mick was unfazed. He sat there throughout the screaming, perusing the extensive wine list with not the slightest sign of annoyance or acknowledgment. He was used to it. "What am I supposed to do?" he asked me.) The promoter Bill Graham always went all out, food-wise. He took over the Trident restaurant in Sausalito after the band's San Francisco show. Backstage at Madison

Square Garden, Bill brought in hot dog carts and egg cream stands. To some of us who just a few years earlier had been going to press parties for the free food, this display was very exciting. However, it soon wore off. Half of these backstage events went unattended; the band couldn't be bothered. And by the time anyone who had actual work to do went to eat before the show, the spinach salad was wilted and the seafood had drawn flies. I always felt slightly sad for these cooks who went to such great lengths to prepare special meals for the Rolling Stones, who never showed up. (Some of the chefs, of course, promoted these jobs on the menus for their own restaurants: "Private chef to the Rolling Stones" and such.) The only band member that I recall ever going and thanking these guys on any kind of regular basis was Mick. But I don't remember any of the band eating anything at all at a venue before the show. And after the show, the band did what the British called a "runner"—which meant race to the cars and beat the traffic while the audience was still screaming for an encore.

o o o

On June 3rd in San Antonio, the band posed for Ken Regan's camera in front of the Alamo, with Mick wrapped in a British flag. Bianca Jagger—who would come on and off the tour—did Mick's makeup and it looked better than when Pierre Laroche had slathered it on. In Kansas City, everyone had to wait to go to the airport because Mick reportedly was in his hotel room, leisurely eating ice cream and drinking champagne. In fact, he was watching Elvis Presley on TV. He made a face. "Owh, he's *awful*," Mick said. I said he's become a parody of himself. "No," said Mick, "he's not a parody, this is what he is." In Boston, I went with Christopher Sykes to the Ritz-Carlton for tea and then to see the movie *Mandingo*. After the Boston show, during the runner, Peter Rudge shrieked, "This is the most untogether getaway since Kennedy tried to drive out of Dallas!!" Charlie Watts

20

said it was hard getting his fabrics together on this tour. People snorted cocaine right in front of me, then slipped me a packet to hold for them. The band arrived at shows in trucks, vans, decoy vehicles. The only one who drove in a limousine was Irving Azoff, the manager of the Eagles—who opened a few of the stadium shows. "We used to have limos," Charlie Watts told me. "We'd have all these limos, like in Milwaukee, for twenty-four hours a day. And then we'd get the bill for $30,000."

Very little escaped Annie Leibovitz's camera. If she heard a food fight going on in the hallway at the hotel in Cleveland at five thirty a.m., she'd get out of bed, stagger to her doorway wearing a salmon-colored robe, and click away. In Los Angeles, Bianca's bathtub over-flowed at the Beverly Wilshire Hotel and Annie took photos. In Toronto, Alan Dunn informed me that Mick had lost his jockstrap, and asked if I had any "knickers" he could borrow. I lent Mick a pair of white, lacy, sheer bikini underpants from Henri Bendel, he wore them backwards, and Annie took a picture. (In 2010, after Keith wrote in his memoir that Mick had a tiny cock, I said to Keith, "You know that's not true. Annie took that photo of him wearing my un-derpants in 1975 and he actually has quite a big one." Keith just looked at me and replied, "Mine's bigger.")

o o o

On June 30th we flew from Philadelphia to Washington, D.C., where there was much discussion about whether or not the band, and Mick in particular, would go to the White House. Bianca had become friendly with Jack Ford, the good-looking, younger son of President Gerald Ford. She was going to interview him for Andy Warhol's *In-terview* magazine and she really wanted Mick to visit the White House. ("Only if they paint it black," sneered Peter Rudge.) There were several backstage phone calls about it, with Mick's continued refusal to go. He ultimately skipped the White House and had lunch with Ahmet Ertegun instead. An assortment of congressmen and other government officials were backstage for the two shows in D.C., and Mick talked to Viktor Sakovich, the Russian cultural attaché. Mick said when he tried to set up a Russian tour for the Stones, he was asked what he would do to improve cultural standards of the Russian youth. "I said I thought they could improve their own cultural standards without any help from me." To which Mr. Sakovich replied, "Oh, that's too philosophical for me." Bianca discussed her research for the Jack Ford interview. She didn't want Andy—who accompanied her to D.C.—to act his usual innocent, wide-eyed, gee-whiz self and make the whole thing too girlish. She said Andy was thrilled that he went to the Oval Office and that David Kennerly, the President's official photographer, took a picture of her sitting at the President's desk, pretending to be writing. Kennerly told her that George Harrison had done the same thing. She said Jack Ford thought Kennerly helped him get girls but in her opinion, it was the other way around. She had taken Jack Ford to dance at Le Jardin in New York City, someone cut in on them, and Jack didn't realize that the guy wanted to dance with him. That's what she liked about him, she said, that he was so straightforward, so naive. But Christopher Sykes privately said to me, "Can you imagine anyone being *remotely* interested in him if he wasn't the President's son?" The day of the second show in D.C., some of us got a private tour of the White House and after that, Christopher, Annie and I went to visit Christopher's friend Maria Shriver at her family's house in Virginia. We sunbathed, swam in the pool, and answered the then nineteen-year-old Maria's questions about what was Mick really like. Onstage that night, Mick wore red shoes, red, yellow and blue striped socks, green trousers, a silver belt, silver bracelets, a pink and green jacket, a white and green top, and a red and gold sash-scarf. All at once. It didn't work.

There was always something slightly . . . off about what Mick wore onstage. A piece of glass would be missing from a chunky necklace. A rip in his pink trousers. An unnecessary scarf. A leather jacket worn over a blouson top over a tank top. As the tour progressed, he really started to pile it on: jackets over other jackets and scarves tied around his waist for no apparent reason. Too much pancake makeup, metallic eyeshadow, mascara and Elizabeth Arden eight-hour cream on his lips. Unfortunate shoe choices. After the tour, he admitted to me that he didn't really look the way he had envisioned. I asked him why he didn't just go onstage looking the way he did every day, which was much cuter. "You don't want to go on looking like some old blues singer," he said. I asked what had he wanted to look like? He wouldn't tell me. "I'll save it for the next tour," he said. Right. Otherwise Bowie might steal it.

Keith had always said that the Stones really were Ian "Stu" Stewart's band. Stu (who died of a heart attack in 1985) had started the Stones as a blues band with Brian Jones in the early 1960s. But he had been pushed out early on because he didn't look the part. I always wondered how he could still work for them. Stu could play fantastic boogie-woogie piano—not only with the Stones onstage and on records, but also with Zeppelin ("Boogie with Stu" on *Physical Graffiti*). Basically, he became their glorified road manager and also arranged all the Stones' recording sessions. When I got to know him better, I asked him if he was bitter about being pushed out of the band. "Well," he said, "it wasn't done very nicely." Stu was wary of most people and outright disdainful of all journalists. I respected him, I knew what he meant to the band and it was important to me to have his approval. At first, it was enough of a hurdle just to get past his disapproval. But we eventually got around to talking about blues and jazz—Lightnin' Hopkins and Thelonious Monk, Miles Davis, Horace Silver—and he warmed up to me a little bit. Then slowly, and possibly because of my previous and ongoing association with Led Zeppelin—who he liked—his distrust disappeared. Eventually, we became friends. Still, it took a long time for him to agree to do the only interview he ever did. He told me that he thought the Beatles were "nice lads who wrote pretty songs, but were horribly overrated." Stu thought that Keith was the best rock and roll guitarist because he didn't do any solos, and, that, even with the interminable twenty-minute solo taken onstage nightly by Zeppelin's John "Bonzo" Bonham, Bonzo was the best rock and roll drummer. He said that Mick got some of his best onstage moves from watching Inez Foxx and Tina Turner. We did that interview in Atlanta, around ten in the morning, and the only reason I managed to wake up so early to do it was because it was Stu. And I'm certain that the reason he set that time was because he probably had a golf game scheduled for right afterwards.

Six weeks into the tour, by the time we got to Chicago, Mick looked tired. Keith appeared invigorated. Bob Greene wrote a column in the *Chicago Sun-Times* that claimed blues legend Howlin' Wolf couldn't get tickets to the Stones show. Wolf eventually came, sat with Buddy Guy and Junior Wells in a backstage dressing room, and fell asleep. But Stu was livid. "When you consider that you've got all these people around," he told me, "and then Bill Wyman can't even get tickets for Howlin' Wolf in Chicago . . . Wolf sat in the dressing room, and they wanted to take him up to the pressbox because there were no tickets. But to get to the pressbox you have to climb a lot of stairs and he couldn't do it. So he just sat in the dressing room, and never saw the concert to this day. But there were a lot of little *Playboy* scrubbers who got tickets and whose friends are they? Not even friends of the boys." (Note: The Stones were always called "the boys." Male musicians in bands are always called "the boys." Men who are now well into their sixties—some in their seventies—when they are on tour, are referred to as "the boys." Sometimes there's an attempt—especially with the Brits and the Irish—to be a bit more graceful. So they say "the lads." Or "the guys." But it is never, ever "the men.")

On show days, the band was awakened between one and three p.m., with the exception of Keith, who either never went to sleep, or got up later, or took hours to wake up. The TOTA staff was instructed to get our own wake-up calls "to suit." Baggage had to be outside our hotel room doors to be picked up by the hotel bellmen and the Stones' road crew and in the lobby by 2:15. The baggage truck left by 2:45, and departure from the hotel was 3:15. None of this ever happened on time. But amazingly, because of "logistics director" Alan Dunn, it always happened. Our bound itineraries had made-up names of doctors on call in each city: Dr. Hyman Stockfish, Dr. Meylackson—it read like something out of a Marx Brothers movie. These were doctors who basically gave out vitamin shots, tended to medical needs, and in return, got tickets for the concerts. The list of lawyers was even longer. Ticket requests were listed for each lawyer who received a laughable $100 retainer in each city. Unbeknownst to some of us on the tour, the Stones were apparently always on the verge of some sort of legal trouble. It took a lot of lawyers to keep things running smoothly. There was always the threat—often whipped up into a frenzy by the overly dramatic and overstimulated Peter Rudge—that Mick would get arrested for singing "Starfucker" onstage. Or that the band would be arrested for having that inflatable cock prop rise up on the stage during shows. In Memphis, the lawyer listed in our tour book was the band's immigration lawyer, Bill Carter, whose address was in Little Rock, Arkansas. That would come in handy. There were many "inside jokes" on the daily memos put under our hotel room doors each night: *"When we arrived in Milwaukee, one security man was on a beer truck, two were on [the] plane drinking and baggage men were talking to girls." "Do not take anything into Toronto that you would not want a customs inspector to find." "Contrary to popular belief, Billy Preston does not like white boys."* Eventually, Keith called the band's office. "Look," he said, "I don't want any more of these jokes on my memos. They're too esoteric."

o o o

On July 3rd we flew from Washington, D.C., to Memphis, in the midst of an electrical storm. Mick, who often kept up with weather charts, was not on the plane; he and Alan Dunn chose to drive instead. At one point during the turbulent flight, the plane dropped 5,000 feet. Or so it felt at the time. Keith and Woody raced to the back to take all the drugs. Annie Leibovitz literally hit her head on the ceiling of the plane. I sobbed in the arms of Christopher Sykes. And I remember thinking then that if the plane crashed, the headlines would read, "Rolling Stones and Others Die in Plane Crash."

We got to Memphis after that scary flight and were greeted at the airport by Jim Dickinson—who played piano on the Stones' recording of "Wild Horses." With him was the old blues guitarist Furry Lewis. But the roots of the blues and Stax Records and Al Green and the Memphis Horns aside, to many of us, Memphis was the place where Martin Luther King Jr. had been assassinated. And the next stop on the tour was Dallas; with all those images of the pink pillbox hat and the Kennedy assassination. It was the South. Just a decade earlier, the black acts from Motown or Howlin' Wolf or Muddy Waters or Ike and Tina Turner—all of whose music inspired the Stones—had to use separate, and unequal, restrooms and often, sleep on their buses because they were denied entry to hotels. So in the

South, even in the 1970s, even with a white rock and roll band and the Rolling Stones in particular, there was always a presumed threat. Long-haired drug takers, faggots, sissies, "girls"—the band had heard it all. For me, coming from a liberal, Upper West Side, New York City background, you hated the South even if you'd never been there. We grew up with those newspaper photos and grainy black and white TV images of police beating black children and Andrew Goodman and Medgar Evers and George Wallace and all that. You didn't want to mess with any of it.

Memphis felt weird from the get-go. First, that plane ride. Then, when we arrived at the Hilton Inn we discovered that there had been some snafu with the reservations and there were no rooms set aside for the entire touring party. The hotel was ominously laid out prison-style, with rooms all around on balconies overlooking the main floor. At the front desk, Peter Rudge went ballistic. He threatened to personally telephone Conrad Hilton, who, at that time, for all he knew, may not have even been alive. When the room situation was cleared up and I finally got to my room, *Gimme Shelter*, the Maysles Brothers' documentary about the Stones' 1969 show at Altamont where an audience member was stabbed and died, was playing on TV. Earlier in the tour, I had asked Charlie about Altamont; how could they have possibly allowed the Hells Angels to organize security, to say nothing of the unprofessional bunch of promoters on that tour. "Well, the Angels just did what they wanted," he said, "especially in San Francisco. That's their home ground. We were lucky to get out of there, basically. We were helpless, really. You could say the same thing about Peter Rudge if he did wrong. Mind you, not that I think he would. But we really didn't know anything about the arrangements until almost when we got there. It was a case of either work with them or have them work against us." Talking to me about Altamont, Mick said, "People tell me all the time that they had a good time there. Kids arriving the day before, camping out and all that. Sometimes I think that the only people who didn't have a good time there were me and the guy that got killed."

The band did the show at the Memphis Memorial Stadium. Then, there was a travel day before the next show in Dallas. This is when Keith decided on that ill-advised drive from Memphis to Dallas. I remember thinking at the time that Keith probably thought about Mick skipping the flight to Memphis, and thought, well, if *he's* going to drive to a gig . . . Maybe not. Perhaps he was lured by the beauty of the backwoods of Arkansas. So Keith, Woody, Keith's security guard Jim Callaghan, and Freddie Sessler all got a head start, with Keith driving a yellow car. The rest of us were scheduled to take the one-hour flight to Dallas. We arrived at the Fairmont Hotel in Dallas and received the news that Keith and Ronnie and a "hitchhiker" (Freddie) were arrested in Fordyce, Arkansas—a town none of us had ever even heard of—for speeding, for drugs, and for knives. All hell broke loose. There was concern that the show in Dallas would be cancelled and that the entire rest of the tour could be in jeopardy. How could Keith survive a night in jail? What if he and Woody were kicked out of the country? But above all, the prevailing attitude among some of us in the touring party was, how could they be so stupid? In a *yellow* car, no less. Mick was clearly pissed off. Peter Rudge was all hopped up. Of course, it didn't take much for Peter to get all hopped up—someone looking at him cross-eyed or rustling a napkin could do it. We all tried to get updates and whispered about it in groups of twos and threes. There was no official meeting, and initially, no press conference. Today, when Willie Nelson is arrested every so often for pot on his bus, or rappers are regularly hauled off to jail for drugs or guns, that arrest in Fordyce seems kind of quaint. But at that time, it was a Very Big Deal. Especially for British musicians, some of whom had been arrested in the past for drugs in England. Visas were at stake. We were all instructed not to talk to the press. The irony of this was not lost on me; I was the press. And many of my colleagues and friends were in the press. Mick, clearly nervous, personally alerted everyone and anyone who might have any drugs to get rid of them right then and there. The police in Dallas might be lying in wait to search the plane. Promoter Michael Crowley was dispatched to Fordyce with bail money; Peter and the lawyers flew there too. Around two a.m., Peter—who prior to this incident had been full of plans for an imminent meeting in Los Angeles with all four Beatles that never materialized—returned to the Memphis hotel with Keith, Woody, Callaghan and Freddie. The judge in Fordyce had let them off with some sort of probation, a fine, and a few autographed photos. There was a big, collective sigh of relief. Everyone went to their rooms and went to sleep.

Reflecting on it now, it probably was either a miracle or a feat of legal wrangling that nothing serious—like an arrest—had happened before this to the Stones in the U.S. (Marianne Faithfull tells me she's still detained at U.S. Customs because of that 1960s English drug bust at Keith's Redlands house.) Occasionally, packages were put together and taken by staffers from one city to another. I personally never understood why any band member would ever carry anything when there were always dealers crawling out of the woodwork in every city, only too happy to accommodate the Stones. But all that holding and hiding and sneaking was part of the ritual. And not everyone was the type to ask people for pills. Just the singer. Talking to me about pills in one of our many hours of interviews, Mick said, "Codeine is so ridiculous in this country. They act like it's such a big deal. Then there are these little pills for diarrhea that have a touch of opium in them; like if you took 300 of them you might get a buzz. So if you want just two, and the doctor is out, you can't get them. It's easier to score heroin in this country. Or guns. My first experience with that was with Keith in Arizona; we wanted to buy a gun, just to see if we could. So we got two guns and then we went into a bar and they asked us for ID. And there we had these two fucking guns that we'd just bought wrapped up on the bar. We didn't need any ID for the *guns*."

o o o

When I was a teenager, my parents, my two sisters and I spent summers at Fire Island. I became friendly with Dick and Jill Kollmar, the children of columnist Dorothy Kilgallen. Once, when I visited their Upper East Side townhouse, I saw their mother at the top of the stairs. She was wearing a nightgown and she sort of floated from one room to another. She was thin and pale and seemed to be not fully awake. It was a bit of a shock to see her; not just because she was famous, or had been on the television game show *What's My Line?* or that her photo was at the top of her column in one of the New York newspapers. It was because she appeared ghostlike. I realize now that I must have sensed that she was probably on drugs, but I didn't understand that at the time. And, except for when he was onstage, in the summer of 1975, that's what Keith looked like to me. Especially during the first part of the day, which usually meant the late afternoon.

People were afraid of Keith, which appeared to suit him just fine. It was a successful method of keeping everyone at a distance. His addictions, vampire hours, elusiveness—all were intimidating. He was a world unto himself, surrounded by reggae music, the exotic beauty Anita Pallenberg, their five-year-old son Marlon, Ronnie Wood, Freddie Sessler and assorted sidekicks. On off days, while Mick toured the colonial houses of Charleston, South Carolina, Keith would do god knows what in his sequestered, incense-suffused, darkened rooms. He'd stay awake for days at a time. He lurched out of the car onto the plane. He swirled into the backstage tuning room. But then, out of the depths of what seemed to be a deep stupor, he would walk onstage and was all swing, all muscle, every night. Years later, Keith would tell me, "My life then basically was, do I have the dope to start this day off? Can I make it until the next fix? You think you're in this elite club. You could be wallowing in the gutter and think, I'm elite. It was an adventurous experiment that went on too long."

Whether they sold the most albums or not, and mostly they did not, the sort of royal status accorded the Stones was unparalleled. The only thing that could have challenged it was if the Beatles ever decided to get back together. But John Lennon told me many times over the next five years that he wouldn't do it. He was having more fun, he said, working with Yoko, and also, he said, the Beatles could never live up to everyone's expectations. Looking at photos of the Stones' 1975 tour now, everyone looks so young. And compared to the tours of today, that 1975 Stones tour was done literally on the fly, by the seat of Peter Rudge's pants. The band stuck to the songs that got the best response: "Rip This Joint," "Brown Sugar," "Tumbling Dice," "Jumpin' Jack Flash," "Street Fighting Man." In one of our interviews, Mick told me that they didn't do new songs in concerts because "It always dies a death. Really, the kids just sit there and stare. Then of course, when you come back the next time, they scream for the stuff they didn't respond to the last time around."

That summer of 1975, from Sunday, June 1st, to Friday, August 8th, there were forty-five Stones shows in twenty-seven cities. Very little escaped my tape recorder, or my pink Beverly Hills Hotel note pads. I blatantly stuck that tape recorder right in people's faces all the time. But I wouldn't jot things down in front of anyone. Instead, I'd race into a bathroom or someplace around a corner and furiously scribble down what someone said, what I saw, what was going on. I did make note of the fact that it was strange to wake up and see Mick Jagger and Keith Richards every day. To this day, those notes are surprisingly legible, kept in separate envelopes labeled for each city on the tour, in one of six storage spaces that house the photographs, notes and memorabilia from my four decades of experiences in rock and roll. During the concerts, Annie's camera was always focused on Mick. All my pink pads are filled with notes about Keith onstage. Because he was so elusive, he became more interesting to me. In interview terms, he was the harder "get." Mick did much more of the business work, of course, and as the frontman, he was the face of the band. But by the very nature of his mystery, Keith was the one I always watched in concert. I'd occasionally watch Mick and admire the way he'd draw out a word—like "soooohhh-daaa" in "Can't Always Get What You Want." Or, I'd cringe at one of his self-conscious, awkward, interpretive dance routines. But within minutes, I'd once again be fixated on Keith. At the indoor arena shows, I stood in the photographers' pit, and I'd look up. For someone who was supposedly always so stoned at that time—certainly he's owned up to it—Keith's entire performance, his direction and control of the band appeared effortless. Every so often, I'd take a break and wander around backstage, holding an open bottle of white wine—my drink of choice that summer. But if I was backstage, and heard the strains of "Happy," the song that Keith sang at every show, I'd say to Freddie Sessler, "Let's go—it's Keith's song." And Freddie would reply, "Are you kidding? They're all Keith's songs."

When the band was in Los Angeles for a week in July for several shows at the L.A. Forum, Lorna Luft followed Bianca around the Beverly

Wilshire Hotel. Finally Bianca said, "I find it strange that all we ever talk about is me." Annie said that Mick and Bianca seemed "madly in love," adding, "That's one of the best marriages I know," and it might have been. Mick told me, "From what I've seen, your articles aren't bitchy enough. Aren't you going to put in my remarks about Robert Plant?" I mentioned that I wrote something nice about Bianca. "You should write something bitchy about her," Mick said. "She's very rude to people. If I have a photo session I don't make people wait for four hours, and she does that all the time." The phones in the band's office at the hotel rang nonstop with celebrity ticket requests. Ryan O'Neal declined tickets when he was told he'd have to pay for them. A meeting was held to draw up a guest list for the party that Diana Ross and her then-husband Bob Ellis—Ronnie Wood's manager—were giving for the band. Their party, at their big white house in Beverly Hills, was the first time I ever saw people set up bathrooms outside, on the back lawn, with no one allowed in the house. The guest list included Barry Diller, George Harrison, Berry Gordy, Sonny Bono, Lou Adler, Ron Kass, Joan Collins, Candice Bergen, Sara Dylan, Joan Didion, Elliott Gould, Sue Mengers, Elton John, Bette Midler, Cat Stevens, Ronee Blakley, Garry Trudeau, the Billy Wilders, the Neil Diamonds, the Swifty Lazars—Stones fans all. After awhile, Keith and Woody got fed up with the idea of using a portable toilet, went inside and started playing pool. Everyone followed. Back at the hotel at three a.m., Keith Moon was on the phone in the tour office. George Harrison wandered around looking for Mick.

On a night off (which meant no show) in L.A., we all went to see Bob Marley and the Wailers at the Roxy on Sunset Strip. Bill Graham had organized the outing and reserved the balcony for the Stones and their guests. He looked as proud and happy as the father at a bar mitzvah. Bill, the flamboyant rock promoter who had escaped Nazi

Germany, could be a bully. He yelled. He was often in a purple rage. He could be really scary. To me, he was smart and tough and hilarious; a total mensch who became a beloved friend. None of us had ever seen anyone perform quite like Marley—an inspired, stoned shaman. People were screaming. I taped his set on my ever-present Sony cassette tape recorder and the tape still sounds great today. We lined up tequila shots along the edge of the balcony and Annie and I probably had about ten each. The next day she realized she'd left all of her cameras at the club.

Freddie Sessler was having a barbecue at his house at 1981 North Coldwater Canyon, where Keith had taken up residence for the L.A. stay. On the mantle at Freddie's house were enlarged photos, taken by Annie, of Mick and Freddie, and Keith wrapped in paisley sheets with a rifle on the floor of his bedroom. It was late in the afternoon on a show day, and Freddie was trying to get rid of two girls who were waiting for Keith to wake up. One, a blonde, was wearing patchwork leather jeans and a matching jacket. She sat on a small amp she brought with her and played a Chuck Berry song on guitar. Keith reeled downstairs. Wearing a mustard-colored leather jacket and pants, which he probably had slept in, he muttered hello to the girl, whom he'd apparently agreed to meet. She had written a letter saying she was a great guitarist, and added that she was a great fuck. Keith executed his trademark swirlaround and fled out of the room, out of the house and into a waiting car while she shouted, "I just want to strut. I know if I played with them it would take them into a whole other thing. They would dig it. I've jammed with Fanny. Isis asked me to be their guitar player. I'm not a groupie. I'm not impressed. I'm a player. I thought I was at least going to jam with them."

I accompanied Keith in the car to the Forum. I turned my tape recorder on and Keith talked in his trademark slur, which I was able to decipher later on by speeding up the tape. "For me, the band is only alive if it's doing what it's supposed to be doing," he said, "which is to play in front of a lot of people—and then to sell a few records on the side." With Keith, it was kind of like that old joke: I didn't really know how stoned he was until I saw him sober, and that would be years later. Listening back to those 1975 tapes now, there was a high degree of slurred words. And yet, when I asked him then if he was taking care of himself, he said, "I couldn't possibly be able to be two hours on a stage if I didn't take care." When I said that people worry about him, he replied, "They should worry about themselves. I haven't heard much about that on this trip, actually." That's because you and Ronnie smile a lot at each other onstage, I told him. "Well," he said, "does a smile mean you're healthy? I mean you can be dying of cancer and raise a smile occasionally."

Several years later I would "meet" the unaddicted, lucid, hilarious, clever, and shy man that is the real Keith Richards. We talked many times. He'd often be scathing, always brutally honest. He referred to Mick as a "nice bunch of guys," and would either be getting along with his oldest friend and bandmate or not. Obviously, after the publication of Keith's best-selling book, with its barbs at Mick, there was tension. But if Keith hurt Mick with that book, Mick hurt him over the years too. I clearly remember that, in the 1980s, when Keith got off heroin and was ready to actively participate in band business, he told me he felt unwelcome. Understandably, Mick had a point: in addition to enjoying the control, he had carried that burden almost singlehandedly for years. Even in the 1980s, when one or more of the band members were having problems staying sober, I asked Mick if they were planning a tour. He replied, "Tour?? They can't cross the *Champs-Elysées*, much less go on tour." But in 1975, Stu told me,

"Keith cares basically about the music, and he can't be bothered to go to any of these meetings. If we're not recording or on tour, the phone in the office will go all day, every day, with accountants and lawyers who have to speak to Mick immediately. The others care, but they have neither the ability or the desire to be involved. Mick never stops. He's always on top of something on behalf of the other four. I sometimes wonder why he takes on all the responsibility of the Rolling Stones."

In 1975, both the rock press and the "real" press attempted to analyze the Stones' deep, dark impact. Some of the writeups were nonsensical. Mick told me that he never read any of the analytical ones; he just looked at the pictures on the front page. One of my favorite "reviews" was from San Francisco which was, and I quote: "The great thing about Mick Jagger is that he knows the audience knows that he knows that they know he's great." Unusually forthcoming with me during the 1975 tour, Mick would still skirt questions and affect a modest, blasé air. I asked him how he felt being thought of as the world's greatest rock star. "I don't consider myself the best rock star," he said, "and I never have." When I asked the obvious followup question—who then, was the best—he replied, "There are a lot of people who are very good, but since I'm not really interested in white rock and roll, I don't ever see them. But I'm sure there are people who are better than I am. There must be, because I'm not very good. I don't really care, and I don't consider myself the best at what I do, and I wouldn't worry if people said I wasn't, and in fact, people have said that I'm not. The Rolling Stones have never said they were the best rock and roll band. Find me a quote that says we said we were." Well, I told him, you may not think you are, but Robert Plant not only said he thought Zeppelin was the best rock and roll band in the world, he felt that they were so much better than whoever was Number Two. "Well," said Mick, "he may be right."

In San Francisco, Bill Graham wore a "Bill Graham Presents: Israel in Concert" t-shirt. Mick wore a big jeweled pin, pink jacket, red gloves and matching shoes, red tank top, red and white batik pajamas, a silver belt, rhinestone bracelet, white socks and a blue denim cap. All at once. In Buffalo, a bunch of us put on rubber raincoats and went to look at Niagara Falls. Peter joked: "For christ's sake, don't show this to Jagger, he'll want it onstage." In Denver, Elton John, who was recording at the nearby Caribou Ranch, wanted to join the band onstage. ("Only if he gives us a Rembrandt each," Keith said.) After some to-ing and fro-ing, it was decided that Elton would sit in on piano onstage for "Honky Tonk Women." He did, then continued to play, to the obvious displeasure of Keith, who looked like he was ready to kick him offstage. ("It was strange that he just stayed up there," Stu told me later. "Especially since he seemed to have no idea of the chord changes.")

I was the recipient of a variety of unusual pranks: in Toronto, someone put a live frog in my portable typewriter. In one city, my bed was full of ice cubes. Another time, eggs. A frog appeared in my *purse*. To this day, I still don't know where they got the frog, or who did all this. I always suspected it was a combo of Alan Dunn, Christopher Sykes, and maybe Mick—especially when a mattress was *nailed* to my hotel room door in Buffalo, with dozens of hamburgers put in between the door and the mattress so that when I opened the door, the hamburgers all fell down. And no, even with the shows and the fucking and the drugs and the fine dining and the wine drinking, Mick didn't always have anything better to do. Especially in Buffalo. The boredom of the travel and the hotels eventually got to everyone.

In one of our talks during that tour, Mick told me, "I try to be in control of my ego, because I've seen myself go off the rails on tours. I start ordering people around, I get really . . . difficult to deal with. I'm not moody on tours; I just like to be on my own sometimes. Just like an hour a day, apart from the time that I'm asleep. And even when you're asleep you're not always on your own, you're with some girl. When you're on a big tour, the more you can relax, whatever method you use to do that, the better it is. Because when you're trying to make it, all your energy is put into trying to make it. Then you realize you have to spend a lot of time cooling out. You have to be calm and effective and all your judgments are balanced because after a while the pressure gets so much that a lot of bands just freak out on the road."

In an undated tape that probably was after that 1975 tour, Keith talked to me about ego. "To put yourself up on that stage," he said, "you've got to have enormous ego. But it's what you do with it in your spare time. You can bloat it or put it to sleep; forget about it or just live with it. Unfortunately, with a lot of people, it just takes over. You see it a thousand times, especially in this business. You can just watch somebody who's a good guitar player or singer or piano player become somebody who believes all their press clippings in six months."

o o o

Six shows were scheduled for Madison Square Garden in June of 1975. The New York press would finally get to see the giant onstage inflatable cock. In certain cities there were threats that the band would be arrested for it, but it never happened. Then again, perhaps Peter Rudge spread that threat to create a bit more drama. Since Mick didn't play guitar, he loved having something to play with onstage—a belt, a bucket of water, an inflatable cock balloon. I can only imagine the meetings that went into the concept and construction of this corn-ball prop. This was the side of Mick that I never quite got—along with the glitter on his eyelids and the abstract expressionist dance steps and freezing into yoga poses mid-song. He started to try too hard. Gone were those inspired, stuttering James Brown dance steps that to this day, Keith still says Mick can do on a coffee table.

During the 1975 tour I asked Mick if he thought he was a good dancer. "No," he said, "not really. I didn't dance until I was nineteen or twenty. I was so nervous. I'm hopeless at steps, I couldn't waltz and I wasn't good at a quickstep, which my mum taught me. The waltz, two-step and fox-trot . . . you had to know how to do all that by the age of twelve to be socially acceptable. The Beatles just stood there and played, but I didn't have a guitar, I had to do something else. When I started singing, I used to consistently hit the wrong key. But the important thing about singing is to get the personality across, fuck the notes."

Bob Dylan showed up backstage at one of the Garden shows and Mick—who was constantly teasing me about writing about all of their clothes—came over to me and whispered, *"Lisa, Bob Dylan is wearing a blue and white striped shirt, slightly dirty at the top, and a black leather jacket with beige pants and, I'm sorry, I don't remember the shoes."* After the first Garden show, there was a party at Camilla and Earl McGrath's apartment. Earl was Ahmet Ertegun's best friend and the president of Rolling Stones Records, and their parties were always fantastic—with Camilla's high-Italian sensibility and an as-sortment of friends that at any given time could include Harrison Ford (then a carpenter and struggling actor), Larry Rivers, Bryan Ferry, Jim Carroll, Stephen Bruton. In attendance at this after-show party for the Stones were Diana Vreeland, Lee Radziwill, John Phil-lips, Genevieve Waite, Andy Warhol, and Peter Wolf with his then-wife Faye Dunaway. After the socialites left, around five a.m., there was a jam session in the master bedroom with Keith, Mick, John, Woody and Eric Clapton. Annie got photos of that too.

o o o

We were in Buffalo for the second time that summer. August 8th was the final show of the tour. Mick sheepishly asked me if I remembered what he wore at the first Buffalo show. I told him yes, sadly, I did. The night before the last show was one of maybe two or three times I hung out in Keith's room. First, you had to be invited. Then, you needed to be really hardcore to put in the time. There was no way you could respectably leave before dawn. On that night in the Sheraton East Hotel, Mick was in Keith's room—along with Woody, Annie, Billy Preston, Christopher and me—and we were listening to the new Rod Stewart album. Slow songs, Stax Records' influences. "It sounds a bit old fashioned," said Mick, who clearly was making a pitch for Ronnie to stay with the Stones rather than go back to the Faces. Listening back to the tapes I made in the room that night, there is a clinking of glasses, reggae music, Frankie Valli on the TV, shrieks of laughter, a water pipe being passed around, coughing and general hilarity. I taped hours of this stuff; what was I thinking? Mick made jokes about a variety of things on TV: Jim Dandy, Frankie Valli—then he spiralled into remarks about Ian Anderson, Eric Clapton and John Lennon. My notes note that Mick danced around by himself. At eight a.m., I must have called room service for breakfast for everyone, because I still have the order written out on a piece of the hotel stationery: *four orange juices, one half grapefruit, two poached eggs on toast, two corned beef hash, two cinnamon toast, two English muffins, two blueberry pancakes, one order fried eggs over easy, one hashed brown potatoes, one order of bacon, and four coffees.* Around nine or ten, after everyone left, still determined to get another promised interview with

Keith, I was going nowhere. Keith went into the bathroom and didn't come out for a very long time. After about an hour, I knocked on the door, concerned that he wasn't going to come out. *Ever.* He shouted something indecipherable. Another hour passed. At around noon, after having been up all night, I called Jim Callaghan and told him he'd better come check on Keith. I went back to my room and went to sleep.

At the end of the tour, I asked Mick why he thought the British musicians had been so affected by American blues and rock and roll. He said that when the Stones first came over to America, he and Keith used to go to the Brooklyn Paramount and to the Apollo to see Joe Tex, Little Richard and James Brown. And Keith, who was then, and is still, obsessed with the guys he first heard play guitar, told me in 1975, "You learn the guitar because you have this burning desire. Nothing matters more in the world than to find out how this guy you heard before played that thing. These guys were gods to you. And the most important thing has always been if you passed a little bit on. It's an incredible reproductive thing, music; you don't have any control over it, you get hooked. It's a very pure ideal, and that's why music has lasted. And whether you perverted it later on from your own needs, or to make a living, or became successful, or gave it up, the fact is—to start doing it is very pure."

o o o

"Any art that comes from rock and roll is accidental," Mick told me. "It's entertainment, funny entertainment. It's played now in these sports arenas, which makes it a very un-artlike event. But no, I don't want to go back to those small clubs; we are too big for them and I have no nostalgia for them at all." Mick may not have wanted to go

41

back to playing small clubs, but every time they did—like the El Mocambo Club in 1977, or Toad's in New Haven in 1989, they were great. They were great too in rehearsal—whether at that airplane hangar in Newburgh in 1975 or fourteen years later at a school gymnasium in Massachusetts. Stu, who was always cynical about the "caravan" that traveled with the Stones, might have preferred for them to still be in a van on the English M1 highway, slogging around to club gigs. In 1975 he told me, "In rehearsal, or on a good night, when you get a concert that swings the way a good one does sometimes, you realize how good a band they are. What doesn't get to me is all the bullshit that goes with it. Mick believes in it all and obviously he's right, but to me, when it all becomes a big machine, it gets to be a routine. It certainly takes some of the excitement away from it. I wouldn't want it to be chaotic the way it was when we first went out, but at least all sorts of unexpected things used to happen. You'd get yourself in a lot of trouble and you'd have riots and all that sort of thing. It used to keep it interesting."

That summer of 1975, Mick was often funny, and, especially around me, very campy and gossippy. Once in awhile he was drunk, and not very good at holding his liquor. And sometimes he was just another musician who was capable of staying up all hours of the night with Billy Preston discussing synthesizers. I once asked him what it meant when the songs said "Written by Jagger/Richards." He replied, "It means we share the money." Jimmy Page had talked to me a lot about money, often bitching that he was paying ninety-eight percent tax. "One day you're playing the blues," Jimmy told me in 1973, "and the next day there's a knock on the door and you're in the realm of high finance." In my 1975 interview with Ian Stewart, he said, "The Stones are getting to be part of showbiz now, which I don't think was ever the idea in the first place. But that's the way Mick wants it—he wants to have a theater production. I suppose one can be very proud of the stages in New York and L.A. They spent a million dollars and it opened up and the kids loved it and the Stones were on the stage and then it closed up and it is the best rock and roll prop. But . . . so what? The money's got them in trouble. They can't even live in their own country."

And Mick talked to me about the band's peripatetic life. "I'd love to be England's biggest teenage idol, which I've already been, but I can't. I mean, I love England, but I can't see why I should give them all the money I earn. If you're not careful, you can pay 102 percent in tax. I don't mind paying half of what I earn but I don't see why I have to give them all of it, I think it's a little bit unfair. The unfortunate thing is, the whole thing we all built up over the last ten years—first the Beatles, then the Stones, Zeppelin, Elton John, the Faces, Eric [Clapton]—that whole group of London musicians has broken up. We all interchanged ideas living in London, which is where we'd like to live, but the tax laws hit London so much that you can't anymore. If I do fifty-five concerts, I have to give the proceeds of fifty-four of them to the English government. All we want to do is live and have our musical community there—however banal it is. Maybe they're right, maybe we should just be content with earning $8,000 a year. But you can't tax people [so much] so that they leave. Then you get nothing."

"In the early days," Mick continued, "the '60s working-class kids didn't have a lot of money. There was this hangover idea of ideal English country life, which was to buy a house, and have land around it to support the house, and support you. You have cattle, wheat, whatever. The idea continued so far into the 20th century that English rock and roll singers dreamed not just of having cars, but of having estates in the country. All the [musicians] you know have them, but now they're being taken away because they don't have enough money to run them. That dream was sold by the upper classes and it just continued. We all did it, we all got big houses in the country we would come to when we were really young—like twenty-two, twenty-three—huge houses. And the plan was to live there when we retired . . . like at thirty-five. . . . I was thrilled when I got mine, what do you think? And I've spent ten days there in the last eight years."

A year after the 1975 tour, I was talking to Mick, when suddenly he said, "You know, I defend you all the time." I beg your pardon? "Yes," he said, "you know all these rock singers who don't want to be taken too seriously, but when they're taken frivolously, they get very upset," he laughed. Well, I said, you're the one who likes to gossip and agreed with me that rock and roll should be fun and it should be about pink socks and white suits. . . . "Well," he said, "it definitely needs that. And it's not a personal thing with you—it's that level I'm talking about." That's OK, I said, I defend you all the time as well. "From what?" he asked suspiciously. From all the people who say you were much better ten years ago.

Two

At first, I wasn't interested in Led Zeppelin. Then, I was scared. In 1970, when they performed an afternoon concert at Madison Square Garden, I sat way in the back. The sound mix was terrible; they were loud, and the singer was screeching. It wasn't dark and sexy and interesting like the Velvet Underground; it didn't seem . . . smart. It sounded like music for boys. Then, when the respected music journalist Ellen Sander went on the road with them to report for *Life* magazine, she wrote about how they attacked her and tore her clothing. She compared them to animals in the zoo.

So, in 1973, when their publicist Danny Goldberg asked me to come see the band in Jacksonville, Florida, and write something about them for my column in *Disc and Music Echo*, I initially declined. Most of my so-called colleagues dismissed Zeppelin as a cheesy heavy metal band. They got terrible reviews. Clearly, I was invited on tour with the hope that I would just write some softball, complimentary stuff about them, which they wanted—no, needed—back home in England. But when Zeppelin started selling out stadiums, I was intrigued. Plus, in those days, to get a free airplane ticket someplace—anyplace—was a treat for a rock writer such as myself who was earning about $40 a week. So, in May 1973, I went to Florida to see Led Zeppelin up close, in concert.

I will never forget the stench in Jacksonville, Florida, when I got off the plane. The city had paper factories or something like that, and the smell and the heat were overwhelming. I took a taxi to the arena, and, for the first time, witnessed a band with an entourage, a security detail, and passes that allowed all-access from the main hall to the band's dressing rooms. Backstage, the band's manager, Peter Grant, was yelling his head off at someone about bootleg t-shirts being sold by someone outside the venue. There was a kerfuffle too, about the cops using undue force to throw someone out of the arena, and Peter was in a fury. (Years later, Peter would tell me he remembered meeting me that day, and said he was angry because the cops had dragged a girl out by her hair and were beating her up. It had, he said, made him question touring in this country. This, from a man whose staff famously beat up a member of Bill Graham's staff at Oakland Stadium four years later.) An angry Peter Grant was a really scary man. A baroque, bearded, 300-pound former rock bodyguard, tour manager and professional wrestler who had gone by the name of Prince Masimo Allessio, Peter was straight out of the sleazy, East End of London, *Expresso Bongo* school of music management. (In that classic 1960s British movie about the music business, the manager, played by Laurence Harvey, said to the "act," Cliff Richard, "From now on, half of everything you make will go to you.") Peter was a foreboding, intimidating presence who reportedly once held someone out of a window upside down by his heels until the guy agreed to whatever Peter wanted. Real thug stuff.

o o o

I was the only journalist to go with Led Zeppelin on and off the road for all five of their U.S. tours between 1973 and 1977. I heard about the shenanigans that went on before I ever accompanied the band, but I never saw anything like Jimmy Page being wheeled into an empty hotel ballroom on a room service table—covered in whipped cream to be licked off by groupies. Nor was I there for the famed shark episode, when a girl reportedly was violated with a shark in 1969 at Seattle's Edgewater Inn. ("It wasn't a shark," Zeppelin's tour manager Richard Cole told me years later. "It was a red snapper. And it wasn't some big ritualistic thing; it was in and out and a laugh and the girl wasn't sobbing, she was a willing participant. It was so fast, and over and done with, and no one from the band was there. I don't think anyone who was there remembers the same thing.") The offstage things I remember were scenarios like Jimmy Page sitting in the dark, on a sofa in a corner suite at New York's Plaza Hotel in 1975 with a cadaverous David Bowie by his side, watching the same fifteen minutes of Kenneth Anger's film *Lucifer Rising* over and over again—snorting line after line of cocaine. Like that.

At the time of their ascent in the early 1970s, Led Zeppelin's reviews were devastating. One critique of the band's first album stated, "Robert Plant sings notes that only a dog can hear." Zeppelin was labeled derivative, a joke. But in Jacksonville, when I saw them perform onstage, I was, frankly, shocked and surprised to discover that I actually loved their music. I thought it was exciting, complex, and majestic. I did. My notes are filled with superlatives—as if I'd never seen a big rock show before. In fact, I hadn't seen a big rock show like this before. At the very beginning of my relationship with Richard Robinson, I'd seen the Stones at Madison Square Garden in 1969 from the third row, and again from the audience in 1972, but it wasn't like this. The Stones were a great, raucous, blues band. This was . . . massive. I heard strains of blues and American roots music and a combination of everything from the 1960s Eastern-influenced British band Kaleidoscope, to the acoustic, hippie-ish Incredible String Band, to Willie Dixon—who, of course, they blatantly ripped off. They were bigger and more complex than Pink Floyd or Cream. Today, because Led Zeppelin's music is used in car commercials and "Stairway to Heaven" is played at weddings and funerals, it seems hard to imagine that then, it sounded like something new. It was a heavy, sexy, hard rock spectacle. Of course, now, forty years later, Led Zeppelin is almost universally considered the greatest and one of the most innovative hard rock bands of all time. But at that time, this was not the majority opinion. Onstage, Jimmy was the embodiment of the foppish, decadent pop star. He wore bejeweled chokers and velvet suits embroidered with moons and stars and all sorts of symbolic, astrological nonsense. He had a cigarette dangling from his lips. He looked angelic. He wasn't. Robert Plant wore a blouse (it could be called nothing else) unbuttoned to his waist. His blue jeans were faded and extremely tight. He was all twinkly and sparkly with a slightly born-too-late flower child persona. From the getgo, I thought all of his hair-flinging and chest-baring was hilarious. Despite the mystical references, the posing, and that nightly shtick—the plaintive "Does anyone remember laughter?"—his charm was evident. But because Jimmy would prove to be the more elusive and mysterious of the two, and because it really was Jimmy's band to begin with, I initially underestimated Robert. Forty years later, Robert would wind up as the one with all the power.

Following the show in Jacksonville, Zeppelin went to Miami and was ensconced in the Fontainebleau Hotel. In the 1960s, Miami was the place where rich Jewish families from New York City went for winter vacations. My family wasn't rich and my left-wing, intellectual, Upper West Side parents wouldn't have dreamed of going there. But once, on a school vacation, I was invited to go with a friend and her family and we stayed in the Fontainebleau. The Morris Lapidus–designed, curved, white hotel had large modernist glass lighting fixtures in the lobby, a grand winding staircase, the Court of the Sun King restaurant with elaborate blue and gold painted wallpaper, and a huge pool with bikini-clad waitresses bringing tropical drinks to oiled-up, tanned sunbathers. To me, this was the height of luxury and glamour. But by 1973, it was fading—no longer Frank Sinatra and sleek kitsch. It would take almost thirty years for Miami to become happening again with its nightclubs packed with rappers and basketball stars. Still, for rock and roll, it was a big step above a bare-bones Holiday Inn. (Mind you, in those days I was thrilled to even stay in a Holiday Inn; any hotel or motel was fun. It still is.)

In the 1970s, those of us who worked primarily for rock magazines couldn't afford to stay in hotels or buy plane tickets to get to a hotel. If a band wanted you there to write about them, and they had enough money to pick up the tab, they paid. So, on May 7, 1973, I was in my room at the Fontainebleau courtesy of Led Zeppelin when I got word that the band thought I was hiding, afraid to meet them. I went down to the pool. Robert Plant, dressed in a red nylon Speedo, was holding court, along with the band's tour manager Richard Cole, members of their crew and a fully dressed Jimmy Page. They were thin, they were sexy, they were in their twenties. They couldn't have been more adorable. And they were in the U.S. to make music, to make money, but also, to go crazy. They were randy. They marauded. They were rough. These were not people who had been positively affected by women's liberation.

The entire history of rock music in the last forty years would have been different with the existence of cellphones, email, or texting. The absence of such telecommunication devices served Led Zeppelin—who rarely traveled in the U.S. with their wives and children—well.

49

Especially in a warm location, and especially around a pool or in a nightclub or near cute girls. There was nothing new about girls waiting in hotel lobbies, jumping into limousines, hanging out at clubs until the musicians had closed the place. Not new either was accompanying them back to their hotel rooms for some quick, or more elaborate, sex. More often than anyone cared to admit, the musician, drunk or stoned, passed out. All of this has gone on in show business and sports—and politics—for years. But what was probably novel at that time, and with Zeppelin in particular, was the level of decadence (high or low, depending on your point of view), especially in the U.S.— which this band viewed as a candy store. It was impossible for anyone at home in England to get in touch with these guys on tour. To even make an international telephone call at that time was a performance. Especially with the time changes: Los Angeles was three hours (and, in those days, three years) behind New York and nine hours behind England. The math alone was confusing. There were no websites for wives to check out photos of nightclub hijinks; no online gossip sites to track the comings and goings in and out of hotels or bars. When the band entertained teenage girls at Rodney Bingenheimer's English Disco on Sunset Strip, they did so in relative privacy—until the black and white photos of such gatherings made their way into the English music papers. Once, Robert Plant returned home to his farm on the Welsh border, and his wife Maureen raced down the hill, brandishing a copy of the British music weekly *Melody Maker* with photos of Robert and John Bonham with six Sunset Strip groupies. Robert merely joked, "Maureen, you *know* we don't take that paper."

It's possible that when I first met Led Zeppelin, that day in Miami, I may have been the only journalist who ever told them anything favorable about their music. Since the words "male chauvinist" could have been coined with Led Zeppelin in mind, the fact that I was female probably made my opinions count less. Still, they—and Jimmy in particular—were pleased that I noticed all the various musical references in their songs. In Miami, we taped some hesitant, guarded interviews; they hadn't done many and really didn't trust anyone from the press. Robert, who was a constant flirt, teased me with innuendoes and double entendres. This would go on for years and wasn't serious—he just couldn't help himself. With my cassette tape on, he told me he wanted to do something as notable as Beethoven's Fifth Symphony. He said this with a straight face. We talked about Sam the Sham, Snooks Eaglin, Otis Redding, Tommy James and the Shondells, and Yehudi Menuhin. He said "Stairway to Heaven" might be one of the things that would still be written down "after he was gone." (To me, the lyrics of that song were utter nonsense; years later Robert would alternately refer to it as a masterpiece or "that wedding song.") He said he could never be bored onstage, because he never forgot that he could just as easily have become a "chartered accountant." He referred to Zeppelin's tours as "the crusades." He said he had been told that Zeppelin was responsible for twenty percent of Atlantic Records' business. I asked him about their reputation. "When we do something, we just do it bigger and better than anybody else," he said. "When there are no holds barred, there are no holds barred. I like to think that people know we're pretty raunchy and that we really do a lot of the things that people say we do. But what we're getting across [onstage] is goodness. It ain't 'stand up and put your fist in the air, we want revolution.' I'd like them to go away feeling the way you do at the end of a good chick, satisfied and exhausted. Some nights I look out and want to fuck the whole front row."

o o o

After traveling a few more times with Zeppelin in 1973, I understood that if you wanted to interview Jimmy, you might often have to wait three hours—or three days—for him to appear. Robert was easier: more accessible, no less smart, quick with a quip, and immensely quotable. But it was always all about Jimmy. Everybody was always wondering and worrying what kind of mood he'd be in. Whether he'd had enough sleep. Whether he was eating. If he'd seen a particular bad review. Of course, he'd set it up that way. Drugs had a lot to do with it. Later, when I traveled with the Rolling Stones, I came to consider this the Keith Richards school of keeping people at a distance. As a former guitarist for the Yardbirds, Jimmy was a highly paid 1960s London session guitarist who formed Zeppelin with another highly paid London session musician, John Paul Jones. Robert and John Bonham were in a band called the Band of Joy, and they came down to London from wherever it was that they lived on the Welsh border and joined up. With the guidance of Peter Grant, they changed the rules of the music business. When Peter worked with Jimmy and the Yardbirds, concert promoters split the take 50-50 with the band, but the band rarely made a dime. Peter signed Zeppelin to Atlantic Records for the then-unheard-of sum of $200,000, before anyone at the label even heard a note of the first album (which was recorded for $3,500 and which Jimmy paid for out of his own pocket). Early on, Ahmet Ertegun told me, "We knew Jimmy Page and we knew he was a genius and he'd be the driving force of the group. We were happy to sign them even before we'd heard any music. I knew it was going to be a success. I'd already had a big success with Eric Clapton and Cream, and I knew this would be another extension of a blues-inspired British rock and roll phenomenon. They were coming, and they were coming in droves. They weren't ripoffs of the blues, they were extensions. Well, maybe a couple of songs sounded close. But they sounded like . . . Led Zeppelin." Because Peter Grant refused to let the band release singles, fans were forced to fork over more money and buy the entire album. He wouldn't let

Zeppelin appear on television where people could see them for free; if fans wanted to see the band, they had to buy tickets to the concerts. And, in a move that forever changed the rock concert business, he forced promoters to give the band ninety percent of the gate—take it or leave it. They took it. Instead of employing the usual local promoters, Grant hired Jerry Weintraub's Concerts West to oversee all of the band's tours. (Weintraub, now the colorful movie producer of the *Ocean's Eleven* franchise, was then the manager of John Denver and concert promoter for Elvis Presley and Frank Sinatra.) Peter and Jimmy (for Peter clearly worked for Jimmy) encouraged a mystique. But, eventually, they were irritated that while Zeppelin broke stadium attendance records, the Rolling Stones got all the good press. And so, after I'd seen their concert in Jacksonville and talked to them a bit in Miami, I was invited to join them again, this time in New Orleans.

In 1973, New Orleans was a party town at a party time. The French Quarter was a tourist destination, full of drunken fraternity boys throwing up in the streets. I had never been there and I was excited to be right in the middle of the Quarter. For me, it was all Tennessee Williams and those lacework balconies and all that important music. I wanted to talk to Robert and Jimmy about the music: about Fats Domino and Ernie K. Doe and the Meters and Professor Longhair. After I arrived and checked into the Royal Orleans Hotel, I walked around by myself—down Bourbon Street to the corner of Iberville to the Gateway club, where Frankie Ford sang "Sea Cruise." Clarence "Frogman" Henry and Ernie K. Doe were alive and well and performing in such spots as the Nite Cap Lounge and the King's Castle. Broken bottles and malt liquor cans filled the gutters in the streets of the Quarter and there were a number of people wandering around mumbling to themselves. Bars served something called "Hurricanes"—a drink I had never heard of in Manhattan. The Deja Vu was an appropriately named club that drew local teenage talent and visiting rock stars. The whole city seemed like a perfect place to just get drunk and throw caution to the winds. (Years later, Nine Inch Nails' Trent Reznor would talk to me at length about living and recording in New Orleans' Garden District and how he hadn't had a sober day in the entire time he had lived there.) After Zeppelin's show at the New Orleans Municipal Auditorium on May 14, 1973, the next morning—which meant the early afternoon—the entourage assembled around the "observation deck" at the rooftop pool at the Royal Orleans. I brought a tape recorder to talk to "the boys." Everyone except Jimmy oiled up for the tanning rays. Piña coladas were served. Millions of dollars, hundreds of thousands of concertgoers and endless logistics were involved in this tour. But at that time, when there were really only ten big bands in the world and there was this sort of semi-tropical, festive atmosphere, it didn't feel like work. Robert Plant was parading around in the same red nylon bikini he'd worn in Miami. Even offstage he was all twinkly and hair-flinging. The rest of the band addressed him by the nickname "Percy." To be around any English band in the 1970s, but especially around Zeppelin or the Who, was to constantly hear nicknames: Robert was Percy, John Bonham was Bonzo, John Paul Jones was Jonesy, and many of them had campier, or far nastier nicknames for their bandmates. There was a wide range of English accents—from Cockney to upper class. (Mick Jagger, I would eventually discover, could switch from one to another in a flash and did, depending on who he was talking to.) The roadies, and Richard Cole and Peter Grant in particular, sounded like total ruffians. Some of the far-northern English accents sounded like a foreign language. But almost to a man, they engaged in that Cockney rhyming slang: from the naughty—"Bristol" or "braces and bits" for "tits" (Bristol City, titty, etc.)—to the more benign "apples and pears" for "stairs." This would quickly lose its luster.

At the Royal Orleans rooftop pool, Robert told me that the English press had put Zeppelin down for trying to do reggae by recording "D'yer Mak'er," while Emerson, Lake and Palmer—who Robert referred to as "a bunch of old queens"—were considered good musicians. About ELP, he asked, "Where is the *magic*?" Despite the oppressive, humid heat, Jimmy Page, pasty-faced and thin, wore white trousers and a red and black silk print shirt. When I took out my tape recorder, he put on a wine-colored velvet jacket. He said he hadn't eaten in three days. He told me he was becoming increasingly afraid of flying. He told me he got weird letters and death threats, probably because he was a known collector of memorabilia relating to the English satanist Aleister Crowley, and especially because he bought Crowley's house in Scotland and the occult Equinox bookstore in London. He said he dreamed of traveling around the world in a sort of motorized caravan, just going somewhere like Morocco and recording with local musicians. He'd done a bit of it, "But the problem with that," he said, "is that you stand out as the rich European. You could be dressed in rags, and you still stand out as a European, the way an American does in London. And bang—they'll come over for the money and you can just forget your recording." We talked about how some of the press had decided, once again, that rock was dead, and Jimmy said, "Every time it gets weak, someone comes back and just goes 'fuck you' and gives it a kick in the ass again." He bitched about the band's bad reviews. This was, I would learn, a constant refrain. When I offered more of my personal opinions about their music, Jimmy was pleased. "That's it," he said, "you get it. But the rest of the press doesn't give us a chance. I wouldn't mind constructive criticism. . . ." I told him I didn't think any musician believed there was any such thing. "But they seem to be losing the essence of what's important, which is music, purely," Jimmy complained. "They wallow in rubbish. And while I may be a masochist in other regions, I'm not that much of a masochist that I'm going to pay money to tear myself to bits—*reading*."

During the week that Zeppelin was in New Orleans, on a night off, Ahmet Ertegun gave them a party at Cosimo Matassa's studio, where Allen Toussaint had recorded local musicians for Minit Records. We all went in limousines to a building that resembled a warehouse and took a wooden freight elevator hauled by big ropes down to a basement. A portable air conditioner with a long plastic tunnel was set up from the hallway into the large room. Inside that room, the Mardi Gras Indians danced alongside Dejan's Olympia Brass Band. Ernie K. Doe was there, wearing white linen trousers, a pink sport coat and a white tie. Art Neville was at the organ, ready to perform with the Meters. Ribs, red beans, rice and hot apple cake were served. And then the great blind blues guitarist Snooks Eaglin played with the legendary pianist Professor Longhair—who wore brown slacks, a brown jacket, white shoes and had Band-Aids on his fingers. Jimmy and Robert and John Bonham and John Paul Jones all beamed. "Ah, it's one of those dreams," Robert said to me, "like when I used to have the radio under the covers too late at night. Chris Kenner, Jessie Hill, Benny Spellman, those records were a part of me." It was two in the morning when we all filed out of Cosimo's. In the car, on the way back to the hotel, John Bonham talked to me about his cattle and his home in Stratfordshire.

I once asked Mick Jagger what was the most important thing in a rock band. "The drummer," he said. John Bonham, called either

Bonzo or "the Beast" by the rest of the band, was a Gemini with a true dual personality. Drunk, he was a madman. At the first sign of his temper, everyone got out of his way. But sober, to me, he was a sweetheart—articulate, and a gentleman. He lit my cigarettes, opened car doors for me, and once showed up at my hotel room wearing a suit and tie for one of the few interviews he ever did. It's hard to imagine now, when drummers sit high on the stage on setups that resemble spaceships, but in those early days, Bonzo didn't even have a drum riser. His solo, the twenty-minute "Moby Dick," was a crowd-pleaser and an opportunity for Jimmy to go back into the dressing room if he so chose, for some quick sex. (Once, Jimmy reportedly went back to the *hotel* during the drum solo.) Bonzo is the one who was credited with driving a motorcycle down the hallway of the Continental Hyatt House in L.A., but it was probably Richard Cole who did that; no one who was there remembers it the same way. During a full moon—of which there were many on Zeppelin tours—Bonzo went wild. As the years went on, he had really bad stomachaches, became increasingly drug-addled and extremely homesick. But with his love of R&B and especially Motown, he probably was the greatest rock and roll drummer of that generation or maybe ever, and was never given credit for it during his lifetime. (Charlie Watts was primarily a jazz drummer, Keith Moon was overrated, and as for Ringo, when John Lennon was asked if Ringo was the best drummer in the world, he reportedly replied, "In the world? He's not even the best drummer in the *Beatles*.") Bonzo would go nuts and bang on people's hotel room doors in the middle of the night, so Peter Grant eventually instructed some of the staff to get two rooms—a secret one to really sleep in, and another kept empty to deflect Bonzo's four a.m. rampages. Once, on a street in Dallas, Bonzo saw a Cadillac he wanted (although it's been written about as a Corvette; again, no one remembers it the same way). He told Richard Cole to wait until the owner showed up and insist that "Mr. Bonham from Led

Zeppelin wanted to buy him a drink." He paid $30,000 for the car, which was worth $20,000, shipped it to L.A., and put it in the basement of the Hyatt House while the band's lawyer went through a rigamarole to get the insurance transferred. Bonzo then dragged musicians from other bands over to admire the car, drove it for two days, and sold it.

In January 1975, before the band was due to go onstage at the Chicago Stadium, Bonzo—who had debuted his *Clockwork Orange* boilersuit and bowler hat on this tour—was roaring mad and flinging furniture in the band's dressing room. "I'd like to have it publicized that I came in *after* Karen Carpenter in the *Playboy* drummer poll!" he bellowed. "She couldn't last ten minutes with a Zeppelin number!" But later that night, he sat in a booth at the gay disco The Bistro, and while Robert and Jimmy stood around listening to whispered propositions from the local talent—including a few drag queens—Bonzo talked quietly to me. "You know my wife is expecting again in July," he said. "She's really terrific, the type of lady that when you walk into our house she comes right out with a cup of tea or a drink, or a sandwich. We met when we were sixteen, got married at seventeen. I was a carpenter for a few years; I'd get up at seven in the morning, then change my clothes in the van to go to gigs at night. How do you think I feel, not being taken seriously? Coming in after Karen Carpenter in the *Playboy* poll . . . *Karen Carpenter* . . . what a load of shit." To this day, I cannot hear "The Crunge" or "Trampled Under Foot"—both underrated Zeppelin songs and still my favorites—without hearing his superior rhythmic talent. In 1975, during the Stones' summer tour, Ian Stewart told me that while Bonzo could be a "right evil bastard at times," he said: "Everything with Zeppelin rocks and rolls. That's because

Bonham, who is probably the best drummer in rock and roll, will always see to that."

You take guys in their twenties, put them on their own private jet, with tons of money and more drugs than they can handle, at a time when life was pre-AIDS, and they turned nothing down. It would be hard to find anyone in that situation who didn't react with a sense of entitlement and grandeur, but rock stars especially were treated like children and encouraged to behave badly. However, there can be no question that along with all the drugs and the sexism and the bad behavior, the perks—like the plane—couldn't have been more delightful. If you were going to shlep to a concert in, say, Pittsburgh, it certainly made it easier and more fun to travel on a private plane. Or to have a police escort to the hall (I had no idea then that you could apply for that, like a permit). So even though it was my husband's birthday on July 24, 1973, we weren't sentimental about such things and so I accompanied Zeppelin on their plane for the first time—to their show in Pittsburgh.

The limousines were lined up outside the Plaza Hotel in New York City, and our seven-car motorcade made its way out of Manhattan to Newark Airport where the band's 707 jet would take us to Pittsburgh. The plane (the same "Starship" used earlier by Elvis and later by the Stones and Elton John) was painted gold and bronze with the "Led Zeppelin" logo along the side. I cajoled the band into lining up by the wing (no easy feat) so that Bob Gruen could take the photograph that would eventually become a postcard. Robert's shirt was, as usual, unbuttoned. So, sadly, was John Paul Jones'. The stewardesses were Susan, dressed in maroon and pink, and Wendy—who wore a blue feather boa and whose uncle was Bobby Sherman's manager. The plane was garish. I thought this was what all private planes looked like. The interior walls were orange and red, there were circular maroon and patterned velvet banquettes, white leather swivel chairs, a mirror-covered bar, something that looked like a fireplace and a white, fake fur–covered bed in the back bedroom. Four off-duty policemen who made up Zeppelin's security team sat together on a sofa. Food was served: steak, string beans, radishes, celery, salad. Nearly everyone smoked cigarettes, and everyone drank. I have many photos of me, sitting with the band or with Ahmet Ertegun or Jerry Weintraub or Peter Grant on that plane, and there is always a drink or a cigarette, or both, in my hand. Or my tape recorder stuck in someone's face. That summer, I wore little halter tops and open-toed platform shoes and flared jeans. I wore huge sunglasses. I never wore a watch and I remember thinking that it was corny if a musician ever wore a watch onstage. Sometime around the 1990s, when life got busier and more deadlines loomed, I started to wear a watch. But I still think it's corny if a musician wears one during a show. At that time, I was thin enough to go out wearing tube tops and bright red satin camisoles—underwear, basically—trimmed in black lace. I wore fur jackets in the winter. (I was not yet wearing only black clothes. That came later. First of all, as hard as it is to believe, no one really made good black clothes then. Towards the very end of the 1970s, when I was spending more time in clubs and Studio 54 and such, and people were constantly spilling drinks, black clothes seemed a good, defensive idea.) When I went on Zeppelin's plane, I carried a bag with my tape recorder, note pads, pens, and makeup. There was no check-in situation; we went right onto the plane, which was right on the tarmac. After landing, we went straight from the plane in limousines to the backstage door at the venue. These days this is all routine, but then, it was brand-new and felt special. There were cases of wine (usually Blue Nun) in Zeppelin's dressing room, along with bottles of vodka and Jack Daniel's. There were potato chips and occasionally, those "deli-trays" made famous in *Spinal Tap*. (*Spinal*

Tap was so on the money in so many ways that my favorite comment about it came from Tom Petty, who once said, "I've seen *Spinal Tap*. It's not funny.") There were terrycloth bathrobes for the band when they came offstage soaked with sweat and had to go straight into air-conditioned cars for the "runners" back to the plane, or to the hotel. Considering that I felt cossetted and privileged during these excursions, imagine what it was like for "the boys."

July 29, 1973, was the final night of Led Zeppelin's sold-out run at Madison Square Garden. The backstage security at the Garden wasn't anywhere near as uptight as it is now. The Garden's been renovated since then, but as I recall, the dressing rooms were still off the rotunda, to the right of the stage if you were in the audience looking at the stage. They were part of the same long concrete hallway that now houses the locker rooms for the Knicks and the Rangers. But at that time, Zeppelin's dressing rooms were more communal. If you were one of the few allowed back there, you could just sort of hang out with the band—except that Zeppelin never really got there early enough to hang out before a show. I seem to recall police escorts from the Plaza racing to the Garden, with very little time between the band's arrival and the start of the show. For these summer 1973 shows, the band was being filmed for what eventually would become the disappointing movie *The Song Remains the Same*. The film crew, hired by the band, got little direction from the band, and seemed confused about what they were doing. (Years later, Jimmy remixed and re-mastered—and for all we know, might have re-recorded—some of the music for the film's re-release.) On July 29th, there were more security men than usual with bomb-sniffing dogs checking out the area underneath the stage. Richard or Peter put me on the side of the stage—as they always did—right by the band's amplifiers. I spent many nights directly next to those speakers and I never wore earplugs; I thought they were for civilians. It's a miracle I still have any hearing left whatsoever. The band did a blistering three and a half hour set and when it was over, the band and a few of us were mysteriously shoved into cars and raced to the Upper East Side apartment of the band's lawyer's secretary's boyfriend. No one told us why we were there, but for some reason "the boys" needed to be kept away from their hotel, the Drake, on East 56th Street. The hotel was crawling with cops and FBI agents, and the roadies rushed to the rooms to get rid of all the drugs. Later that night, at a party hosted by Ahmet Ertegun at the Carlyle Hotel, we learned that $253,000 in cash had been stolen from the group's safe-deposit box at the Drake. "Peter did have a funny expression on his face," Robert said later, "but what were we going to do? Break down and cry? We had just done a great gig." The next morning Peter Grant, Richard Cole and Danny Goldberg faced press accusations that the robbery was faked by the band. The band's position was that someone who worked at the hotel took the money. The "case," such as it was, was never solved. The 1973 tour was over.

o o o

By 1974, Atlantic Records gave Led Zeppelin anything they wanted and what they wanted was their own record label, just like the Rolling Stones had. Zeppelin's Swan Song Records signed other acts—1960s band the Pretty Things, Scottish singer Maggie Bell—but the only one other than Zeppelin that had any real commercial success was Bad Company, led by ex–Free singer Paul Rodgers. On May 7, 1974, Zeppelin came to New York City for a Swan Song launch at the Four Seasons restaurant. They instructed Danny Goldberg to get some swans for the pool and when he couldn't find any, he got geese instead. The band was furious. "We all live on farms!" Robert shouted. "Don't you think we know the fucking difference?" Bonzo and Richard Cole picked up the geese, carried them outside and let them loose on Park Avenue. The band then traveled to L.A. for a Swan Song launch (with real swans) at the Bel-Air Hotel, attended by, among others, Bryan Ferry, Bill Wyman and Groucho Marx. They went back to England to record *Physical Graffiti*, the double album that included the Eastern-flavored "Kashmir," which many still consider the band's real masterpiece and which, more than twenty years later, was sampled by Sean "Puffy" Combs. I went to London as Zeppelin's guest for a huge party they had at the Chislehurst Caves on Halloween to celebrate Swan Song in England. The plan was, after the Christmas holidays, Led Zeppelin would come back to the U.S. to start the next tour.

Led Zeppelin's 1975 tour did not start off on a good note. Right before the tour, Jimmy injured his finger getting off a train in England. Robert had the flu. The first show, on January 20th in Chicago, was mediocre. The second one, the following night, was better. We were all staying in the Ambassador East, the hotel with the famed Pump Room—the restaurant where Chicago columnist Irv Kupcinet did his radio show. The walls of the Pump Room were lined with framed photos of every show business personality who had ever come to Chicago—among them, Frank Sinatra, Eydie Gorme and Steve Lawrence, Don Rickles, Myron Cohen. In his suite, Robert Plant posed for photos. He lit two cigarettes at once, like Paul Henreid in *Now, Voyager*. Everyone around him murmured, "Lovely." Robert appeared pleased. I rifled through the LPs on his coffee table: Margie Joseph, Danny O'Keefe, Otis Redding, the Guess Who. "Don't count that as my taste," he said. "Although the Guess Who are great." I told Robert that Bob Dylan had said his kids listened to Zeppelin. "Well," he said, "that's very nice. But doesn't he listen as well?"

At two in the afternoon on January 22nd, Jimmy came to my

room for a breakfast interview. He was in a good mood because he'd had five hours of sleep, and he felt that the show the night before had been great. But he was slurring his words more than usual and he was scary skinny. The truth was, of course, that his heroin use had escalated, but this was never acknowledged around me. The party line was that Jimmy was a genius, and a delicate, sensitive soul. But that angelic, wasted appearance belied a shrewd, tough, manipulative hedonist. In an interview that lasted several hours, Jimmy and I gossiped a bit about someone setting fire to Angela Bowie's hair in Rodney Bingenheimer's L.A. disco. Jimmy told me he didn't want to see "those girls" get so fucked up. We discussed Iggy Stooge—who Jimmy likened to a sadhu. He said he couldn't believe how much Alice Cooper had stolen from Screaming Lord Sutch. Jimmy said that at the end of the last tour he had no idea where he was, and that he was becoming a recluse. He was increasingly afraid of heights and of airplanes. Jimmy, then thirty-one, said he never thought he'd live past thirty, and that his music was "a race against time." He told me that before the show the previous night, he'd been depressed because of his broken finger: "I wanted to toss myself out of the window, but people kept stopping me." He drew a diagram for me of where the finger was broken, and talked about how he had to develop a "three-finger technique." He ordered scrambled eggs with ketchup, an English muffin and tea. It would be the only food he would have for days. "I'm going off eating," he said. "I'm trying to photosynthesize, like a plant." He was just going to have banana daiquiri shakes which, he claimed, "gave him all the vitamins he needed." Jimmy, who weighed 130 pounds, said he wanted to get down to 125.

Later that afternoon, I visited Peter Grant in his suite—which was all blue brocade drapes and fake French furniture. It was the same one occupied by Zsa Zsa Gabor whenever she came to the city and where, Peter said, her dogs relieved themselves on the carpets. He was told that she never tipped the maids. There were large cases of champagne and Heineken stacked up in a corner, and several floral displays sent by Atlantic Records. Peter wore a satin tour jacket with the Zeppelin "ZOSO" logo and his fingers were covered, as usual, by rings. He reminisced about a Midwest hotel clerk during the band's last tour who admitted that the worst trashing of hotel rooms had occurred during a Young Methodists' Convention. "The guy was so frustrated about not being able to just go bonkers in a room himself," Peter said, "that I told him to go and have one on us. He went upstairs, tossed a TV set against the wall, tore up the bed, and I paid the $490 bill." He discussed his objections to doing a week in the same theater: "It's like vaudeville," he said. "The minute a rock musician wakes up night after night in the same place, it becomes a grind. Pure routine." And then he grabbed my pad and wrote a note in it as follows: *"Lisa Robinson is a lying, cheating, conceited . . . fucked . . . prissy, whoring sweetheart. I love her. Yours truly, Peter Grant."*

On January 31st, on the plane to the show in Detroit, Jimmy argued with a reporter from the London *Daily Express*. The reporter, who wore an ascot, smirked and said to Jimmy, "You're not supposed to make intelligent remarks." Jimmy, who was stoned and drinking Jack Daniel's, was exasperated. "Listen," he said, "I don't just jump up and down onstage. I compose. I've done session work. . . ." Bonzo muttered, "Uh-oh, I know what he's like when he gets like this. He's gonna slug somebody." After landing in Detroit, in the car on the way to the Olympia Stadium, Jimmy was incredulous. "Can you believe that man referred to my guitar playing as a *trade*?" During Bonzo's drum solo, the other band members went into the dressing room. The reporter tried to follow but was stopped by Richard Cole, who said the band was having a "meeting." The reporter was enraged: "I write for ten million people and I won't have you humiliate me in front of a member of my staff!" The member of his "staff": a buxom blonde woman swathed in rabbit fur. On the way back to the plane, the reporter demanded the radio be turned off in the car. "After two hours of that Led Zeppelin racket, I can't stand any more!" Back on the plane, people whispered in groups of twos and threes. Jimmy, who'd been huddled under a red blanket, suddenly came to life and got right back into the argument. "You don't want to know about my music," Jimmy yelled, "all you care about are the [financial] grosses and the interior of the plane. You're a communist!" Meanwhile, Robert was muttering under his breath, "I don't think he's such a bad bloke. Ten million people read the paper. Me mum and dad read the paper. The singer was good. . . ." Jimmy started yelling about the way he voted in the last election, someone threw a drink at the reporter, the reporter became more belligerent and then, suddenly, Richard Cole stood in the aisle, holding a gun. I had never seen a real gun before. We were 25,000 feet in the air. I cowered in my seat. Nervous glances all around. Two of the band's security guys walked over and stood menacingly next to Richard, who threatened the reporter with his silent stare. "FOR CHRIST'S SAKE," Bonzo yelled from the front of the plane, "WILL YOU ALL SHUT UP??? I'M TRYING TO GET SOME SLEEP!"

o o o

In February 1975, Led Zeppelin was in New York City in the Plaza Hotel, where every so often, in the middle of the night, tour photographer Neal Preston had to give them a slide show and present every photo he had taken, for their approval. Shouts of "Flab!" could be heard as they made fun of each other during this cumbersome process that often took hours. I lived in Manhattan, so I'd visit them at the Plaza if we were doing interviews, or accompany them to an out-of-town show, or go see them at the Garden. Today the Plaza is a condominium with a lobby built for tourists. It resembles an upscale Midwestern mall and is full of children. A piano player sits in a corner of the lobby near what was once the real Palm Court restaurant and plays "Happy Birthday" every few minutes because there is bound to be some kid there having a birthday tea, just like Eloise. But in 1975, it was quiet, it was elegant, and had huge corner suites that overlooked Central Park. It was the first time I ever saw a kitchen or a dining room in a hotel suite. Jimmy hated his suite, which he likened to "the fucking Versailles Palace." His TV set didn't work because the black candles he placed on top of it dripped down. The movie projector Jimmy rented buzzed, so his *Lucifer Rising* screenings (he was writing the score) had to be at such high volume to block out the buzz, that he was afraid he'd be thrown out of the hotel. Bonzo demanded that a pool table be brought into his suite, and no one was going to argue with him. On a night off, I suggested that we all go to a party for Leonard Cohen, to which Robert said, "Let's run through it tossing quaaludes around to liven up the place." Instead, we left the Plaza and strolled down the street to Nirvana—an Indian restaurant in the penthouse of 30 Central Park South. Nirvana was one of those restaurants that could have been considered impossibly corny: sitar music was piped in over the sound system (there might even have been live sitar players as well), the place was dimly lit, and covered in floor-to-ceiling Indian tapestries and mirrored pillows. It had an amazing view of Central Park. The band loved it. "Have you got any fresh dania?" Robert asked, showing off to the waiters. "I know about this food, I'm married to an Indian," he added. Jimmy laughed, "So you tell them every time you come here." I told them that John

Lennon told me that he heard "Stairway to Heaven" and loved it. "He's only just heard it now?" Robert said.

By 1975, my life revolved around a diverse assortment of bands: Queen, Roxy Music, the New York Dolls, Patti Smith, David Bowie, the Jackson Five, and many others. I did a lot of interviews for the *New Musical Express*, my syndicated column and rock magazines. I went out nightly to Studio 54 and Max's Kansas City and CBGB's. I went out to dinner, but restaurants were not a destination or a way of life. Dinner was something you had before, or after, you went to a concert or a club. Usually after—like midnight. My social life and my work life were inexorably intertwined. I spent days on the phone with friends, re-hashing the nights before. My musical tastes were to the right—Led Zeppelin—and to the left—Television. But when Led Zeppelin came to town, they were a priority.

In general, Led Zeppelin did not draw a celebrity crowd. In 1972, Truman Capote had followed the Stones around on tour, so, in 1975, Jimmy wanted to enlist William Burroughs to interview him. It was decided that Burroughs would spend some time with Jimmy and write something for the underground rock magazine *Crawdaddy*. Burroughs came to a show at Madison Square Garden, spent two sessions interviewing Jimmy, then wrote mostly about himself and arcane black magic practices. Mick Jagger stopped by one of Zeppelin's Madison Square Garden shows to check out the sound system. When Zeppelin was in Los Angeles, David Geffen visited Peter Grant backstage at the L.A. Forum. George Harrison showed up at one of the band's after-parties and threw some cake at Bonzo—who then threw the former Beatle in the pool. But the band mostly surrounded themselves with pals like Freddie Sessler, or the Irish journalist B.P. Fallon, or the musician Roy Harper. And there was a retinue of girls—especially in Los Angeles—with names like Lori, Sable, Bebe or Connie the Butter Queen. Occasionally, someone would show up from the trendy London scene—like the mysterious, glamorous personality and Roxy Music album cover girl, Amanda Lear. ("I'm in love," she once said to me on the phone after spending some time with Jimmy.) But there was no Andy Warhol or Lee Radziwill or the gang from Studio 54. Led Zeppelin was just not fashionable.

Zeppelin was aware that when the Rolling Stones walked into a room, they created an ambience. So when they went to a club, say the Rainbow on Sunset Strip—down the block from the band's Hollywood hotel, the Continental Hyatt House (which they called the Riot House)—Richard Cole would call ahead. He would alert them that the band was on its way and to make sure the bottles of Dom Pérignon (which Earl McGrath called "rockstar's mouthwash") were chilled and waiting at the table. Richard would personally go in advance to stake out the "talent." When Zeppelin was in Los Angeles, the groupie grapevine went into overdrive. At the Rainbow, bodyguards manned the tables reserved for "the boys." Teenage girls, dressed in what appeared to be no more than two handkerchiefs, with platform shoes and frizzed-out hair, lined up in front of the band's table and just *stood* there. The girls' style, such as it was, was a look made popular by the short-lived *Star* magazine, a publication that publicized and glorified L.A. groupies. At the Rainbow, the girls posed provocatively in front of "the boys," while the musicians and some of the crew drank, chatted up the girls who were actually *with* them, and just generally behaved in whatever loud, drunken, loutish ways they pleased. Lots of Cockney rhyming slang and Monty Python acting-out and shrieking. The mantra was "No head, no backstage pass" among the roadies, who were in a position to get the former and give the latter. A few such evenings went a long way. I often left earlier than any member of the band, which could mean one in the morning. I went back to the hotel, made long-distance calls to Richard or whichever friends were still up at four a.m. in New York, which meant all of my friends. During my times with Led Zeppelin, I didn't have a chance to get too lonely; I never was with them for weeks at a time. It was usually in and out, like a jaunt to Pittsburgh or Detroit for a night, or a week in New Orleans or Chicago, and then back to New York, where they were "stationed" in the same hotel for a week.

Even for those times, the excesses were astounding. During one tour, when Robert got the flu and a show was cancelled, Jimmy considered sending their empty private jet to fetch his then sixteen-year-old tour girlfriend Lori Mattix, to bring her from Los Angeles to be with him in the Midwest. And the cocaine and heroin that was an unspoken fact of life around the band, management and crew became extreme. A doctor accompanied the band to minister to their medical needs. Jimmy reportedly sat in his darkened hotel suite for hours at a time while people—meaning girls or dealers—were brought to him. Years later, his L.A. girlfriend Lori Mattix would paint a slightly different picture: she told me he sent her flowers, wouldn't let her smoke cigarettes, met her mother, and was a perfect gentleman. As far as I could tell, Robert's tour amours were girls who believed that he was, at any given moment, about to leave his wife, Maureen, the mother of his two young children.

On August 4, 1975, I was on tour with the Rolling Stones in Williamsburg, Virginia, when I heard that Robert Plant, his wife Maureen, seven-year-old daughter Carmen and three-year-old son Karac were in a serious car crash while vacationing in Greece. I remember thinking at the time how I hated the first nine days of August. My friend, the Australian journalist and author Lillian Roxon had died on August 9, 1973. The Manson murders were on August 9, 1969. Lenny Bruce died on August 3, 1966. Marilyn Monroe died on August 5, 1962. And Stevie Wonder had been in a near fatal car crash on August 6, 1973. The Plant family was airlifted back to London. Maureen was in intensive care with a fractured pelvis, Carmen had a

broken wrist, Karac a fractured leg, and Robert, who suffered multiple fractures of the elbow, ankles and other bones, was in a cast from
his hips to his toes. He was told he wouldn't be able to walk for six
months. All of Led Zeppelin's 1976 concerts were cancelled.

The next time I saw Robert was January 13, 1976. He came to New
York without a winter coat and, as was the custom of the Royal Family, or, as was rumored, Paul and Linda McCartney, he carried no
money. He walked with a cane and joked, "One small step for man,
one giant step for six nights at Madison Square Garden." We spent
the afternoon at the Park Lane Hotel on Central Park South, then
walked up the street to Nirvana where he was his usual, flirty, sparkly self. He let me take the check. He encouraged me to leave a bigger
tip because "we come here all the time." He told me that he'd had a
lot of time to think about the rock and roll life: "The insanity, the
hours, the flying around, rampaging the way we do. I think I need to
get back to my farm on the Welsh border and be with my family—
which doesn't mean that I've lost the grease off my shoes. I'm still
part of this thing that Led Zeppelin is. But you need to go back to
your corner every once in a while to get the energy that you need to
perform in front of all these people. When Zeppelin first came to the
U.S. in 1969 it was like a little light, flashing inside of me. As the
lights hit my face I started wiggling my hips and I realized this
was all a fantastic trip and I had something to do. I wasn't even sure
what it was, I just knew I had to do it." We talked about Hermann
Hesse, Buddy Guy, the British rockabilly band Dr. Feelgood and Joni
Mitchell—who he'd always had a crush on. He talked about his hometown Wolverhampton football (soccer) team and his local pub, where
he went to throw darts. He said the reason the band didn't play in
England was because they didn't have the proper venues, just "silly
old cinemas." The truth was, of course, that they were tax exiles at

the time, but also, they could make much, much more money playing in the U.S. because there were more stadiums, which meant more people. He said while he knew it was a "punk" thing to say, "I'm just glad to be alive. I remember talking to Mick Jagger one night at the Plaza about the separation, or the lack of communication between one rock band and another. In the early days, there was a sort of jousting for position, a definite ego thing until you got up to a certain point. Basically, you think that the rock and roll scene is lacking a camaraderie, a kinship. But when this accident happened, there was a giant rally around from a lot of people I don't think about that often. Wishes and regards sent, to Maureen, to both of us, from all levels of the music business, and it was a great gesture and an enlightening thing. Before, I was just sort of swept along by the impetuousness of everything we did, everything we are, and what was created around it. The accident gave me a fresh appreciation of things." When I asked him how much longer he wanted to tour, Robert said, "No one knows how long this can go on. Look at Sinatra. He came to terms with his age and the time, and we can do that too. Who do they say is getting old and can't do it anymore—Jagger? Oh, he'll go on forever and ever."

o o o

In 1977, for the heavy rock fan, there was no bigger band than Led Zeppelin who, with Robert recovered, were back in the U.S. on tour. But the British press now liberally referred to them—along with the Stones and the Who and the Faces—as bloated dinosaurs. Self-doubt started to creep into the band's conversations. Things started to go terribly wrong. The drugs were getting so out of hand that there were times onstage when Jimmy would appear to be playing a completely different song than the rest of the band. The audience rarely noticed.

Bill Graham, the larger-than-life San Francisco concert promoter, always thought Zeppelin brought an unpleasant element of male aggression to their shows. When the band performed the first of two shows for Graham outside San Francisco at the Oakland Stadium in July 1977, Peter Grant's nine-year-old son Warren tried to remove a "Led Zeppelin" sign from a dressing room trailer. According to Bonzo, who claimed he saw it from the stage, a guard hit the kid. A hideous, violent scene followed. Peter Grant, Bonzo, and security man John Bindon, a thug who'd been hired for extra muscle, beat up Graham's guy inside a trailer while Richard Cole stood guard outside. Graham's staffer was rushed, bleeding, to the hospital. The band refused to do the next day's show unless Graham signed a paper absolving the band of any guilt in the incident. Graham, fearing a riot if Zeppelin didn't play, signed the paper after being assured that it was legally worthless. After the show, Peter Grant, Richard Cole, John Bonham and John Bindon were arrested at their hotel. Thankfully, when this happened, I was not with them. The lawsuit between Bill Graham and Zeppelin dragged on and was settled out of court for a sum lower than it should have been. Bill Graham devoted an entire chapter to it in his posthumously published autobiography. Reportedly, when a sober, thinner Peter Grant read it, he cried.

The rumors continued. Limousine drivers, always eager to blab, said the band's hopped-up road managers and bodyguards stormed into drugstores and, threatening physical force, demanded that prescriptions be filled. A restaurant was trashed and waiters humiliated in Pennsylvania. With the exception of Bonzo in San Francisco, the band members were never involved in these incidents; Richard Cole told me years later that Jimmy and Robert were "never aware of any of this shit." Whenever I was with the band, most of the drugs, all of the violence, the extreme decadent behavior—whether perpetrated by the band or the crew—was kept away from me. Of course I heard the stories, and I didn't just dismiss them as benign. But I was with them to get a story, not to judge. However, as I've said, when you're not a participant in these activities, you can be, and often are, on a completely different tour.

A few days after Oakland, when the band checked into the Maison Dupuy Hotel in New Orleans, Robert got a phone call at the front desk and went upstairs to take it in his room. He was told that after being rushed to the hospital with a mysterious respiratory infection, his five-year-old son Karac had died. Accompanied by Richard, Bonzo and tour assistant Dennis Sheehan (today, U2's longtime tour manager), Robert immediately flew back to England. The U.S. tour—a tour marked by increasing turmoil, tension, drug use, band estrangement and violence—was over. Robert, devastated by his son's death (and reportedly upset too, that Jimmy and Peter had not attended the funeral), went into seclusion. The press wrote about Jimmy's "bad karma," and implied all sorts of absurd theories about a Zeppelin "curse." There were ridiculous rumors that, like the blues singer Robert Johnson, Jimmy had made a deal with the devil. By the end of 1977, I'd already been on the six-week summer tour with the Stones, spent a lot of time with Michael Jackson, and was immersed in the CBGB's scene. My idea of exciting new music was the Clash. I remember thinking at the time that Zeppelin would never be able to survive Robert's accident, the drugs, and now the death of his child. I would be only partially wrong.

In August of 1979, Peter Grant invited me to come see the band at Knebworth, in Hertfordshire. Zeppelin was going to perform their first shows in over two years on the thirty-six-acre site of one of the stately homes of England. The plan was for a new album, to be followed by another lucrative U.S. tour. The band sent me a round-trip ticket on the Concorde, then put me up in some tacky motel near the site. Typical Zeppelin: high/low. I checked myself into Claridge's in London, then went out to Knebworth on the afternoon of August 4th for the sound check. I stood with Bonzo way in the back as we watched his then thirteen-year-old son Jason sit in onstage on drums. "It's the first time I've actually ever seen Led Zeppelin," Bonzo told me. "Jason can play 'Trampled Under Foot' perfectly." Only a few people were allowed in the closed-off backstage enclave that housed the dressing room trailers. The band appeared paranoid, nervous. "Now don't you go and say this is nostalgia," Robert warned me. In truth, with clubs in London starting to be populated by drag queens in science fiction outfits and everyone in New York having cut their hair three years earlier, this massive long-haired, denim-clad audience, ten years after Woodstock, did look like a throwback to another age. Robert was with Maureen and their daughter Carmen. Their new baby boy, six-month-old Logan, was at home with his grandparents. A half hour before the show, Jimmy Page flew in by helicopter with his longtime girlfriend, Charlotte Martin, the mother of his daughter Scarlet. He no longer wore one of those white satin pop star outfits or wildly embroidered black velvet suits; he was dressed in a more subdued blue silk shirt and baggy cream-colored trousers. He seemed smacked out. The band played for three and a half hours. The audience sang "You'll Never Walk Alone" for fifteen minutes after the third encore. It was all very emotional backstage, and Robert appeared to cry. I hung out for hours after the show with a slightly out-of-it Jimmy Page and a companion who was not his longtime girlfriend. On that night, which was to be a new beginning, Led Zeppelin was not the same band I had seen in Jacksonville six years earlier. They were more than just rusty; the wit and the magic—to paraphrase Robert—was gone. It would be the last time I would ever see them together.

On September 25, 1980, after a night of overeating and drinking, thirty-two-year-old John Bonham choked to death while reportedly asleep in Jimmy's house. I was in New York City at the Dakota apartment building interviewing John Lennon and Yoko Ono when I heard the news. It sounds cold, but I was becoming slightly immune to the deaths of rock stars—with the exception of the shocking murder of John Lennon two and a half months later—because so many of them had been on such druggy, downward trajectories. But I was really fond of Bonzo, and I was sad. And I knew that now, there would be no chance of a 1980 Led Zeppelin tour. Two weeks later, the three surviving members of Led Zeppelin met with Peter Grant at London's Savoy Hotel and issued the statement that said, in part: "We can no longer continue the way we were." Because of the ambiguity of that statement, speculation ran rampant for months that the band would reunite with another drummer. And even though no one involved would admit it, the three of them did get together and rehearse with other drummers to see if it would work. It didn't. None of the other three band members had the heart for Zeppelin without Bonham. Robert, who during the 1980s told me he "refused to be one of the dying embers of poodle rock," always insisted that there could be no Zeppelin reunion, because, he said, "no one could ever replace Bonzo," and "we weren't going to give anyone the opportunity." John Paul Jones also said, "When John [Bonham] died, there was a big hole in Zeppelin. The Who and the Stones are song-based bands, but Zeppelin wasn't like that. We did things differently every night, and we were all tied to each other onstage. I couldn't even think how to do this without John." Two early and brief "reunion" concerts with the three surviving Zeppelin members—1985's Live Aid concert and Atlantic Records' 40th anniversary in 1988—were abysmal. The band was out of practice, out of time, and out of tune. There was no groove. But most of the audience, who had never seen the group in its heyday, didn't know the difference.

In 1994, Plant and Page did an *Unledded* show together for MTV, then toured with Egyptian musicians and released two albums (all without a very unamused John Paul Jones). The show was good, but without Bonzo, it just didn't have that swing. On January 12, 1995, Jimmy, Robert and John Paul Jones stood together onstage at the Waldorf Astoria's Grand Ballroom (where Jones pointedly thanked "my friends for finally remembering my phone number") for Zep's induction into the Rock and Roll Hall of Fame. Peter Grant died in November of that year. At one point during his solo career, when Robert Plant was unhappy that his band was the opening act for the Who on arena tours, his manager Bill Curbishley (who had managed the Who for years) told me he told Robert, "Here's a phone number of a guitarist. Here's a phone number of a bass player. Call them up and you can headline any stadium anywhere in the world." Rumors of Zeppelin reunions surface as regularly as Elvis Presley sightings. When all three came to New York in 2003 for the premiere of the first reissue of archival live sets (featuring material Page bought from bootleggers, then spent over a year synching up, mixing and re-mastering), reunion buzz started all over again. Those of us who knew Page and Plant wondered if their egos could co-exist for a week's worth of promotional activities, much less a prolonged, reunion concert tour. At the Plaza Hotel for a round of interviews to plug the boxed set, a clear-eyed Jimmy Page still wanted to talk only about the music. "I can understand why we got bad reviews," he said. "We went right over people's heads. One album would follow another and would have nothing to do with what we'd done before. People didn't know what was going on." He referred to the band's reputation as "offstage antics," and said: "We were doing three and a half hour concerts. We unleashed floodgates of music. By the end of that, you come offstage and you're not going back to the hotel to have a cup of cocoa. Of course it was crazy, of course it was a mad life." Later, in another room, Robert said, "How can we be reviled in so many different generations and then find out that we were people's favorite band? We were considered underground, and I've got band members now whose parents wouldn't let them listen to us; they thought it was the devil's music. We questioned the whole order of things, and not just for one or two albums, but for ten years. We took a whole core of people who knew we were nothing like Bobby Goldsboro, or Rod Stewart. Led Zeppelin wasn't an aerobics session. It was dealing with the devil; taking all that beautiful blues music and screwing around with it."

In February 2006, I was having dinner at the Tower Bar in L.A. when Jimmy and Robert appeared and came over and sat down at my table. They stayed for hours. We affectionately reminisced. They refused to tell me why they were together or what they were up to. They teased me mercilessly. They had some drinks. They didn't pick up the check. Some things never change. In 2007, Led Zeppelin "reunited" with Jason Bonham on drums for one concert only at London's O2 Arena in honor of the late Ahmet Ertegun. The tickets were scalped for thousands of dollars. This time, the band rehearsed. They reportedly slowed down some numbers and lowered the key on certain songs so Robert wouldn't have trouble hitting the high notes. Those who were there said it was great. I didn't go. I prefer to remember them the way they were. It's been a long time. The song couldn't possibly be the same.

Three

I first met David Bowie in the fall of 1971 at the New York City offices of RCA Records. He had long blonde hair and was wearing a
floppy hat, baggy, pleated trousers, and, as I recall, yellow patent
leather maryjane shoes. RCA's big acts at the time were Elvis Presley
and John Denver. My husband Richard was working for the label as
a "house hippie"; every record company had someone who was in
touch with what was then called the "counterculture," to tell them
what was what and who to sign. Bowie's manager, Tony Defries, had
sent RCA a vinyl demo of Bowie singing the songs that would eventually become *Hunky Dory*. And, as Richard recalls, the B side of that
demo featured a woman—possibly Dana Gillespie, who Defries also
managed—singing the same songs. The message was clear: pick one.
Richard told the label executives that Bowie was an artist who could
get on the cover of *Rolling Stone*. RCA picked Bowie. Richard also
encouraged RCA to sign the Kinks and Lou Reed—who had left the
Velvet Underground and was temporarily working in Long Island
for his father in some accounting capacity. In the late 1960s, Danny
Fields was Elektra Records' "house hippie" who had signed the
Doors, the MC5 and the Stooges. In 1971, Danny brought Lou to our

apartment a lot. The arrangement was that Richard would try to get him signed to RCA as a solo act and produce his first album.

When Richard worked at Buddah Records, he had an expense account, and now he had one at RCA too, so we were able to throw parties. We had a large, rent-controlled apartment on Manhattan's Upper West Side. I had been unduly impressed by the movie *Performance,* so I had the walls of our apartment painted maroon, brown, and red. We had a sofa where people could sleep. This was unique in the world of struggling rock writers. Most of our friends had, at best, one-room, walk-up apartments. Our building had an elevator. Everyone in this set relied on press parties for free meals. Among those who stayed on our sofa at one time or another were the rock critics Dave Marsh—in from Detroit—Richard Meltzer, and, for quite some time, Lenny Kaye, who became a close friend. This was several years before Lenny started working with Patti Smith. Once, in August, when Lenny had already been with us for months—and by now had moved to the floor, where he slept with his girlfriend—he asked if "we" were going to have a Christmas tree. Clearly, it was time for him to move on. Lester Bangs was an ever-present fixture at our parties; he was occasionally loveable and often drunk, but never both. We had no indication at that time that Lester—as opposed to the more talented Richard Meltzer—would wind up as a legend in the world of rock criticism. Death can do that for a career. We fed and occasionally housed others we thought were our friends until some of them wrote really nasty things about us years later. But we by no means ran a "salon," as it was referred to in various recollections by some people who weren't there. Nor did I wield any sort of "power" over the rock press—which, at that time, consisted of maybe ten people. Before I ever took over Richard's column in *Disc and Music Echo,* I wrote an anonymous newsletter called "Popwire" that was mimeographed on brightly colored paper, and I mailed it to people. It was essentially a gossip sheet—similar to a blog today—about people in the music industry. It created a bit of what today would be called a buzz. Then I began the *Disc* column, which quickly led to a column in the *New Musical Express.* I typed those columns on an electric typewriter (or, when I had been on the road with the Stones, a small portable one), put them in manila envelopes, and went to the main post office on 34th Street after midnight to mail the columns to England to meet my deadlines. I wrote for the rock magazine *Creem*, and later, edited *Hit Parader.* But in the re-telling of this time in some books that will go unnamed here, our house, our parties, and even our feeble attempt at creating a group we called "Collective Conscience" (to serve as "youth" consultants to corporations) has taken on a life of its own— as if it had been a rock writer's version of Gertrude Stein's house on the Rue de Fleurus. Basically, we gave parties. We ordered in Chinese food. I made brownies. The record company paid for it. Richard recalls that if he turned in his expense reports by eleven in the morning, they would give him an envelope with cash in time to deposit it in the bank by noon.

That day in September when we met Bowie, he was with his artfully butch, naturally boisterous wife Angela and his manager Tony Defries, who was one of those questionable, *Expresso Bongo*-type English managers. I started to tell them all about how David should meet the Warhol crowd—well, what was left of the Warhol crowd, Andy himself having moved ever upward in the world of society toward those who had the money to have him paint their portraits. I raved about such Warhol "stars" as Penny Arcade and Wayne County and the "underground" actors and drag queens who had performed in London in *Pork*—the play based on the taped telephone conversations of Brigid Polk. Right on cue, the door opened. In came Tony Zanetta—who "starred" as Warhol in *Pork*. With him were photographer Leee Black Childers, director Tony Ingrassia and actress Cherry Vanilla. David grinned. It might have been the first time I saw him pleased that he was a step ahead, but clearly, it would not be the last.

Having been a devotee of mime artist Lindsay Kemp and Marc Bolan and whatever passed for the underground in London in those days, David had already checked out the *Pork* crowd. And, as this was a group who knew a good score when they saw one, they all had quickly signed up to be part of Defries' MainMan company's so-called "staff." It was an association that would, several years later, contribute to a drug-fueled, dysfunctional operation, and one that would deplete Bowie of millions of dollars.

But in 1971, the future looked bright, the rock and roll possibilities limitless. David had already tried several personae: there were some early bands, and an embarrassing novelty song "The Laughing Gnome." He recorded material that sounded suspiciously like Anthony Newley. Then came the always attention-getting, Englishman's penchant for putting on a dress. He'd had an international hit with the corny "Space Oddity." But his musical heroes were Lou Reed and Iggy Stooge, and I was conveniently in a position to introduce him to both. That night, I arranged a small dinner at the Ginger Man restaurant two blocks from Lincoln Center. Some say if the lie reads better than the truth, go with the lie. But such ridiculous nonsense has been written about that "fateful" evening in retrospective articles and some books by people who, again, weren't there. It was even "fictionalized" in the Todd Haynes–directed movie *Velvet Goldmine*. David Bowie meeting Lou Reed and Iggy Stooge has been made to sound as if it was akin to the coming together of FDR, Stalin and Churchill at Yalta. Of course no one who was there remembers it the same way, but the truth is that it was a fairly sedate, uneventful dinner. There were white tablecloths, steaks, and wine. Lou, who was often socially difficult and none too gregarious in the best of circumstances, was with his then-wife, Bettye. Present too were Richard, Tony Defries, Angela Bowie, and an RCA executive to pick up the check. Towards the end of dinner, I called Danny Fields, who had Iggy Stooge living at his apartment. We went to Max's Kansas City so that David could meet Iggy. David and Iggy instantly hit it off. So much so that the next day Iggy moved into the Warwick Hotel, where Bowie and the MainMan bunch were in residence, running up a sizeable room service bill. A few nights later, the Bowies, Reeds and De-fries came to our apartment for one of those Chinese takeout dinners. What I remember most about that evening was, with Lou watching appreciatively, Bettye go-go danced alone in the living room, someone stole a rare copy of *The East Village Other* with an article about the Velvet Underground from our library, and Lou and David locked themselves into a small room at the back of our apartment while Angela Bowie banged on the door, screeching for them to let her in.

o o o

In November 1971, with much fanfare, the drag queen troupe the Cockettes came to New York for the opening of the musical revue *Tinsel Tarts in a Hot Coma* at the Anderson Theater. In the audience that night were society types like Mica and Ahmet Ertegun, Chessy and Billy Rayner, Gore Vidal with Angela Lansbury, Bobby Short, restaurateur Elaine Kaufman, Diana Vreeland and Bill Blass. Fran Lebowitz was an usher, and claims she was never paid the promised $90 for the job. From then on, if there was a rhinestone or a sequin in rock and roll, you could make a case for tracing it back to the Cockettes. Or to Charles Ludlam, or the Lower East Side and the Theater of the Ridiculous—where John Vaccaro directed Warhol "superstar" Jackie Curtis in the low-camp *Heaven Grand in Amber Orbit*—or *Pork*. Andy Warhol influenced a lot of us in the early 1970s. He snapped Polaroid pictures wherever he went, and his pal Brigid Polk taped all her phone conversations. David Bowie might have been the only one so carried away by Andy that he wrote a song about him. But I admit I kept a cassette recorder on my night table, affixed a suction cup on the receiver of my telephone and taped most of my phone conversations. I took Polaroid pictures. Richard was one of the first—along with the filmmaker Michel Auder (who was married to Warhol "superstar" Viva) and rock photographer Bob Gruen—to have a video camera that came with the Sony portapak, reel-to-reel tape recorder. We taped and photographed our parties. Evenings out involved shlepping all of this equipment with us. Eventually, we got fed up and abandoned the whole thing. But we still have boxes and boxes of all this stuff. We have reels of videotape, including, but not limited to: Lou Reed and Richard Meltzer on our sofa, singing an acoustic version of "Walk on the Wild Side" several years before Lou recorded it on *Transformer*; Lou and Velvet Underground chanteuse Nico rehearsing in our living room in 1971 for the first Velvet Underground reunion (to be held in the winter of 1972 in Paris); former Velvet Underground co-founder John Cale in London, conducting a rehearsal with the Royal Philharmonic Orchestra; Ray Davies visiting us in our London hotel room; and a birthday party at David and Angela Bowie's London house in the winter of 1972.

In December 1971, Lou Reed, Richard and I flew to London for the recording of Lou's debut solo album. Lou had some great songs planned for the album—"Walk on the Wild Side," "Lisa Says" and "Berlin." They signed up session musicians, including a variety of guitarists. You could always count on Lou to get excited about a guitar sound. He could talk for hours about amplifiers and cables and microphones. The three of us stayed at the Four Seasons Inn on the Park for four weeks and ran up a huge bill sent directly to RCA Records. Lou's room was down the hall from ours, and there were many—*many*—long nights when he just sat in our room, droning on for hours. As I recall, he was drinking a lot. Valium may also have been part of the equation. He was often paranoid. He talked extremely slowly. He could be nasty. Of course you couldn't have one without the other; those great songs had to come from somewhere, and more often than not, it was anger. During the day, Richard and Lou would go off to Morgan Studios to record the album, and I had lots of free time to wander and play in London. I went shopping with John Cale's wife Cynderella—formerly of the GTOs, the California girl art-rock group put together by Frank Zappa. I did interviews with Ray Davies and John Cale. I hung out with our friend Richard Williams, the editor of *Melody Maker*, host of the TV show *Old Grey Whistle Test*, and author of *Out of His Head*, a biography of the legendary "wall of sound" producer Phil Spector.

We'd only been in London about a week when David Bowie phoned to invite us all to his house for his birthday dinner. I asked him to please not have any Scotch on hand, as Lou was decidedly more fun without it. When we arrived, David greeted us at the door with a brand-new look: the black and gray jumpsuit, red patent leather boots and the short spikey orange hair. Ergo: Ziggy Stardust. I burst out laughing. So, I noted, you've gone from "ground control to Major Tom" and *2001* to *A Clockwork Orange*. He laughed a wicked cackle with a full display of his (then) rotting teeth. (Of course as soon as he had the first flush of success, he got new choppers—as did much of the gang from MainMan.) He dangled a bottle of Scotch provocatively at Lou. My heart sank. It was going to be a long night. I recall that he and Angela lived in a house that had a large, circular staircase that led to nowhere. Their house was full of people: his friends Daniela Palmer and Freddy Moretti—who designed David's costumes—the musical composer Lionel (*Oliver!*) Bart (this explained the Anthony Newley influence), and Angela, who was in the kitchen, cooking. Later that night, the Bowies, their friends, Lou, Richard and I all went to the gay dance club El Sombrero. When Richard and I left several hours later, Lou and David were on the dance floor, slow-dancing.

My best friend, the music columnist and *Rock Encyclopedia* author Lillian Roxon, came to London. We went shopping on the King's Road, and went to the just-opened Hard Rock Cafe to get a hamburger. At that time, London didn't have anything like the restaurant scene that came years later. We were lucky to occasionally get a decent meal (on RCA) at San Lorenzo on Beauchamp Place or Mr. Chow's in Knightsbridge. I bought blue suede sandals at Zapata—Manolo Blahnik's first, tiny shop on Cheyne Walk—and maroon suede, knee-high platform boots at the Chelsea Cobbler. After finishing Lou's album, Richard and I moved to the trendy, but inexpensive Portobello Hotel in Notting Hill, which was not yet a fashionable area. John Cale was staying there too. After the breakup of the Velvet Underground, Richard had tried to get John a job at RCA, but the idea went nowhere when, at his first interview with RCA executives, John suggested that he do the job from inside an oxygen tank. One night in the Portobello, we were awakened by the sounds of screaming as John, crawling naked down the hallway, bit the leg of some passerby. This was not unusual behavior for many of the musicians that we knew at that time. While we were still in London, Richard and I went to Better Books at 136 Charing Cross Road to videotape a reading with Warhol poet Gerard Malanga and his opening act, Patti Smith, who performed her poem about Jesse James. And Lou did not record "Walk on the Wild Side" on that solo, self-titled debut album.

After Lou's debut solo album came—and went—Lou asked David Bowie to produce his next album. We learned this news literally the day before Richard was set to fly to London to work on the record that would eventually become *Transformer* and include Lou's only mainstream hit (but by no means his best song), "Walk on the Wild Side." While Lou's solo debut had been difficult to make and didn't turn out the way either Lou or Richard envisioned, I was fiercely loyal to Richard and royally pissed off at Lou. I stopped speaking to, and writing about, both Bowie and Lou for a while. Of course, teaming up with Bowie—whose star was on the rise—made perfect sense for Lou, whose solo career had not taken off. But horror stories filtered out from those *Transformer* recording sessions—that Bowie's guitarist Mick Ronson was doing all the work and David had to console and placate Lou for hours on end—and it helped ease any of my longterm bitterness. Despite the hit song "Walk on the Wild Side," Lou veered into dodgy territory. He embraced a tacky glamrock phase with messy makeup and tottering high heels. It was sad and inappropriate for one of rock and roll's greatest songwriters. Meanwhile, Bowie's Ziggy persona took off in England, where British fans were entranced at Bowie's performance of "Starman" on TV on *Top of the Pops*—with a tight closeup of his face. The whole Ziggy shtick— the makeup, costumes, feather boas, jockstraps, mimicking going down on Mick Ronson onstage—was cringeworthy to some of us in New York, but drew a generation of glitter queens dressed just like Ziggy to David's shows. It sent him on his way to fame, fortune, success, drugs, retirement, more success, more drugs, more fame, some absolutely great albums and retirement once again. Over the years I did many, many interviews with David. They ranged from lucid, funny, charming and insightful, to strange encounters and mumbled gibberish. He was rarely dull—except for the period when he rode around in a convertible, making sure he was photographed giving some sort of salute while extolling Hitler. Or when he was coked out of his mind in the Plaza Hotel with Jimmy Page, watching Kenneth Anger films. Or when he looked like a skeleton backstage with John Lennon and Yoko Ono at the Grammys in 1975 in New York City. Or once, when we were in San Diego or Phoenix, I can't remember which, and our scheduled interview never got done because he literally was making no sense. Then, from an adjoining room, out came a surprise: Iggy, who was also speaking in tongues. This was around the time they both decided to clean up, detox, and together, they departed for Berlin—the heroin capital of the world. Still, Bowie made two of his best albums there: *Heroes* and *Low*. David used to tell me that he wasn't really a rock star, he was an actor playing a rock star. I always thought he was a rock star playing an actor playing a rock star. He had a whole philosophy that he had clearly thought out and would trot out during interviews. "To create an art movement," he said, "you have to set something up and then destroy it. Do what the Dadaists or the Surrealists did. Complete amateurs who were as pretentious as hell . . . create as much ill feeling as possible. Then you have a chance of creating a movement. You'll only have a movement if you have a rebellious cause. And you can't have a rebellious cause when you're the most well-loved person in the country. What you've got there is . . . well, a chance of being the most well-loved person in the country."

In the summer of 1972, David invited a bunch of American journalists to come see his "Ziggy Stardust and the Spiders from Mars" concert at the Friars Club in Aylesbury, outside of London. I couldn't resist. Performing separately in London that same weekend were Lou Reed, the Stooges, and the high-energy, roots rock band the Flamin' Groovies, who Richard had produced a few years earlier at Buddah Records. In addition to David, MainMan was now "handling" Lou and Iggy, and in the famous photo of the three of them taken that weekend by Mick Rock in the Dorchester Hotel, David looks like a gorgeous vampire. As for all the talk about his "bisexuality," I always thought it was fun, no big deal, a clever marketing ploy, or all of the above. Years later he would tell me, "People ask me if I'm bisexual and I tell them it's none of their business. It's so trite, and I will not give in. I think I talked about my private life twice. Then statements were thrown at me. But I don't regret any of it. It was a way for me to get my music over. On the other hand, I was an experimenter. Particularly during those years, I was experimenting with my emotional life. I threw myself a test of absorbing every possible experience that I could while I was young, with no realization of what happens later."

By the mid-1970s, the symbiosis that marked Bowie's relationship with Lou had fully embraced Iggy, who had dyed his hair platinum blonde, was supported by MainMan, and was rumored to be taking heroin with the rest of the Stooges in the Hollywood Hills. Leee Black Childers had been dispatched by MainMan to be the Stooges' "minder," and it couldn't have been a pleasant task. On my recommendation, Leee had initially installed the Stooges in the Beverly Hills Hotel, but either unpaid bills, slovenly habits, bad behavior or all of the above forced the band to move into their own house, where they rehearsed for shows that never materialized. The entire MainMan staff was living the high life—lavish hotel suites, catering, plenty of drugs—and traveling hither and yon. Years later, Bowie would tell me, "I didn't choreograph the MainMan situation. I'm not quite the mastermind people would have me be. Like a fool, I thought Defries would be a good manager. It wound up as 'We are MainMan, and we also have David Bowie.' I was supposed to be the star; my money ended up being the star. It wasn't a pleasant time of my life." And many years later, when Iggy was in better shape, he told me, "You know, when I met you and a lot of people from New York, well, you know where I come from [a trailer park outside of Detroit, Michigan], and I was thrown into a scene that was very . . . mondo. I think it turned me a little bit evil." Still, the records he made with Bowie, specifically *The Idiot* and *Lust for Life*, are among his best. And as for his association with Bowie, he told me, "Bowie didn't have an influence on me other than friendship. Friendship is an underrated influence in these modern times. Basically, David and I exchanged information. It's great to meet somebody else who thinks they're always right."

o o o

Some say the 1970s New York rock scene really started in the 1960s with the Velvet Underground. Others think it was when Danny Fields brought the Stooges and the MC5 in from Ann Arbor, Michigan, in 1968. Or with Lou Reed's reconfigured Velvet Underground at Max's Kansas City in 1970. Or with the opening of CBGB's in 1973. What really happened is that several things happened, all at once. But what no one can dispute is that in early 1972, when the New York Dolls performed every Tuesday night at the Oscar Wilde Room in the Mercer Arts Center (in the Broadway Central Hotel), the 1970s New York rock scene was born.

In 1971, the lower Broadway area was abandoned at night. We used to joke that it felt like Poland. The Mercer Arts Center (on Mercer between Bleecker and West 3rd Street) was a place where people went, usually after eleven p.m., to hang out, drink, pick people up, and watch avant-garde plays and "happenings." The appropriately named Oscar Wilde Room was a little theater: there was a stage that was no higher than a platform, and there were seats for the audience. Performers included the drag queen Wayne County and actress/ singer Ruby Lynn Reyner. But mostly, everyone went to see the New York Dolls. At this time, there was still such a thing as a "New York sensibility." Every new thing—whether it was fashion or music or theater or a magazine—was not discovered, or available, or co-opted, or perverted, by everyone. Very few writers wrote about what was still considered "underground." Before they were the Ramones— whose singer Joey had an early glamrock band called Sniper—the Ramones went to see the Dolls. Patti Smith read poetry as an opening act for the Dolls. Richard Hell and Tom Verlaine went to the Mercer to see the Dolls before they formed their own band the Neon Boys, the precursor to Television. In the dismal atmosphere of the early 1970s, while the rest of the country was lulled by "soft rock," or numbed by radio rock bands—like Styx and REO Speedwagon—in New York City, every Tuesday night was New Year's Eve with the New York Dolls.

Charles Barkley has said that in basketball, the statistics don't always show who had an impact on the game. The Dolls had an impact on the game. With their extraordinarily sloppy, R&B-style songs, funky, glammed-up appearance and sophisticated performances, they were the wittiest rock band that ever stepped on a stage. Ultimately misunderstood, unsuccessful and self-destructive, they were initially the house band for those who loved the nightlife, and what was left of the Warhol set. To see the New York Dolls in the midst of the rest of the rock world at that time was like seeing Miles Davis in a roomful of Wynton Marsalises. They were immediately appreciated by a handful of rock critics—James Wolcott, Ellen Willis, Robert Christgau, and Paul Nelson, who signed them to Mercury Records. Still, there were the predictable music snobs who said they "couldn't play"—that they were a low-rent version of the Rolling Stones. In fact, "couldn't play" is a description that certainly had once been levelled at the Rolling Stones. And "couldn't sing" was most definitely a term that had been applied to Bob Dylan. Comparisons to the Stones were understandable given lead singer David Johansen's androgynous sex appeal. But the level of wit was on another planet. Jagger, albeit more successful, never sang anything like "I ain't no golden shower queen." (The Dolls certainly appealed to David Bowie, who loved them, and for better or worse, we certainly know who he wound up influencing. And there would have been no Sex Pistols had the Dolls not come first. But that comes later.) In an early interview, David Johansen asked me, "What is all this talk about being musically proficient? I saw *Monterey Pop* and if you look at the Who or Janis Joplin at that stage of their careers, well, we're just as musically proficient as they were then. Besides, we know in our hearts that we're hipper than anybody else." The New York Dolls never had a confidence problem.

In 1971, the New York Dolls—David Johansen, Johnny Thunders, Sylvain Sylvain, Billy Murcia, and Arthur Kane Jr.—came to my apartment for the first of what would be many interviews. They collectively wore: platform wedgie shoes, hot-cha green-trimmed sunglasses, sequined hot pants, transparent chiffon blouses, and pink denim overalls covered by a dragon-appliquéd apron. (My father, a lawyer and a judge and a serious man who re-read Proust every summer, lived across the hall from me at the time. He found my life amusing. When the Dolls came to visit me, my father phoned me later that night to say he had seen "my friends" in their full regalia in the elevator. It was just assumed that they would have been visiting no one else in the building.) "When we formed our band, we knew we had the best rock and roll band," David told me. "When the record companies come to see us, I think they get turned on. Their wives get drunk and start dancing and they go crazy. But then they think about their kids . . . and that's what stops them. They start thinking about their kids."

David was swagger personified. He wore pumps. Or a tube top, shorts, knee-length leather boots and a cowboy hat. Apropos of nothing, he'd burst into "Diamonds Are a Girl's Best Friend" in the middle of some rock number. Or he'd introduce a song as "inspired by Batista, who used to run Cuba." Once, onstage at the Whisky in Los Angeles, he pointed to a table and shouted out, "At the celebrity table over there—[Manson girl] LINDA KASABIAN!!" He'd dedicate a song to Kitty Genovese—a girl who screamed as she was stabbed to death in Queens while no one came to help. In the South, or even west of the Mercer Arts Center, David's onstage patter sailed above the heads of the audience, much of the press, and, quite possibly, his own band. "I'll say something fantastically funny, like I can't believe I said it," David told me once in Los Angeles, "and maybe I'll get a snicker from the fifteenth row. I think maybe the ones who get the jokes are too stoned, and the rest of them are tourists. I guess I'll have to go to a Grand Funk concert and see how they relate to the masses." I said it was different in New York. "It's *really* different in New York," he agreed. "The audience at the Oscar Wilde Room is so fabulous, we're just a reflection of them. That dance floor . . . well, all my favorite people were out there, so we had to be incredible. I'm still doing them. I've taken them on the road."

In those days, no one went to a gym. We all smoked. No one went to Brooklyn; there was no reason to. We didn't talk about money except to bemoan not having any. No one—ever—mentioned, or cared about, the stock market. I wore huge sunglasses. I wore black and maroon nail polish and carried Bakelite pocketbooks. Along with others, I imitated the campier styles of the 1940s. Platform shoes were the norm and, at 5'2", I loved being tall. Well, taller. No matter what time of day or night, if I had to call a musician, my opening line would be, "Did I wake you up?" I never went to sleep before four a.m., woke up around noon, and spent half the day on the phone discussing what had gone on the night before and what was planned for the night ahead. We hung out. We didn't use the term "rock star." Of course, because of the Beatles and the Rolling Stones, the concept was there. But the use of the term—the way people use it today to refer to the likes of Bill Clinton or Oprah Winfrey, as if it was the highest thing someone could be—was unheard of. To be a musician was not considered a good career choice. Most of them went into it because they felt they had no choice. And to the rest of the world, to be a rock musician then, was still thought to be one step above a criminal.

On August 9, 1973, my severely asthmatic friend Lillian Roxon died. After not hearing from her for twelve hours—an unheard of amount of time for people who spoke four times a day—I broke into her apartment with the police and discovered her dead body. I arranged her funeral, and packed up her belongings to ship back to her family in Australia. I was devastated. I needed to get out of town. I decided to join the circus and accompanied the New York Dolls to Hollywood. The band drew stares at the airport. They were considered freaks. I was writing an article about the Dolls in L.A. for *Creem* and for *New Musical Express*, so I hung out with the band for most of the week. They were booked into the Whisky on Sunset Strip, and it was a scene. The groupie grapevine had been buzzing for weeks about the imminent arrival of the Dolls. The girls from *Star* magazine were out in full force. David Johansen was bored and lonely and too sophisticated for this bunch. In New York, he was living with Cyrinda Foxe, who was a Marilyn Monroe lookalike, one of the inspirations for Bowie's song "Jean Genie," and a role model for her contemporaries Angela Bowie and Debbie Harry. But she was having a moment as the "trois" in the Bowie ménage, and did not accompany the Dolls on this trip. I recall David drunkenly calling her, imploring her not to run off with the Bowies. She did anyway. (Years later, she permanently ran off with what, at the time, seemed to her a much better offer, and wound up as Steven Tyler's wife—but that's another story.) David and I just sort of gravitated towards each other. It was a like-minded sensibility, nothing sexual, and it didn't hurt that I was staying in a patio room at the Beverly Hills Hotel, as opposed to the funkier Continental Hyatt House on Sunset where the Dolls occupied several rooms. Steve Paul, who had run the rock club The Scene and was now managing Johnny and Edgar Winter and Rick Derringer, was also at the Beverly Hills Hotel. He was residing in splendor in Bungalow 5—the 1960s home away from home for the likes of Elizabeth Taylor and Marilyn Monroe. Steve had waited all his life, he said, to be able to stay in Bungalow 5, and now he wanted to give a party to celebrate the achievement. He thought it would be chic to serve just chocolate soufflés, strawberries and champagne. We rounded up whoever was in town—John Cale, Cynderella, Jonathan Richman, Danny Fields, Rick Springfield, Rick and Liz Derringer, Lance, Kevin and Delilah Loud from *An American Family*, and, of course, the Dolls. David, who had impeccable taste, immediately warmed to the pink bungalows and the luxurious smell of the jacaranda and hyacinth on the winding paths of the hotel. So he just sort of moved in to my room for a few days. "Passed out" would be more like it, and, as he put it, it was a way to get away from what he described as the "bitches" at the Hyatt House. "I don't mind them hanging around," he said about the groupies, "as long as they don't get *traumatic*." During an interview we did at a cabana above the pool (videotaped by Bob Gruen, bits of which made their way into Gruen's Dolls documentary), David wore sunglasses, a white bangle bracelet and a red nylon Speedo. I asked if the Dolls' first trip to Hollywood had met his expectations. "Well, they have a definite style here," he said. "Low camp. I guess when you're in New York, everything you get from L.A. is so filtered—so it sounds more glamorous than it really is. Although," he looked around the Beverly Hills Hotel pool, "I must say *this* is very nice. This is *lovely*." It certainly was a far cry from the Hyatt, where the band's rooms were filled with opened suitcases, overflowing with shiny outfits strewn about on the floor. Unmade beds. Beaded necklaces, bangle bracelets and bottles of cheap perfume on top of the Formica dressers. Styrofoam coffee cups filled with stubbed-out cigarettes. Empty beer cans. Room service tables with days' worth of rotting food. Teenage girls. Teenage boys. Drug dealers. "Whenever I go on the road, I feel like Fidel Castro in the Hotel Theresa," David said. "Remember when they were plucking the chickens?"

o o o

One day, in 1973, for no apparent reason, the Mercer Arts Center (and the entire Broadway Central Hotel) collapsed. As in, the building just fell down. Sometime that year, Neil Bogart called Richard and me and asked us to come to either the basement of the Hotel Diplomat or a rehearsal space to see a band he considered signing to his new Casablanca label. He wanted our opinion. I could not believe what I witnessed in that small, cramped, brightly lit space. Four hairy, sweaty boys, wearing makeup and costumes. It was literally like that line from *Spinal Tap*: *"Do you know how much it will cost to dress the band as animals??"* I was appalled that this foursome, dressed as cheap cartoon superheroes, were ripping off the music of the adored New York Dolls. Badly. Without a modicum of wit. I told Neil they should be ashamed of themselves, they'd never make it. That they were, basically, criminals. Richard's opinion: Kiss would make Neil a fortune.

In 1975, after *Transformer* and several other albums, Lou Reed asked Richard to have another go-round at producing one of his albums. By now, Lou was signed to Clive Davis' Arista Records, which was distributed by RCA. Despite the fact that Lou could be difficult, scary, and mean, he was still Lou Reed. The man who wrote "Sweet Jane," which is, in my estimation, perhaps the greatest rock and roll song of all time. He was the songwriter who told me he just wanted to "elevate the form." In one of our many interviews, Lou told me, "I've been studying Delmore Schwartz for years, and his short stories were incredibly clever and succinct, in a very efficient vernacular. And it makes me think of Raymond Chandler, when he said, 'You know, that blonde was as pleasant as a split lip.' They had these amazing images and I just thought, put a drum to that." Of course, Lou admitted, "It's interesting, because it's just a rock and roll song. And you may have contempt for the form, but then you go and stick something into it and expand its horizons, and you get criticized for it twofold."

So in the winter of 1975, Richard and Lou and his then-paramour Rachel (who today might be described as a member of the transgender community) went off to Germany in search of one Manfred Schunke, who had invented "binaural sound"—a process that involved a gray foam head with microphones sticking out of each ear. While in Germany, Lou did concerts that were recorded live, with two of the foam heads hanging above the audience. Lou made phone calls on a daily basis to a New Jersey kennel just to hear his beloved dachshund Baron bark into the phone over the transatlantic wires. He refused to believe Richard's suggestion that he was, in fact, listening to a tape. After not hearing from Richard for almost six weeks, I tracked him down and arranged to meet him in Paris. I walked into L'Hotel—the hotel where, in Room 16, Oscar Wilde had died—to discover my husband twenty pounds thinner and bursting into tears. Apparently, he had been taking a lot of over-the-counter German speed. It had been a rough trip. According to Richard, whenever Lou would put on his sunglasses at midnight, it would signal the beginning of Lou yelling at his "minder" from the record company that they were doing "nothing" for him. Once, Lou was so incensed that he told Richard that he threatened the president of the English record company with a knife, then called Richard to come and get the knife before the arrival of the police. Of course, again, nobody who was there remembers this the same way. Back in New York, they finished up the recording that would ultimately become *Street Hassle*—one of Lou's best albums. Bruce Springsteen and Joe Perry, also working in separate rooms at the Record Plant, stopped by and played on some tracks. The then-president of Arista Records, Clive Davis, who prides himself on his ability to pick hit singles, showed up at the studio once, said, "Hoist your petard," and left.

One night in the mid-1970s, Lou and I walked into CBGB's before Television was about to play. Lou was carrying a cassette recorder. Television's Tom Verlaine was, quite possibly, even more paranoid than Lou. He muttered to me, "What's he doing with that tape recorder? Should I ask him to keep it in the back?" I suggested that he ask Lou to take out the cassette, or the batteries. Tom said to Lou, "Hey buddy, whatcha doing with that machine?" Lou replied that the batteries were run down. "Oh yeah?" Tom said. "Well then, you won't mind if I keep it in the back." Lou handed him the cassette, then said, "You'd make a lousy detective, man, you didn't even notice the two extra cassettes in my pocket." Tom was not amused. "Okay, then give me the machine, I'll keep it in the back for you." Lou handed it over, then looked at me and burst out laughing: "Can you believe that guy?" he asked. I said that there were many musicians who would be thrilled if they thought Lou Reed wanted to tape them. I mean, it wasn't as if Lou didn't know how to write a song. Of course, years later, I wondered if Tom would be mad had he known that I gave Bono and the Edge some of those Television tapes that, like some fan of the Grateful Dead, I made nightly at CBGB's. Of course he would have been. I mean, just listen to U2's guitar sound.

In 1976, Lou and I had a New York telephone conversation (also the title of one of his best solo songs), and I reprinted it verbatim in one of our rock magazines. This was the sort of thing that you could only get away with if you yourself were editing a small rock magazine. Basically we discussed Clive Davis: Lou said Clive wouldn't have signed and hugged him for a publicity photo if he wasn't "white." Lou thought it would be funny for me to write that, but added that he didn't think Gil Scott-Heron would find it amusing. I asked him what he would be doing had he not gone into this line of work. He said he'd either be selling shoes at Thom McAn's or he'd be really bitchy. As opposed to the way he was normally? I asked. We segued onto a discussion of his concerts, and past performances that included his pretending to shoot up during "Heroin." Lou said, "If they want to see someone make believe he's shooting up, and they get their rocks off at age fifty, well, at that time in my life I was happy to stand there like a ghoul and do it." Did he have contempt for his audience? "Certain segments of it, yes. That's why I'm playing smaller halls. I hope the barbarians won't be there. I want the show to be for people who aren't interested in my pretending to shoot up during 'Heroin.'" Lou told me he had moved apartments several times in the past year, that he'd gotten an incredible bargain on a loft, but then learned that it was an incredible bargain because it turned out to be above a methadone clinic. "It wasn't a place for me and my dachshund." He admitted that he took the Baron everywhere. Even to the recording studio. "I brought him down there, but just to take a look, because he gets cranky."

By 1980, Lou was engaged to Sylvia Morales, a woman who was rumored to have been a former dominatrix, and they invited us to their wedding. I went. Richard skipped the ceremony, which was held at Lou's apartment on Christopher Street with a reception afterwards at the Greenwich Village restaurant One If by Land, Two If by Sea. At the restaurant, in elaborate, drunken detail, I told Lou's father how important I felt Lou was to the culture. He listened quietly as I went on and on about how, if there was a space capsule a thousand years from now, Lou's "Sweet Jane" and "I'll Be Your Mirror" should be inside it to truly show the greatness of rock and roll. Not Jimi Hendrix, not the Beatles, not Bob Dylan. Just Lou. Mr. Reed listened. Then he looked at me. "You know what makes me happy?" he asked. "Guess what Lou and Sylvia wanted for their wedding present?" I waited. "Storm windows," he said.

o o o

We started *Rock Scene* magazine because Richard thought it would be amusing to do a magazine of just photos and bitchy, funny captions, like the "Eye" section in *Women's Wear Daily*. It was an irreverent, cult music magazine that documented and glamorized the rise of glamrock and punk rock. The first issue, in March 1973, had David Bowie on the cover, and the magazine lasted until the end of the decade. Richard was on the masthead as Managing Editor, and Doug Thompson, a name he made up, was the News Editor. A heading on the cover read "Alternative to the alternatives," which meant it was not *Creem* or *Crawdaddy*, which were the alternatives to *Rolling Stone*. The concept of only captions was an attempt to avoid large writing tasks. Longer articles came later. Part fanzine, part tabloid, *Rock Scene* was where you could see what happened before or after the show, particularly at parties and backstage. I used to drag Bob Gruen and Leee Black Childers around backstage to take the pictures. Richard, Lenny Kaye and I put the magazine together at our dining room table over the course of a few nights every other month. Then we shipped the issue—with all the photographs—to the publisher in Connecticut. We never thought anyone saw it other than the crowd at Max's, then later, at CBGB's. But it made everyone in that small scene think they were huge stars. Among the photo spreads were "David and Cyrinda At Home," "A Subway Ride with The Ramones," and "David Byrne in The Supermarket." Peter Hujar took the photos for "At Home with Fran Lebowitz," which I "art directed"—except that no one called anything in any rock magazine "art direction." Peter and I moved her few pieces of furniture around so that in the photos, her one-room apartment appeared to be four rooms. There were plenty of backstage photo spreads of Bowie, or Roxy Music, or the Stones, or me on tour with Led Zeppelin or Aerosmith. Wayne County wrote an advice column. While Wayne's onstage material—"Rock and Roll Enema," "It Takes a Man to Be a Woman"—escaped mainstream attention, in *Rock Scene* he was a very big deal. Years later, as Jayne County, he sent us postcards from Germany describing his sex change operation in graphic detail. He thought we would be providing a public service to baby transsexuals if we printed them. We declined. Clearly, she was way ahead of her time. And, there can be no doubt that years later, *Hedwig and the Angry Inch* was more than just a bit influenced by Wayne's memoir, *Man Enough to Be a Woman.*

We had a regular column called "Know Your Rock Writer" which featured, among others, James Wolcott, Cameron Crowe, and Lester Bangs. Lillian Roxon wrote a food column. Robert Plant won our "Chest-O-Rama" contest for "Best Chest." Coverlines, at one time or another, included "Holly Woodlawn: The New Cher?" and "The Stones Have Lunch!" Every so often, we would try to hold an editorial "meeting," with friends such as Danny Fields, Donald Lyons and Fran Lebowitz—all of whom would suggest potential coverlines. Some of Fran's were: "Average White Band—I'll Say," "Bryan Ferry Ill—In Quality Hospital," and "Queen, Just Another Bunch of Limey Queers." My favorite fan letter to *Rock Scene* was: *"Dear Richard, Your magazine sucks. I'm tired of glitter. Glitter nauseates me. My god, your magazine is depraved. Please, for the sake of keeping mankind di-*

vided into two sexes, stop exploiting the actions of a handful of musically innocuous homosexuals. Name withheld, Medford, New York."

Rock Scene was printed on cheap paper and the ink came off on your hands. The few ads we got were for things like "The Astonishing Power of Automatic Mind Control!!" It quickly became a shameless promotional vehicle for me. There wasn't an issue without numerous photos of me, grinning, with Freddie Mercury or Bryan Ferry or at a party for the Rolling Stones. A picture of me and Bowie and Iggy and Danny Fields in the back room of Max's was accompanied by the caption: *"Lisa and Dave can hardly contain their delight as Iggy and Danny Fields discuss an old Holiday Inn hotel bill."* And then, in the middle of nowhere, we'd stick in a review of something we liked—like cabaret singers Mabel Mercer and Bobby Short at the Carlyle and St. Regis Hotels. Patti Smith was one of *Rock Scene*'s main subjects, and an avid fan. "I read some of the stuff that's written about me," she told me very early on in her rock and roll incarnation, "but I think people like to hear the human side. The rest is for school. I mean, they can put books out about that stuff if they want to analyze it. When they start writing that stuff about Norman Mailer's white negro and penal envy, I don't even know what they're talking about. I just like to look at *Rock Scene* or *Creem* to see what I had on, or if the pictures are good."

Years after *Rock Scene* was out of print, musicians—Michael Stipe, Duran Duran's Nick Rhodes, Pearl Jam's Jeff Ament, Thurston Moore, Chrissie Hynde and many others—would tell me that they grew up trying to find it in their small towns, reading it, and wanting to come to New York and go to those parties and backstages that they saw in those grainy black and white photos. It's like that old joke about the Velvet Underground: *Rock Scene* didn't have many readers, but it seemed as though everyone who bought it formed a band. (It also had a little-known, but far-reaching influence. We once had a photo caption identifying Lenny as "rock genius Lenny Kaye." Apparently, the fledgling fashion photographer Steven Meisel and his pal, transsexual model Teri Toye, were *Rock Scene* fans, and thought this so hilarious that they would go around pronouncing certain things "Genius!!" as a dramatic, Diana Vreeland–like declaration. It was the first time that this term was used in the fashion world as an adjective, and Meisel's influence in the 1980s was such that it caught on—with models, hairdressers, makeup artists—and it was only a matter of time before it was everywhere.

o o o

When Bowie first came to New York he wanted to go to Max's Kansas City to see Andy Warhol, not realizing that by then, Andy had moved on from Max's back room to . . . oh, I don't know, certainly well on his way to the Reagans. But in the early 1970s, when I went practically every night—because if you didn't, you felt as though you were missing something—Max's was still fun. It was filled with the likes of Lou Reed and David Johansen and Cyrinda Foxe, Warhol regulars like the witty Dorothy Dean and Donald Lyons, who famously said, "No one ever goes to Max's when they're happy." And Lillian Roxon and Fran Lebowitz and Ruby Lynn Reyner and Danny Fields and Warhol "starlets" Geraldine and Maria Smith, Donna Jordan and Jane Forth. Patti Smith has written about how she never felt that she really belonged there, but I recall her being there almost every night. After all, she dated Bobby Neuwirth and Sam Shepard and those guys were welcome anywhere. Years later, photographer Steven Meisel told me that as a teenager, he and his friend Richard Sohl (who would later play piano in Patti Smith's band) would come in from Long Island and stand outside and watch people go in and out. We sat in the booths with the bowls of the grayish white, chalk-like chickpeas on red, polyester-clad tables and some sort of rough wall covering that felt like mouse hair. But by the time bands started playing upstairs at Max's, it was almost an afterthought. The fake Velvet Underground (with lead singer Doug Yule, the band that Danny Fields called "the Velveteens") and Wayne County all, at one time or another, performed upstairs. So, apparently, did Bob Marley—although I must have missed that night. And Bruce Springsteen. Most infamous and memorable were the Stooges shows, especially when Iggy fell on broken glass. Or cut his chest until it bled just to get a reaction. Or threw up. Years later, Iggy told me, "In my live work, I was going for the quick thrill, rather than spend time concentrating on my voice. I figured I'd get on, make as many quick movements as I could, dance my ass off for five minutes, then move into the insult portion of the evening. Then, at the end, create some kind of chaos until the forty-five minutes were up." But no one really went to Max's for the bands. Nothing upstairs could ever compete with that crowd downstairs. Towards the end of Max's, bands like Tuff Darts or Lance Loud's Mumps played there, and the place was on its way out. But for a while, we all felt as though Max's was the center of everything. Until it wasn't.

Then one day in 1974, guitarist Tom Verlaine, who had formed Television with the writer/bassist Richard Hell, wandered into a tiny, ratty club next door to a flophouse on the Bowery. He asked owner Hilly Kristal if his band could perform there. Hilly had wanted to showcase country and western music—hence the CBGB, which stood for Country, Bluegrass and Blues—but he reluctantly agreed. Later, Hilly would tell me, "Television was terrible. And the Ramones were even worse." CBGB's was a dump, but it was our dump. Many of us who went there on a regular basis were so wary of the unsanitary conditions, we only drank beer straight out of the bottle. Hilly's dog Jonathan was always slobbering, or asleep, or both, on the floor by the front desk at the entrance. It's hard to imagine now, but often, after midnight and desperate with hunger, we would order and actually eat hamburgers cooked on a questionable grill and served with potato chips on paper plates.

CB's has been well chronicled as a graffiti-laden, long railroad-like room with a pool table, long bar, tables and chairs, and a disgusting restroom downstairs. The backstage area, such as it was, consisted of a few rooms with no locks on the doors, some sagging, filthy sofas, and not much else. The backstage door led into an alley strewn with broken bottles and needles and worse. If you were with a band that had what passed for a soundcheck on the day of a show, you arrived in the afternoon and were greeted with the smell of stale beer and cigarettes, not unlike any bar in any city, anywhere in the world. Except that there was an undercurrent of change in this club that made us feel we were taking part in bringing rock and roll out of its doldrums. We were naive enough, at that time, to think that this would change the world. The music of the 1960s actually had changed the world; in the 1970s, the New York bands were just trying to change it back. And after all the mellow, big business rock coming out of Los Angeles, and the fluffy hot pink and orange concoction that had been David Bowie, bands like Patti Smith and the Ramones and Television were our own little black and white eight millimeter movies that affected the world. It seemed like the center of the rock and roll universe. Until it wasn't.

At that time, New York City was still affordable for misfits who came from somewhere else: Lou Reed from Long Island. Debbie Harry and Patti Smith from New Jersey. Tom Verlaine (né Miller) from Delaware. The Ramones from Queens. They were drawn to Manhattan to get famous, don't think not. But it really was for the music; the music was the scene. "Any group that gets onstage, even at CBGB's," Blondie's Chris Stein told me, "dreams of becoming as big as the Beatles." Still, no one really admitted that they went into this wanting a hit. No one thought they would ever get a hit. There was no radio station that would play this stuff. There was no cable TV. There were no television shows catering to these kinds of rock bands. The closest these bands got to television was when Richard directed the first Blondie video and videotaped the first Ramones set in a studio. Or when Bob Gruen chronicled the New York Dolls with his portapak. Or when Amos Poe filmed nights at CBGB's. The entire New York band scene started with five to ten bands who basically all hated each other, were jealous of each other, had nothing in common with each other, and yet, were lumped together in the mainstream press as "punk."

None of these bands had any money. They all lived in semi-squalor. There was a lot of jockeying for position: who got signed first (Patti), who got more pages in *Rock Scene* (Patti, Television, Ramones) and who had hits (at first, only Blondie). Patti wasn't punk; she defied categorization. Television thought they had more in common with John Coltrane—and their lengthy improvisational jams probably, in actual fact, had more in common with Pink Floyd or the Grateful Dead. Blondie, with its adorable lead singer/star Debbie Harry, started out as an art project by Debbie and Chris Stein—who wanted to create some sort of performance art piece around a blonde lead singer who had pop hits (sound familiar?). Blondie was ahead of their time when they embraced disco and rap. The Talking Heads were an arty trio from the Rhode Island School of Design. If anyone could legitimately be called "punk" it was probably the Ramones, four boys from Queens, none of whose name was Ramone, who wore jeans, leather jackets and sneakers. But then again, I always thought the Ramones' songs sounded melodic—sort of like the Beach Boys on speed. Early on, Tom Verlaine told me, "We definitely are part of a New York atmosphere, but within that atmosphere, there are eighteen ways of saying the same thing. I don't know if we're associated with Patti or not. There are some people who come to see her when she plays with us, and there are some people who come to see us.

Probably more people come to see her, because she has records out. But it's better than being associated with the Ramones." Debbie Harry put it this way: "We never did anything as serious as Patti did. She came from a poet's background, she made a statement, she came on as an artist. Blondie was always more of an entertainment type thing." And years later, singer, songwriter and undisputed leader of the Talking Heads David Byrne gave a left-handed compliment to Alice Cooper. "Before our band was together," he told me, "I got the idea for 'Psycho Killer' from that Alice Cooper album *Billion Dollar Babies*. I thought it was real funny stuff. So I thought, Hey, I can do this. But rather than make it dramatic and theatrical the way Alice Cooper would, I would underplay it and go for what's going on in the killer's mind. It came out okay, it was pretty popular, and so after that I thought, yeah, I guess I can write songs. Being lumped together with the punk scene in New York really annoyed me at the time, and I know it annoyed a lot of other people. But looking back on it, I guess it helped draw attention to all of us." These bands, and CBGB's, immediately rendered everything else that was going on in the rock scene obsolete. Most of these bands cut their hair short, which instantly looked right. I recall one year, maybe two, when Richard and I went to CB's practically every night. Whenever I would return to New York from an out-of-town trip with another band, I would immediately go to CB's, especially to see Television. And always when they performed there on New Year's Eve.

o o o

In November 1973, Lenny Kaye started to accompany Patti Smith on guitar for her poetry readings. These dovetailed into some 1974 cabaret appearances at Reno Sweeney's—the nightclub where Manhattan Transfer and the delightful Genevieve Waite and her junkified husband John (Mamas and the Papas) Phillips also performed. Patti wore a feather boa (yes, she did), sang Kurt Weill's "Speak Low" and paid homage to Anna Magnani and Ava Gardner. This did not catch on. But there would be no holding her back. Patti and Lenny's first record was "Piss Factory," a single that was a little poetry, a little rock and roll. Soon, she and Lenny formed the Patti Smith Group with keyboardist Richard Sohl (who they called DNV after the adorable boy in the Visconti movie *Death in Venice*), guitarist Ivan Kral, and drummer Jay Dee Daugherty. But Patti's energy, her immediate embracing of the form, was euphoric, exhilarating, and new, especially coming from a girl. It wasn't Appollinaire's "Zone," or Allen Ginsberg's "Howl," but the way she punched the air with so much attitude (some said artitude) and combined her poems with the music behind her, created a sense that something was happening here, and whatever it was, it didn't happen often. She was pretentious as hell. She rambled onstage for a long time, then would catch herself with a flirtatious, little girl smile, and say, "There have been a few art forms throughout history: housecleaning, sculpture, rock and roll. Listen, I talk a lot of crap up here. If you don't like it, talk amongst ya." She'd lose me for a minute or two with the Rimbaud rants, or the William Burroughs tributes or the references to Blake (and Richard would move towards the bar) but then she'd reel us back in with "Do the Watusi/do the Mashed Potatoes" or "G-L-O-R-I-A" or "The boy looked at Johnny" or "Jesus died for somebody's sins but not mine." It was joyous rock and roll: part circus, part dance party, part political rally. It could not be explained to tourists. And in fact, you couldn't have had one part of her without the other. Without the cringe-inducing Rimbaud references or the poetry or the earnest rambling prior to the music, it wouldn't have been Patti. No one else had done anything like this before. No woman, certainly.

Because of our friendship with Lenny, and our editing *Rock Scene* and *Hit Parader* magazines, and my syndicated column, syndicated radio show, columns in *Creem* and—a few years later—my column in the *New York Post*, I became close to Patti, who certainly knew how to work the press. But we also became friends. We confided in each other. We did hours and hours—and *hours*—of interviews. Patti always joked that we could do the long, stream-of-consciousness interview or the "snappy, showbiz, Earl Wilson gossip column interview." Basically, to interview Patti was a breeze; all you needed to do was to turn on the tape recorder and she would talk. Words like Haile Selassie and Brian Jones, Sam Shepard and Verlaine and Keith Richards and Simone Signoret would fall easily and constantly from her lips. She claimed that she never thought she would go very far, that she was honored to be in rock and roll. That she just wanted to inspire other people who would see that if she—a fan of Brian Jones and Brigitte Bardot and Keith Richards and Marianne Faithfull and Bob Dylan and Jim Morrison and Jeanne Moreau—could do this, so could they. She wanted people to say "Fuck her" and go off and do it themselves. "It's like Surrealism," she said, sounding very much like David Bowie, who had a similar rap at the time. "Someone writes the manifesto and then other people run with it."

She told me she only thought a show was bad if nothing happened. If she wasn't hated or loved. "If you don't either flower or self-destruct onstage, then there's no point. That's why I always try to do something—even if it's stupid or I make an ass of myself, as long as there's some part of the show where I do some parachuting. I never want to do something like . . . a ranch house. A middle-class show would be a bad show. And it's not always me, it's the guys too; the cool thing about having a group is that one night Lenny might step outside himself and do a really cool solo." And, in 1975, she said, "The neat thing about performing, is that for the first time in my life it gives me the chance to live for the moment. Before, even if I was having sex with someone, we'd be turning down the sheets and I'd be writing the poem in my head."

I traveled with Patti and her band in a van to shows in Boston, Chicago, Cleveland. She was romantically involved at the time with Allen Lanier from the Blue Oyster Cult and then later, with Television's Tom Verlaine. She was always worried about her boyfriends. But when it came to the work department, she had no lack of confidence. On a trip to Cleveland, she told me she and Keith Richards (who she hadn't met) should do a version of her song "Pumping"— that it would be their first hit single. John Cale, who was producing her debut album *Horses*, accompanied us to Boston, where in between her two shows, we went to a restaurant called Clams on the Half Shell. Patti drank warm milk and John accidentally swallowed a Herco guitar pick. She called her mother, who told her that her Washington, D.C., shows were all sold out for the following week, and also, that she had sent her eight new pairs of underwear. A year or two later, when Richard and I went to Paris to see her perform at the Bataclan Club, she said to me, "Wouldn't it be great if we broke really big in Europe?" She talked about how, just four years ago, she sang on the streets of Paris with a fire-eater. Of course, who knows how many times she really did that. But that night in Paris, after what had been a triumphant show at the Bataclan, we arrived in a big limousine at La Coupole when it was still La Coupole and we ate escargots and drank champagne. Record executives picked up the check. It was a long way from CBGB's.

One night in 1976 at the Bottom Line in New York City, the management of the club wouldn't serve Patti a drink while she was onstage. So she walked from the stage across the tables, took my hand, marched me up to the bar with her, had me order her a drink, and took it back with her onstage. Right in the middle of the show. Once, during one of her concerts in Central Park, she asked me to shield her on the side of the stage so she could quickly urinate—out in the open—without anyone in the audience seeing her. It wasn't a big deal; these were just those kinds of times. She told bad jokes. She paraphrased the Declaration of Independence. She improvised a version of the 23rd Psalm. I don't remember her exact words.

Patti was developing her look. It started out as very Bob Dylan in his *Don't Look Back* period. Then there was the addition of a Lion of Judah t-shirt that read "Love Rastafari and Live." Or Ivan Kral's red and black Milwaukee Braves baseball jacket. Wildly colored striped Peruvian wool socks. Moroccan scarves, like the one worn by Keith Richards and the one she gave Bob Dylan when they met, possibly when he showed up at one of her early shows at Gerde's Folk City. (I wondered at the time if someone had told Dylan, there's this girl who's doing you. Much in the same way that someone might have once told Ramblin' Jack Elliott in the 1960s, hey, there's this guy who's doing you.) Patti also wore: a mint green cashmere sweater, a Bob Marley button, a conservative man's black suit, green khaki army surplus pants tied around the ankles, a gray cashmere pullover, and Richard Sohl's cashmere black coat. Not all at once.

We talked a lot about clothes. Patti said she liked getting more money and buying more clothes: "I'm a girl, after all," she said, "but I can never find anything that I like. All that stuff about being beyond gender—that's great for art, but when it comes to *presents* . . . I felt so great yesterday because I was in a store, looking at cashmere sweaters and the man was real snotty and he didn't want me to look at them. So I just said, 'Give me these two—a green one and a black one—and don't even bother to wrap them, just put them in a paper bag.' I turned over all my money; I gave him a hundred dollars. I felt so good. And then I had to walk home. When I have a lot of money I want a mink jacket. Mink, you know, 'cause it's status. That's all. A dark mink jacket, lots of Rastafarian t-shirts and twelve pairs of custom-made pants."

In the mid- to late 1970s, we talked and talked; I must have hundreds of hours of tape with just Patti alone. She told me, "When I met Robert [Mapplethorpe], my ambitions in terms of the outside world were really oriented towards Robert. I wanted to be able to do great work, but it was really because of Robert, because when he was young it was important to him to be famous and to know Andy Warhol. To be accepted, to be adored, to be rich. And it just became a sort of mutual intertwining of work or energy to develop Robert's situation. He was extremely shy and nervous and had difficulty communicating. None of which was my problem." She said that she always thought she had a cool band, but when they got into the studio with John to make her first album, it was hell. She literally said they experienced "agony and ecstasy." Fighting and screaming and pain; but that they became a "real band" after that recording experience. For people who may not know, or understand what it's like within a rock and roll band, no matter who they are, especially in a recording studio, no matter how much they supposedly get along, let me tell you: it's warfare. Whether or not the drums are miked correctly, or if the hi-hat is loud enough or too loud can throw off the entire rhythm of a song. Or, the mood of the drummer. Or worse, the mood of the lead singer if the vocals aren't loud enough. If the guitar sound is too tinny, or the bass isn't solid enough—what might seem like minor details to the uninitiated can make or break a song, a record, a band, a career. A musician is fully capable of pulling you aside, making you sit down and listen to something and telling you in confidence, "Steve's not on this track," even though you don't know, nor do you care, who "Steve" is.

In 1977, after Patti fell from the stage during a concert in Tampa,

I visited her while she was recovering in her apartment at One Fifth Avenue. She wore a neck brace and lay back on her queen-sized bed with its green and white checked sheets and a Moroccan cotton bedspread. I noted at the time (because I always took notes) what surrounded her on the bed and in the room: Styrofoam containers with half-eaten hamburgers, drawings and pages filled with writing, records, books, fan mail, a 1920s picture of Antonin Artaud, a photo of Brian Jones circa the *Beggars Banquet* album, a Brian Jones scrapbook, a pearl-handled stiletto given to her by Dee Dee Ramone, the complete works of Rimbaud, an 8×10 glossy photo of Rimbaud in Paris, the signed works of William Burroughs, a bronze incense burner, Ethiopian baskets filled with silk rags, a royal babuka rug, a globe that glowed in the dark, a Smith Corona typewriter, the complete works of the 16th-century Japanese warrior Ninja Han, a full-color map of Ethiopia, six copies of Jimi Hendrix's *Electric Ladyland*, a hand-combed hair shirt from Abyssinia, several pairs of ballet slippers, twenty-two copies of her new album, *Radio Ethiopia*, a transistor radio, a lion pipe made from the clay found at the bottom of the Mediterranean Sea, postcards with dervishes on them, a cardboard fretboard to learn guitar chords, a box filled with something she called "radiant dirt," thirty photos of Jim Morrison's grave, crime magazines, a Raggedy Ann doll dressed like Patti, old Rolling Stones Hyde Park newspaper headlines, a big empty white bird cage, Charles Lindbergh's autograph (signed, she pointed out, on Brian Jones' birthday), a sacred ritual belt from Morocco given to her by Paul Getty III (the one who'd been kidnapped and had his ear cut off, and had been one of her flings), and a pale green silk party dress. "Some kid must have stolen it from his mother," she said about the dress, "it looks like a Balenciaga." It all spoke volumes to what she was about; her personal art direction was a direct line to her art. She and I sat there and she talked in a perfectly normal voice, straightforward, strong and direct. And then, the phone rang. It was her new boyfriend, Fred

"Sonic" Smith, the original guitarist of the MC5, calling from Detroit. She said, "Hi honey," and in an instant, her voice had turned into giggly, girlish mush.

Patti wrote me letters and sent postcards from various tours. In Cannes, she said the boys in her band were in heaven, because all the girls were models. She said she hadn't left her room. She seemed lonely. And so, to those of us who knew her well, it wasn't a surprise when, at the height of her fame, after her only Top 10 hit "Because the Night" (the song she co-wrote with Bruce Springsteen), she moved to Detroit to start a new adventure: to marry Fred Smith and raise a family. She disappeared for fourteen years. But, as she wrote in letters to me during that time, she was still working on her art.

o o o

In 1976, I was traveling to London on a regular basis to do interviews with Rod Stewart or Pete Townshend or Peter Gabriel or Freddie Mercury for my *Inside Track* syndicated radio show. I stayed at the Ritz Hotel, had dinners with Bryan Ferry at Mr. Chow's or San Lorenzo, and scoured flea markets looking for 1940s Clarice Cliff painted dishes to add to my ever-growing collection; at that time, they cost next to nothing. It was on one such trip, in December, that I saw Rupert Murdoch boarding my Pan Am morning flight. He had just bought the *New York Post*. I was sitting in what was the forerunner of business class—a section between first class and coach—and he, of course, was in first. My syndicated column was carried in the newspapers he owned in San Antonio and Boston, and my friend, the late Lillian Roxon, had worked for him as the New York correspondent for his *Sydney Morning Herald*. I never did anything like this before (or since), but I asked the stewardess (they were definitely called stewardesses then) to bring him a note that said some of his newspapers carried my column, and if he wasn't sleeping or working on the flight, I would like to buy him a drink. He came back to my section and sat down next to me. He ordered a bottle of champagne. We drank and talked our way across the Atlantic. He told me the story of his life, and while my memory about this is hazy, I recall he also talked a lot about his first marriage. The minute we got off the plane, I promptly and on purpose forgot everything he said. On his direction, I sent some of my work to an editor at the *Post*, and in 1976, I got my column "Rock Talk" in the *New York Post*, where I would write about music for the next two decades.

And still, whenever I returned to New York from anywhere, if Television was performing at CB's I wouldn't miss a night. They always lifted my spirits. They reminded me of why I went into all of this in the first place. Along with the Dolls, Television was underappreciated and commercially unsuccessful. Eventually, they self-destructed. But their first album—with the songs "Marquee Moon" and "Venus de Milo"—still sounds as good as it ever did. And Tom Verlaine did the best live version of anyone (including Bob Dylan) of Bob Dylan's "Knockin' on Heaven's Door." Today, Patti Smith, Talking Heads, Blondie, and the Ramones are all in the Rock and Roll Hall of Fame. Television, along with the New York Dolls, are not.

o o o

The lie, which is more fun than the truth, is that one night, Danny Fields and I decided to "divide up" bands we would go and see, and I "discovered" the Ramones. Like Diana Ross and the Jackson Five. (Except that she didn't discover them either; Suzanne de Passe did.) No one remembers this the same way, but what I recall is that the Ramones were pestering us to cover them in *Rock Scene* and *Hit Parader*. So finally one night, I told Danny I'd go see them at CB's and would give him a report. They took my breath away. I called

Danny the next morning, which meant the next afternoon, and told him that he had to see them. They rushed at breakneck speed through the shortest, cutest, and loudest songs I'd ever heard. The best thing was that all of the songs were under two minutes. Their entire set at that time was only about twenty minutes, which, at that volume, was a huge plus—but also, refreshing. And their humor was, as Joey Ramone referred to it, "dark and dry." I especially was fond of the lyrics in "Beat on the Brat"—which basically consisted of repeating "beat on the brat" numerous times. Joey told me this song came from personal experience; he saw undisciplined, annoying kids in his Queens neighborhood playground, and, he said, he just felt like killing them. "Everything's kind of a joke with us," Joey told me. "You can't take things too seriously or it doesn't pay to live." To civilians, the Ramones had the kind of reputation that the Stones had when they first came to the U.S.—that "lock up your daughters" thing. Danny Fields, who eventually managed the band, told me that when the Ramones checked into a Cincinnati hotel, the register read: *This is a punk band. Strange and violent.*

By 1977, there was a strong cult of European rock fans enamored of what they called "the New York Underground": Patti Smith, Lou Reed, Television, the New York Dolls, John Cale, Iggy, the Ramones. Included in this scene was the French couple Michel Esteban and Lizzy Mercier who lived in Paris and had a clothing store, a punk fanzine called *Rock News*, and eventually, Michel had a small record label. In April 1977, when I traveled to Paris to see the first Ramones/Talking Heads European tour, it was obvious that the Ramones were not about to return the love. In Zurich, their amps broke. In Geneva, the customs and telephone company were on strike. It took two days for them to drive to Marseille, only to discover that the club didn't have a stage. In Le Havre, the musicians got severe electric shocks onstage. In Holland, Johnny Ramone's leather jacket was stolen and Danny Fields had to have another one shipped from New York. The contrast was great between the Ramones—four boys from Queens, all of whom went to bed early and wanted to watch TV—and their tourmates, the Talking Heads, who opened the show and traveled on a bus with the Ramones throughout Europe. Talking Heads singer David Byrne likened the tour to a vacation, saying, "Everything is so scenic." The Ramones were not enthusiastic. "Nobody talks English," Johnny told me. "It's not like America. I miss home. We can't find lasagna or ravioli, and I miss milk. All the milk here has stuff floating on top of it." Joey added, "Even the orange juice and the Coca-Cola tastes weird." Dee Dee chimed in, "But I'd like to find an apartment here in a crooked old building."

The Ramones never really even got along with each other. They'd play for forty minutes, but half of that time would be spent yelling at each other onstage. Years later, Joey would tell me, "The Ramones were our own breed of band. We were classified as punk, but it came about spontaneously. When we started, there was Donna Summer and 'Disco Duck.' And then Boston, Journey, Foreigner, Kansas and REO Speedwagon. They were all the dominant force of faceless, spineless, radio rock. We were rebellious, annoying, alien. Everybody wanted us to disappear. They didn't know how to deal with us. Except for the people who found us refreshing—like yourself or Andy Warhol—those outcasts."

o o o

Epilogue: More than thirty-five years later, this world has completely changed. Lou Reed died on October 27, 2013. It was Fran Lebowitz's birthday and she and I were on our way to a private screening of a new Marty Scorsese movie when I heard the news about Lou. And I thought about how these three New Yorkers—Lou, Fran and Marty—

made such important cultural contributions to the culture of this city. And how the music Lou made forty years ago sounds as good today as it ever did.

I interviewed David Bowie a lot, well into the 1990s. After the heart attack he had while on tour in Germany in 2004, his public appearances have been scarce. He has released only one new album and so far, has not performed in concert. We've seen each other socially only rarely. But we email each other about various bands and new music. He seems to be on the Internet all the time and doesn't miss a trick. He's one of the few who has managed, so far, to gracefully get off the stage. The Ramones continued to tour the world until Joey Ramone died of lymphoma on Easter Sunday, 2001. Supposedly Bono phoned him on his deathbed in the hospital. A year after Joey's death, the Ramones were inducted into the Rock and Roll Hall of Fame, where Johnny said, "God bless President George W. Bush and God bless America," and Dee Dee thanked himself. Three months later, Dee Dee died of a probable drug overdose. In 2004, Johnny died of prostate cancer. Today, there's a "Joey Ramone Place" street sign on the Bowery and 2nd Street. When I see it, I'm reminded of those lyrics in Bob Dylan's "Desolation Row": "They're selling postcards of the hanging." Richard (DNV) Sohl died in 1990. Fred "Sonic" Smith died in 1994. Patti's beloved brother Todd died one month later. Patti came back to New York and resumed her performing career. Her children are grown up; her son Jackson is a fantastic guitarist married to former White Stripes' drummer Meg White. Patti is now an award-winning author, and has been a sort of muse to her good friend, the actor Johnny Depp. She continues to tour the world with pretty much the same band—Lenny Kaye, Jay Dee Daugherty, and Tony Shanahan. (Years ago I heard Patti's onstage tirades against President George W. Bush during the Iraq War and wondered if I was the only one who remembered that she campaigned for Ralph Nader—who, of course, helped George W. Bush win the

2004 election.) But I still get excited when I hear her song "Horses." When the Stooges were finally inducted into the Rock and Roll Hall of Fame in 2010, Pearl Jam's Eddie Vedder and I were jumping up and down and singing along as Iggy performed "I Wanna Be Your Dog." When the band came off the stage, I greeted Iggy in the kitchen (which serves as the "backstage" at the Waldorf Astoria Grand Ballroom) and thanked him for reminding me why I got into this racket in the first place. The young Iggy—born Jim Osterberg—from a trailer park outside of Detroit, was one of the most amazing live performers ever. Intense and sick and full of wild, misunderstood rock and roll abandon. Two years ago, Iggy appeared on *American Idol*, performing "Real Wild Child" shirtless. He had that body of an eighteen-year-old and the face of someone closer to seventy. I thought about how Lillian Roxon would have called it a "perversion of culture." Was it good that "America" got to see Iggy? I'm not sure. Certainly, with the exception of the *Idol* judge Steven Tyler, they couldn't have possibly understood who the hell he was or what Iggy had meant to us. These days, Iggy's great song "The Passenger" is the soundtrack for a rum ad on TV. The backing track of Lou Reed's "Walk on the Wild Side" is used in a TV ad for computers. When Alice Cooper was inducted into the Rock and Roll Hall of Fame in March 2011, Rob Zombie said that Alice was the band that drove a stake into the heart of the love generation. Of course that's just not true: the Velvet Underground did that—they just didn't have any hits. And in 2007, Hilly Kristal, owner of CBGB's, died of cancer after his club was shut down by rent issues, and while he was trying to make a deal to bring CBGB's to Las Vegas.

Four

On December 8, 1980, I was, uncharacteristically, watching *Monday Night Football* on television. Sometime around ten p.m., Howard Cossell interrupted the play-by-play to announce that John Lennon had been shot outside his apartment building—the Dakota, on West 72nd Street off Central Park West—in New York City. I immediately picked up the phone to call the Lennons' close friend, photographer Bob Gruen. The line was busy. I frantically changed channels on the TV, searching for more information. Finally, one of the stations broke in with the news that John had been rushed to Roosevelt Hospital, where he was pronounced dead. I called my friends Loraine and Peter Boyle (Loraine was a music columnist and the first New York bureau chief at *Rolling Stone* magazine, Peter was the actor and John was best man at their 1977 wedding). Peter answered the phone. He was crying. Sometime after midnight, Bob Gruen came to our apartment. He was devastated, and I spent several hours consoling him. The city editor at the *New York Post*, where I then wrote a weekly music column, called to ask me for the Lennons' home number. I said I didn't have it (even though I did), and I didn't answer the phone for the rest of the night.

∘ ∘ ∘

The first time I was ever in a room with John Lennon was when Richard and I took one of our regular trips to London. It was around the end of 1969, or maybe early 1970. As the '70s progressed, we went often, because Richard—who had very long hair for years—decided it was time to cut it short. He found a hairdresser he liked (which meant I liked) in London, so we went every few months for him to have a trim. Seriously. This was not as decadent as it sounds. The flights were cheap, the Portobello Hotel was cheap (we stayed in a tiny room the size of a ship's cabin). Plus, he still had those record company expense accounts. He "needed" to look for new bands in London, and I "needed" to meet with my editor at *Disc and Music Echo*. It was on one of our very first trips that we had a drunken lunch with Derek Taylor, a friend who had worked with the Beatles throughout the 1960s and was currently the press officer at the Beatles' Apple Records. Richard recalls that an interview with JohnandYoko (at that time, they were always referred to as one word) was offered to Richard, who hadn't even asked for one. We assumed that Derek needed to deliver a member of the U.S. press to the couple, who were intent on getting out their message of Peace and Love. I accompanied Richard to the interview at the Apple Records offices in the famous white building on Savile Row. JohnandYoko sat behind a large desk in a large room on the main floor. Richard set up a tape recorder. But it was immediately apparent that Richard's questions were pointless. For almost an hour, John babbled on about giving peace a chance. He was arrogant, slightly snide—in keeping with the way he'd been described by people who knew him when he'd been in the Beatles. He had his peace and love rap down pat. Yoko, who wore her trademark sunglasses, occasionally chimed in, murmuring something or other that reinforced what John had said. (Years later, it occurred to me that they might quite possibly have been stoned—on what, I have no idea. And it probably was one of the few times in my life that I sat in a room for an hour, listening to people talk without my saying one word.) I do remember thinking then, in that room in the Apple building with JohnandYoko, that if I ever did interviews, I needed to participate more. Just letting them go on and on was boring.

In 1971, JohnandYoko moved to New York City, to 105 Bank Street in Greenwich Village. Considering his great wealth, they lived modestly, in a fairly small ground-floor, two-room apartment. It might be hard to understand today, but John Lennon, at that time in his life, new to what he considered the New York City art and political scene, was fairly accessible. The post–flower power, anti–Vietnam War fervor was in full force. The world—at least our world, by which I mean young people in the music and art scenes who went out every night—was divided into two categories: us, and them. The longhairs, and the straights. The evil Richard Nixon was on one side—in the White House—and rock fans, students, liberals, Black Panthers and Democrats were all lumped together on the other side. People actually used words like "right on," "dig it," and "brothers and sisters." Johnand-Yoko had been made fun of in newspapers all over the world for their bed-ins and their naked album cover for *Two Virgins*. They also were the targets of great anger over Yoko's presumed role in breaking up the Beatles. Now, in New York City, they found a home. And not just a physical home, but an artistic, creative and political home. They took up with (or were taken in by) the likes of political activists

Abbie Hoffman and Jerry Rubin, and various political bands such as Elephants Memory and street singer David Peel—whose one "hit" song at the time was literally titled "I Like Marijuana." At the urging of Abbie and Jerry, JohnandYoko traveled to Ann Arbor, Michigan, to perform at a benefit concert for John Sinclair, the manager of the hard rock band the MC5 and the head of the "White Panther Party." This sounds absurd today, but at that time, and in certain circles, the White Panther Party was taken quite seriously. Sinclair had been jailed for ten years for giving an undercover policeman two marijuana joints. And such was the power of the Lennons that the day after the concert, Sinclair was released from jail. (Going out on a limb for John Sinclair appeared heroic at the time, but it might have surprised Yoko, who purported to be such a feminist, that communal living at the White Panthers' house in Ann Arbor was marked by the women cooking food and rolling joints for the men.) But the Lennons certainly could command an audience, and they knew how to manipulate the media. And they appeared to be having the time of their lives living as beatniks/activists (albeit dilettantes) in New York City's Greenwich Village. Despite having been the leader of the world's biggest and best-loved band, John always considered himself a rebel and an outsider. He took Black Panther Bobby Seale with him on the Mike Douglas TV show—which today would be akin to something like the Ellen Degeneres show. John seemed ecstatic to be free of the Beatles and with the woman he adored at his side. *Constantly* at his side. The Lennons tried to do good deeds: on August 30, 1972, they performed with Elephants Memory at Madison Square Garden for the Geraldo Rivera–hosted "One to One" concert to raise money and protest substandard conditions at Willowbrook—a state facility for retarded children (and yes, you could use that word then). But because of John's outspoken remarks, his newly discovered political fervor, and his association with Jerry Rubin and Abbie

Hoffman, he became a person of interest to the U.S. government. (Some of us, despite their good work in rabble rousing at the 1968 Chicago Democratic Convention, considered Jerry Rubin and Abbie Hoffman a vaudeville team. But it would take awhile for John to become disenchanted with them.) As bizarre as it sounds now, President Richard Nixon, Attorney General John Mitchell, Senator Strom Thurmond and their ilk became semi-hysterical about John Lennon. They eventually wanted him thrown out of the country. In the Beatles, John was a witty and brilliant songwriter and performer. With Yoko, in New York City, he became a political threat. In the 1960s, the Rolling Stones were considered "dangerous"; they were overtly sexual, they had urinated in public at a gas station, and were portrayed by the press as filthy louts. They also had a clever manager in Andrew Loog Oldham, who took full advantage of a "lock up your daughters" marketing campaign. But the Rolling Stones were never a threat to the U.S. government. Mick Jagger, when in New York City, lived on the Upper East Side with his "socialite" wife Bianca and went to parties with the Ahmet Erteguns. A political "artist" was Neil Young singing "Four dead in Ohio" about Kent State. Or earlier, when Bob Dylan wrote "Masters of War"—despite his protests that he was not a protest singer. And, even though, as Gore Vidal noted at the time, "Give Peace a Chance" wasn't exactly the "Battle Hymn of the Republic," it became a catchy, easy, singalong, anti-war anthem. It certainly wasn't Elvis Presley, long past his prime, shaking Nixon's hand at the White House. Excessive marijuana use may have had something to do with the all-pervasive paranoia of the day, but many of us suspected that there were FBI or CIA informants, or "narcs" (narcotics agents) among us. We were concerned that they worked at record companies, joined us at parties, infiltrated the rock press. When John talked about being wiretapped at Bank Street and how J. Edgar Hoover was after him, we initially thought he was paranoid and/or naive. He turned out to be right.

It is also hard to imagine now, but not only was John fairly accessible in New York City, to those of us who were more into the New York Dolls, or Max's Kansas City, or David Bowie, the solo John Lennon just wasn't that big a deal. Notations in my journals from 1973 onwards, when I spent time with, or interviewed the Lennons, were fairly small. They were scribbled on pages that had—in much bigger letters—"Wayne at Max's," or "Dolls at Mercer," or "Patti at Reno Sweeney's." Yoko's shtick—the bed-ins, the bag-ins, the shrieking—seemed to be not much more than nutty cries for attention. She advertised herself as a famous avant-garde performer; but many of us who regularly attended performances of the Living Theater, or other "performance artists," had never heard of her before she hooked up with John. The Lennons rounded people up to be in the Warhol-influenced, eight millimeter movies (*Bottoms*, *Legs*) that they made with filmmaker Jonas Mekas, and, depending on your point of view, the films were amusing or cringeworthy. The lawyer Nat Weiss, who had been a close friend of the Beatles' manager Brian Epstein and had helped run the Beatles' fan club in America in the 1960s, told me that John had asked him to help Yoko with her films. "She arranged for me to see this movie she had done, called *Bottoms*. I saw it at the Rizzoli screening room. Afterwards, she asked me what I thought, and I said, 'Well, it's not exactly *Gone With the Wind*.' She never spoke to me again."

Photographer Bob Gruen first set me up with the Lennons. Without Yoko's stamp of approval, or a compatible astrology sign, you could not get to John, who clearly wanted to distance himself from the world of *Billboard* magazine. He didn't want to hang out with Mick Jagger or Eric Clapton. In fact, when I got to know him better it was apparent that, aside from gossip, he wasn't at all interested in any of the music being made by any of his contemporaries. I recall a party at Loraine and Peter Boyle's house where Paul Simon brought his new album for us all to listen to in its entirety. *Twice.* John paid attention for as long as he could, but pretty soon it became an eye-roll moment. Despite his millions of dollars and his fabled past, John was living the life—or playing the part—of the bohemian artist with his woman in a garret. By 1973, I was writing for London's *New Musical Express* as well as *Creem,* and I was editing *Hit Parader* magazine. I was plugged into whatever was going on in the rock scene. Bob Gruen's then-wife Nadya was an assistant to the Lennons, and Yoko had an album (*Approximately Infinite Universe*) about to be released. It was, I was assured, her most "commercial" work to date; she sang actual words, in actual songs. She wanted to do some interviews. She wanted to do them with women. I was happy to comply. I had written some complimentary things about her singing—comparing it to the early stages of punk rock or some such—and, as this was not the majority opinion, she was pleased. So on January 8, 1973, I went down to Bank Street with my little Sony cassette recorder to talk to Yoko. It was made very clear to me that the interview was to be with just Yoko, not John, and we would only discuss her *twenty-two* song album.

The evening started out slowly. Bob Gruen sat in or was around during the entire time. There was a fire in the fireplace. There were a lot of books in the large living room. There were several phones and they were constantly ringing. John was nowhere in sight. We sat at a round table in the living room, and I asked Yoko questions about her album and about her singing career. I asked her if she felt people hated her because the Beatles broke up, and if she felt the antagonism towards her was racist because she was Oriental (yes, we could still say that then). But mostly, I talked about specific songs on the album. At first, she was guarded, but when she realized that I had really listened to all twenty-two songs, she warmed up to me and talked. And talked. She said that she had had early operatic training, but, she said, "It was not my bag." She said she had always been eloquent (her word), but when she was going through a bad time in her private life, one day she started to sing. She had a tape recorder and she taped her singing and played it back. Much to her surprise, she told me, she realized she was out of tune. Also, she said, the microphone was so close to her mouth that the sound became distorted. "This should have upset me," she said, "it sounded like a song sung by someone who was mentally deranged. Or someone at the limit of their emotion. But, it was very interesting." After an hour or so of this sort of thing, she appeared satisfied that she had talked enough about herself, about the role of women in society, and her new album. Then she brought John out from the back room—like he was dessert. He came bounding out, seemingly pent-up and ready to talk. (For all I know, they were high—on what, I have no idea. But I've learned that except for groupies, drug dealers and Keith Richards, almost no one in the music world has ever been honest about their drug use while they were using drugs.) John seemed eager to talk about Yoko. "[At first] I put up as much fight as many other people about Yoko's ideas," he said. "I'm from the sticks, and when somebody keeps pointing to the light . . . I mean it's all right to do it yourself, but when it's somebody else doing it, well, it's eye opening. On her new album, I like the rock songs, that's my scene. But I also like the howling. I think she should have done more howling. I've been taking off the howling but now I want to go back to it. Because it was so new before, it was like the first abstract painting you ever saw. When someone starts going 'WOOOOOOOGGGGHHH,' I mean, you'll accept Little Richard doing it in the 1950s, but someone who eliminates all the words altogether, it's quite a trip. To write, that's easy. But to bloody howl, that's hard."

o o o

In all of John Lennon's career with the Beatles, he was part of a foursome that was mostly always "interviewed" together. They had "press conferences." They gave sarcastic quips or sound bites. On his own, John had a forum to really talk. And, being as bright as he was, and having seen a lot of the world but now wanting much less of it, he was happy to have Yoko by his side, who nodded and smiled beatifically at every gem he uttered. Correction: he was *determined* to have Yoko by his side—in the studio, on his records, in his band—even when she just stood next to him onstage and banged on a bongo drum. It has been well-chronicled how mesmerized he was by her and what he perceived as her worldliness and her artistic sensibility. Because I was a woman who had been sympathetic to Yoko, I was allowed in. No less important was the fact that I wrote for a major British music weekly. And that I could gossip with John about the Stones, Zeppelin and Bowie—at a time when he was psychically removed from that scene. He always enjoyed a good gossip; they all do. And I kept secrets. When Yoko kicked John out of the house in 1973 because he allegedly had been sleeping with other women, I never wrote about that aspect of the estrangement. It was well known that John fooled around—including with, among others, a photographer who was the wife of a famous folk-rock singer. But I never would have written about that, nor would I have written about Yoko's affair with musician David Spinozza. This is all ancient history now, and has been recounted elsewhere, but at that time, it was considered someone's "private life." When I was aware of drug use, I didn't write about it. But to this day, unless people are practically nodding out in front of me, or babbling uncontrollably, I am the last person who can tell, or care about, or would report about, drug use. I never felt like a "combatant," or a reporter; I felt like an ally. The writer Pete Hamill once said that rock journalists were like prosecutors, but I was the defense attorney. As far as I was concerned, we were on the same "side," because our lives had all been so changed by the music. But also, I was unaware, for example, of the rampant heroin use in New York's CBGB's scene—much less that of the Lennons, who were rumored to be involved with the drug until Yoko got pregnant in 1975, when they cleaned up. No junkified musician will own up to drug use while using for two reasons: privacy and shame.

o o o

In the 1970s, no one from the New York music scene took Los Angeles seriously. With all that constant, bright sunlight and those palm trees, it seemed like a vacation spot. For English musicians, it was a sexual playground. If you had money, you stayed at the Beverly Hills Hotel or the Beverly Wilshire. If drugs were your priority, you'd hole up at the Chateau Marmont. The lower rung of musicians stayed at the Continental Hyatt House (except for the spectacularly rich Led Zeppelin, who stayed there because they were allowed to run amok and they couldn't get in anywhere else). Even lower was the truly seedy Tropicana Motel. There were clubs, of course; the Laurel Canyon and Sunset Strip scenes had such venues as the Troubadour and the Whisky a Go Go. Older Hollywood types had discos like the Daisy. But there was no restaurant scene like there is today. There was Chasen's for the Reagans, and Barney's Beanery and Duke's for rock musicians. Or the coffeeshop at the Beverly Wilshire Hotel, where I once had breakfast at three in the afternoon with Chuck Berry who was "dating" Diane Gardiner. Diane was the publicist for the Jefferson Airplane, a friend of Jim and Pamela Morrison's, and an old girlfriend of my husband's. I met Jim Morrison only once, at Diane's two-story bungalow in Los Angeles, at a later stage of his life. He was fat, bearded, drunk, and babbling about the blues—which, it seemed, he had only recently just discovered. He and Pamela lived upstairs from Diane, and they were, as usual, fighting. Pamela probably said it more than once, but I distinctly recall that Richard and I were there when she screamed at Jim that he always ruined her birthday. When I met Diane and Chuck Berry—or "Charles," as Diane called him—Diane wore an orange minidress and white high heels. "Charles" wore white trousers, a white undershirt clearly visible underneath a black lace shirt, and white shoes. He had the biggest hands I'd ever seen. I recall there was a lot of discussion about "property"— Charles was telling Diane she needed to have some, and she was trying to get him to purchase some for her. He ate scrambled eggs, bacon, sausage, hash brown potatoes, a chocolate milkshake, and apple pie a la mode. He let me pick up the check.

Chuck Berry's black lace shirt aside, people in Los Angeles didn't wear black clothing then. There were no cheese shops, not even in Beverly Hills. There were no nightclubs with lists, or ropes at the door. There were no vintage clothing stores. There were some antique stores where decorators shopped, but none of this was part of the "culture." Even in the early 1990s, when I went to Los Angeles for some interview or other and was friendly with Phil Spector and he would send me a car and driver for the week, it would be a block-long white stretch limousine. That was either Hollywood fantasia or Phil's idea of a joke. Or both. To me, the city just was not a serious place. And, except for Sue Mengers, it was not run by agents. Or museum directors. Or cooks. At least the music business wasn't; David Geffen ran the music business. With the exception of those who actually lived there, it was a place musicians went to play, get high, have sex, and make records. And so, it was to this Los Angeles that Yoko Ono banished John in September 1973, when they were having a rough time in their marriage. He ostensibly went to finish up the recording sessions for *Mind Games,* and then to record the *Rock 'n' Roll* album with Phil Spector. He went, at Yoko's direction, with the Lennons' assistant May Pang by his side. He stayed for ten months, a period he would describe later as his "lost weekend."

o o o

Despite the party line of this "lost weekend," and how miserable John would later say he was without Yoko, on September 9, 1974, when he was back in New York City and I visited him in his penthouse apartment at 434 East 52nd Street, John was relaxed, fun, ebullient. Some who knew him well during that time felt he was happier than he ever let on. When I went to talk to him, he was living with May Pang; he was still "on leave" from Yoko and the Dakota. In Los Angeles, he had been wildly and publicly drunk. Wearing a Kotex on his head, he was thrown out of the Troubadour for heckling the Smothers Brothers. Years later, he would tell me he had wanted to "go home" to Yoko. But when we talked that day in 1974, he couldn't have been more delightful. We talked about the Beatlefest convention that had been held the week before at the Commodore Hotel in New York City. He said he'd contemplated attending, but decided against it because, he said, "I still get nervous in crowds." But did people in New York really bother him? "Well," he said, "people try to be cool. They're not quite as bad as the Parisians, who try so hard to be cool you can feel the vibe from a mile away. I'm always aware of everybody in the room. So I can feel them trying to not take notice of me. But people in New York are pretty cool." I asked if he felt he was able to be more anonymous in New York. "Well," he said, "I guess it's about the same everywhere. It's been a long time since we were really hassled by people. I mean people see you and look at you, but it's not like Beatlemania." We discussed the Beatles memorabilia sold at the convention.

I told him I had four enamel trays with photos of all four Beatles on them. He said—almost plaintively—"I haven't got a tray." (I now have three trays.) I told him I had a lunchbox. "I *wanted* a lunchbox," he practically whined. "I told them, get me a lunchbox, something *practical*." (I still have my Beatles lunchbox with matching thermos.) He said Brian Epstein had made "some mad deal," that someone made millions on all that stuff and none of the band members ever got a dime from any of it—the dolls, the trays, the toys, the buttons. I told him that the singer in the Beatles cover band at the convention said, "We're all going to sing along, because we know these songs, don't we? We know them as well as we know the Lord's Prayer." John laughed. "Isn't that nice," he said. He likened it to Rudolph Valentino. But, he added, "It's good for business, isn't it? It goes to the family. And if we ever did anything together again, it keeps the fires burning. There they are. Waiting." Had he been concerned that they wouldn't be there waiting? "No," he said, "but things like that, a convention with 3,000 people a day . . . it just reminds you. It's a lot of people to look at pictures."

We talked about Los Angeles and the incident at the Troubadour. "For one period," John said, "I was getting really manic—as you might have noticed by a few press clippings. But only half of what was reported in the papers about L.A. was true." The Kotex on his head in the Troubadour? "Oh, that was true, but nobody took a cryin' bit of notice of it. It was only in retrospect when I was heckling the Smothers Brothers that they noticed it. Actually, all that happened was that they dragged us out. But the Kotex thing, nobody really noticed it. It was just something I stuck on me forehead; like the way people stick pennies on and say, 'look at that.'" Who sticks pennies on their forehead and says, "Look at that?" I asked. "Well," he said, "I just found it in the toilet, clean as a whistle, and I stuck it on and it stayed on all night. It was rather splendid. And [gossip columnist] Rona Barrett didn't want to mention it. An 'unmentionable,' she said." I said that that made it sound even worse than it was. "Well, it may be unmentionable to her," John said, "but they advertise them on TV. I was having my first night on Brandy Alexanders. Right? Brandy and milk, and it tasted like milkshake, and the next thing I knew I was out of me gourd. And Harry Nilsson was no help feeding me them; saying, 'go ahead, it's great John,' one of those scenes, come on, give it to him. All that's true, and I was wildly obnoxious."

We talked about his escalating deportation problems; it was turning into the U.S. vs. John Lennon. He wanted to stay, the government wanted him gone. "I've been through emotional stress and manic depression. And also, it costs a fortune. Just to stay here. Most expensive holiday I've ever had." I asked him how he felt about the possibility of becoming a martyr. "I think it's daft. Look, they never liked me in school, either. They didn't like me face. They used to say 'he's *looking* at us.' They used to call it 'The Look.' It really was just that I was shortsighted and I'd be glaring at the teacher. It's *exactly* the same, only the school's bigger now." He said he was "allowed" to perform in concerts, but that he didn't feel like doing it. "When I think of all that . . . thirty-eight bloody cities and sweating around . . . the average good fun at the end of a tour is two shows out of ten. I know it's different now than when I was with the Beatles, but it ain't all that different when you're up there. I couldn't do what George Harrison is doing, thirty-eight cities. The highs aren't worth the lows. I have the feeling that sometimes I'd like to get up and do it, but not quite enough to get me out there." The "One to One" concert in 1972 had been the last time he had been onstage, and, he added, another time "I staggered around the stage with Dr. John, but I wouldn't call that a performance. I played organ and he played harmonica. Neither of us could play anything. But we stood up there."

I asked what it would be like to perform with the Beatles now. "It would be harder," he said, "because no one would ever be satisfied. We'd never be good enough. Everybody's got this . . . *dream* about how wonderful it was. Imagine if we went on; they'd all say, 'not as good as they were.' Actually, if we all got together, it would sound exactly the same, only better. Listen to all the solo records and you'll hear the same people, the same stuff. Just that there's too much Paul, too much George, too much Ringo. You're not getting enough variety." John was harsh about George Harrison's 1970 double album *All Things Must Pass*. "I can't stand double albums," John said. "Too much mixing and listening to it and putting them in order and then who's going to sit down and listen to forty bloody tunes?? I can't. I can hardly bear to listen to eleven or ten or nine."

We talked a long time about his associations with what he referred to as "certain types": Abbie Hoffman and Jerry Rubin. "They got what they wanted from it," he said, "and I got what I wanted." He admitted that after just two and a half years in New York, his life was different: he got back into music. "I've always been interested in politics, but I've got to do it the poetic way. It just doesn't work any other way. I took it too literally. Because all of us singers are minstrels anyway, right? And we're saying what's going on in the world, one way or another. Rock and roll was really folk music. But I think I got too literary about it, thinking well, if that's what I'm doing, then I'll say it about specific issues. And when that happened, I think it limited my self-expression. So, I just went back to being me again. It's like going through the Maharishi or something. As long as I'm going through something, I've got something to say. If it all gets cozy, then there's nothing to say. If it becomes a happy life with the dog and the cat, which I can't bear, then there's nothing to say. I have to bang me head against the wall and then write about how good it is to stop. Otherwise, I think you die as an artist. I can't deal with that settling down business. I'll never settle down. I always have to keep moving or falling over just so something's happening to me. I've died artistically a few times. I didn't like it. As long as I'm writing songs, I don't care where I am, unless I was in prison." Was prison an imminent possibility? "Nah. Not unless I kill somebody." He talked about his new album (*Walls and Bridges*) and how it would help his image with the government. "It's all showbiz," he said. "That's why I never get really depressed about reviews. . . ." Reviews? He reads reviews? "I eventually read everything," he said, "because all your best friends send you your lousy reviews."

o o o

When John and I talked that day in 1974, he told me that the recording sessions he did with producer Phil Spector in L.A. were "pretty mad sessions. My sessions are usually pretty straight, but those were weird to say the least. Phil and I were at the height of eccentricity." In Martin Scorsese's documentary about George Harrison, *Living in the Material World*, there is an interview with Phil Spector about the production work he did with George on George's double album *All Things Must Pass*. It was filmed after Phil's arrest but before his trial for the murder of Lana Clarkson. In the documentary, Phil looks the way he did in court; a red pocket square in a dark blazer, a matching red shirt, a blondish, almost mop-topped wig. Behind him was the white piano that I believe was the same one John Lennon played in the video of "Imagine." Phil may look weird, but he talks as lucidly and on point about George as he always did when I knew him and we were friends in the 1990s. It made me sad. For those who know only of his reputed violent streak, or the murder conviction, or who saw him shaking on Court TV, it's probably hard to understand how funny and insightful he was.

I first met Phil in 1991 at one of the interminable meetings of the Rock and Roll Hall of Fame nominating committee—when I was the only female on the committee. He, Ahmet Ertegun and I agreed on, and argued for, many of the same people who were not yet in the Hall of Fame and, in the case of some 1950s doo-wop groups, are *still* not in. Or, we agreed on black blues pioneers such as Howlin' Wolf, who, after years of arguments, finally got inducted in 1991 as an "Early Influence." One night, following one of those lunchtime nominating committee meetings, I was at the Bottom Line to see a performance by the gospel group the Blind Boys of Alabama. Phil was at another table with bandleader/musician Paul Shaffer. A bottle of champagne was sent to my table, courtesy of Phil, and thus began a friendship that lasted until a year or so before his arrest. Despite some occasional erratic behavior, I spent many entertaining nights on the town with Phil and his coterie. Among his New York friends were Paul Shaffer, other journalists, some female companion or other, and two bodyguards who, I recall, Phil introduced as the sons of jazz guitarist Barney Kessel. We went to hear jazz—at Eddie Condon's and the Village Vanguard. We went in large groups to dinners, and Phil always picked up the check. He stood every time a woman got up to go to the restroom or returned to the table. He did spot-on impersonations of George Harrison, Ahmet Ertegun, John Lennon, and songwriter Doc ("Save the Last Dance for Me," "Viva Las Vegas") Pomus. Phil always used the expression "We'll double cross that bridge when we get to it." He was furious about the Rock and Roll Hall of Fame nominating process—saying that he just knew one day we'd be voting on Phil Collins and Billy Joel. We did. They're both in.

On June 6, 1991, I went to a recording studio on Greene Street to watch Phil, with his longtime engineer Larry Levine, re-master the songs from his catalogue for what would become the Phil Spector boxed set. He talked about John Lennon in L.A. with the Kotex on his head. He talked about Yoko, Mama Mae Thornton, Esther Phillips, Screamin' Jay Hawkins. The studio was dark, there were barely any lights on and it was freezing—the air conditioning was on full blast. I listened to "You've Lost That Lovin' Feelin'" and Phil told me that when the song was first recorded, music publisher Don Kirshner told him he couldn't use that title, that the title was too *negative*. I heard "He Hit Me, and It Felt Like a Kiss" by the Crystals for the first time; Phil had never felt he could release it before. While I watched Phil and Larry re-master those songs—"River Deep—Mountain High," "Be My Baby," "Walking in the Rain," "To Know Him Is to Love Him"—it was like watching Picasso re-paint his masterpieces. "I don't care if it sells a lot of copies," Phil said to me that day with a straight face. "As long as every man, woman and child in America buys one."

Once, in his suite at the Ritz-Carlton in New York City, Phil had assembled a group of friends, including Paul Shaffer, the globetrotter/art collector Jean Pigozzi, and lawyer Marvin Mitchelson. Several books written about Phil were on a table next to a sofa, and a book about Meyer Lansky was on the coffee table—along with bowls of Tootsie Roll lollipops, candy bars, nuts, cookies and potato chips. There were framed photos of Phil with the Rolling Stones, with Doc Pomus. He told many stories, many of which I had heard previously—at least once. About how Charlie Chaplin wrote "I'll Be Loving You Eternally" for the movie *City Lights* because Irving Berlin wouldn't give him the rights to Berlin's "I'll Be Loving You [Always]." He marveled at how Berlin could write an Irish song ("Alexander's Ragtime Band"), an Easter song, a Christmas song, then "God Bless America." How Berlin wanted to be Cole Porter so he wrote "Puttin' on the Ritz." Porter couldn't do Berlin, Phil said, but he wrote the best country and western song ever written: "Don't Fence Me In." Phil seemed to know every song ever written (a level of knowledge that in my entire career I have seen matched only by musician-producer-composer Jon Brion). Phil talked about how, as a teenager, he had met Oscar Hammerstein and Jerome Kern and their wives. He asked Mrs. Hammerstein, "How did your husband write 'Ol' Man River'? And Mrs. Kern broke in, *My* husband wrote 'Ol' Man River,' *her* husband wrote—she sang—Da-da-da-da." He told me how he and Doc Pomus went to Joe Marsh's Spindletop restaurant when Phil was eighteen, and how they ate great big salads and steaks night after night. One night, a man came into the restaurant wearing a raincoat, pulled out a gun and shot someone sitting next to them. Phil was astounded, horrified, he couldn't stop thinking about it. Later, he said to Doc, "Can you believe this? Someone got murdered. In the restaurant. While we sat there. I never saw anything like that in my life." Then Doc said, "Phil, they have such big steaks, such delicious salads . . ." And Phil said, "But Doc, someone got *murdered. I mean, excuse me,* a man came in and shot someone while we sat there." And Doc said, "So that's the down side of it, baby. They've got great steaks . . . great salads . . ."

On November 4, 1991, some of us were gathered in one of Phil's hotel suites. Phil talked about the boxed set of his early songs and productions, the reviews it got, his reputation. He said that at first, no one ever took his work seriously. He was doing production numbers, he said. Each song was like a Broadway show. He told a story about how Ike Turner stayed at the Waldorf Astoria for one of the Rock and Roll Hall of Fame induction ceremonies and told Phil he needed $920 cash for "dry cleaning." He talked about being in a restaurant with John and Yoko and how the violinists came over and played Beatles songs—"Yesterday," "Michelle"—all the McCartney songs. John was holding his head, mumbling that he hadn't written any of them. I said Cole Porter couldn't have written with Irving Berlin—one of them was the sophisticated one, the other the sappy one. Phil said that was exactly the point—John and Paul hadn't written songs together either.

On November 12, 1992, I went with Phil to *Rolling Stone* magazine's 25th anniversary party at the Four Seasons restaurant. Phil, who was an amazing mimic, spent quite a lot of time that night doing his impersonation of Ross Perot. Then Martin Scorsese came over to the table. He started to tell Phil how much Phil's music meant to him growing up in Little Italy in New York City in the 1950s and '60s. Phil stared straight ahead, refusing to acknowledge Scorsese. I kicked him and hissed, "Phil, this is the greatest living movie director standing here talking to you and you are being rude." He whispered to me, "He stole my music for *Mean Streets*." I said he should be honored that his music was *used* in *Mean Streets*. Marty, who became increasingly more uncomfortable with Phil's snub, eventually edged away. Later in the evening, Marty was standing and chatting with Lou Reed and Keith Richards. Phil looked over at them and asked me to "Go get Scorsese." Oh no, I said, I'm not getting in the middle of any trouble. He assured me it would be all right. So, I went over and relayed the "invitation," and asked Keith to accompany us. Scorsese went over to Phil Spector. Phil Spector hugged him. And that was that.

I thought about all of this while recently watching Scorsese's George Harrison documentary, and reading over my notes and transcripts from that day I spent with John Lennon on East 52nd Street. There were many—*many*—nights when I sat up very late listening to Phil Spector talk about John. I have many letters from Phil about his feelings for John. Phil revered Irving Berlin and Stephen Foster and Cole Porter and Jerome Kern. Often, when we were out, we would literally sing the songs from the Kern musical *Show Boat* together. We both idolized Lenny Bruce—whom he had known well, had recorded for Philles Records, whose daughter Kitty was a friend of ours, and whose routines Phil and I could both recite word for word. But I don't think anyone was as meaningful to Phil as was John Lennon. When I took Phil to Yankee Stadium on August 29, 1992, to see U2 (and he corralled a phalanx of policemen to escort him onto the field to the soundboard, where we watched the show), he became obsessed. After the show, he talked to me about U2 until around five a.m., comparing Bono to John Lennon. The following day I received several faxed letters from Phil that basically said he had not met anyone since John who had the insight, imagination, fire, enthusiasm, intelligence, voice and pure innovative rock and roll roots in his heart and soul that Bono had. He went on to say that he rarely got excited about anything, but as a songwriter himself, he saw that talent in Bono, as much as he had with John. He wanted to record Bono in mono. They never did work together. My good friend, the great producer Rick Rubin, a Beatles fanatic who has worked with Bono, always wanted to meet Phil. I never could get them together.

o o o

Tony King, who ran Apple Records from 1970–1975 and who organized the recording of John's *Mind Games* album, was in Los Angeles during John's crazed period and the Spector sessions. Later on, Tony became friendly with John and Yoko when John went back "home" to the Dakota. Tony was a good friend of Elton John's and he brought John and Elton together to record "Whatever Gets You Through the Night." John promised Elton that if the song went to Number One, he'd sing it with him onstage at Madison Square Garden. It went to Number One. So, on November 28, 1974, John performed it onstage with Elton at the Garden. Yoko sent gardenias backstage, but she didn't want John to know she was at the concert. Tony King escorted her to a seat in the eleventh row. John was a nervous wreck, but he would have been worse had he known Yoko was in the audience. At the midnight supper after-party in the Grand Ballroom of the Pierre Hotel, John told me, "I had a great time. But I wouldn't want to do it for a living." Among the guests at the party were Loraine and Peter Boyle, Peter Rudge, Elliott Gould, Cheech and Chong, Angela Lansbury, Atlantic Records co-founder Jerry Wexler, and Yoko, wearing white. Uri Geller was there, bending spoons. It was clear to anyone who saw the Lennons that night that it was only a matter of time before John would move back "home," to Yoko. By February, he was back in the Dakota.

And, despite the fact that years later he would tell me he never phoned anyone, ever, in 1975 John called, saying, in that unmistakable voice: "Hello, it's me, John, Beatles," and invited me to the Dakota for a chat. He wasn't pushing an album at the time, but the *New Musical Express* wanted an update about his deportation problems, and it was to John's advantage to keep his name in the papers. We talked on February 19, 1975—I noted that it was my mother's birthday. The Lennons' seventh-floor apartment had the tall, mahogany doors that still mark the Dakota's hallways. You left your shoes at the door outside their apartment; this was a Japanese custom but practical as well—there was white carpeting in the apartment. There were Persian carpets, art deco objects and Yoko's "art." The art included life-sized Barbie doll mannequins kneeling in front of vases filled with roses, a bandaged chair, and an empty glass on a white column. At the time, it was amusing. Today, some sucker would probably pay a fortune for it. And if I were to tell Yoko today that she was a precursor to Damien Hirst, Matthew Barney and that bunch, I'm sure she would wholeheartedly agree. In fact, it's not that far-fetched a comparison. All of this stuff co-existed in their apartment with John's tape recorders, guitars, a jukebox, and a white baby grand piano. Gold albums lined the long hallway that led to the large kitchen where John and I sat and talked. By now, I had enough of a rapport with the Lennons that Yoko was comfortable remaining downstairs in their office—in one of the several apartments she had purchased in the building—while I spoke to John for hours, upstairs in their kitchen.

I told John he seemed ecstatic to be back home with Yoko. "I am, I am," he said. "This is no disrespect to anybody else I was having relationships with, but I feel like I was running around without me head on, but still functioning. You don't want to admit it while it's happening, that's what was making me go barmy. You think you're just going to a party but you end up throwing up in the toilet. Now I feel I've got me head back on. Yoko and I were always in touch, either on the phone or one way or the other, but I just sort of came home, is what happened. I feel like I went to get a coffee and a newspaper somewhere and it took a year."

He described his deportation situation as "hellish." Basically, he said, the government stance was that he had to leave the country. "It started because of my conviction in England for marijuana, which was planted by Sergeant Pilcher—which everybody knows by now because the guy's in jail for some other case." (This was the same policeman who busted Mick Jagger, Marianne Faithfull, Keith Richards and others at Keith's house in Redlands, England, in the 1960s.) "We were busted by about twenty people," John said, "there was dogs, it's a whole *film*. They wouldn't let us get dressed, they threatened to break the door down. It was [even] questioned in the Houses of Parliament: why were so many people needed to bust two people? It took them hours—they were all over the house, they could have planted us with *diamonds* and we'd have had no chance of controlling them. I was a wreck, just panic stricken. *Cops*. In jolly England. I still half believed [that stuff] about the good old 'bobby' helping you down the street. And I was really nervous about Yoko, because we'd just got to living together, it was all in public, and I thought they'd deport her, they'd deport us, so I just copped a plea, thinking what the hell, it was a misdemeanor. But they still write letters to the papers, claiming that Lennon is a convicted criminal . . . he wants to live in this land of milk and honey and that's too bad. No mention of how much *taxes* I'm paying. It's been going on since 1971 and it's just crazy." I asked him where else he would want to live—Canada? "You know they always say that," John laughed, "because whenever I talk to Canadians, they ask me if I like Canada. And I say yes, I like Canada. I like Toronto, and Montreal, I don't know much about the rest of it. Then the next thing I know, they say I'm going to *live* there. Every country I've been to I've thought, could I live here? So I was always answering on that level. It's that old bit where if you're in some small town people say to you, 'what are you doing *here*?' Like, 'surely you don't want to live with us or even *visit* our town.' When I was driving through America or if I'm *anywhere*, people say why are you *here*?? Of all *places* . . . Everybody's always thinking our place is nowhere, nobody would want to be here not even for a *minute*."

He went on and on about Senator Strom Thurmond and about how he and Yoko had been wiretapped on Bank Street and how many famous Nazis were living in America and no one hassled *them*. "There was two guys following me around in the car," he said. "This was before Watergate, remember, and people were thinking, Oh that crazy Lennon . . . what an egomaniac, who's gonna follow *him* around? Why would they want to bother with him for? They were bothering with me because we were associated with Rubin, Sinclair, these little rallies and being seen around with them people. It's like a mini-

Watergate case." (My transcripts of just this conversation run over eighty pages.) He offered me tea. "Want it with milk or what?" Then, back to the Nazis. "There's a list of Nazis as long as your *arm*, with all the things they'd done—one of them even ended up holding a service in Congress at one time. It's just ludicrous, it's *Kafka*." I asked if the President was aware of this? "You bet," he said, then added, "You can't have one junkie in the White House and try and kick another out." What? "Well, George [Harrison] passed through, you know. No, I'm being flippant, neither of us are junkies." (Except that on some level, they probably, at that time, were.) I asked how long this political harassment could go on. "As long as they can go on. As long as I've got the money. If they don't stop it, it'll go to the Supreme Court. I mean if they can take [Australian singer] Helen Reddy, they can take me, is what I say."

I asked John how much of his time was taken up with the deportation case as opposed to, say, music. He said it was on his list of lawsuits. "People sue you if you just bump into them on the street. Just ask any rock musician how many lawsuits he's in. The more money there is, the more lawsuits there are. The bigger the artist, the more lawsuits. I mean, people sue me for anything. I don't know how it happens. One minute you're talking to somebody, the next minute they're suing you." I burst out laughing, then apologized. "No, it is funny," he said. "You have to laugh about it, it's just so ludicrous." He talked about how it helped to be visible, to have a record out. "Because," he said, "it reminds the powers that be of me and what I represent. Power is power to those people, and whatever power I have, they're aware of it. Power doesn't frighten power, it makes it respect it in their business. You've got the bomb, we got the bomb, everything's okay. If you ain't got the bomb you don't even get a look in. So I'm always aware of keeping my bomb. Even though I blow it a few times, I always manage to put my bomb back together again, because that power is necessary." I asked if he thought this would all have a happy ending? Would he one day be knighted by the Queen of England? "I'm not really interested if I get knighted at seventy," he said. "I want it now. Not the knighthood; I'll take a green card and a clean passport. And cash I earn in the bank, in my own name, and I'll let my music, or my art, speak for me. If they give me a knighthood, I'll deal with it then. Sir John." He laughed.

We talked for hours about whether Brian Epstein was the mastermind who packaged the Beatles. "Everything is true and not true about everything. That's one thing I've learned. Both things are both true." I told him that was a very Yoko answer. Wasn't there a time, I asked, when the Beatles were naive? "Oh, we weren't naive," he said. "We were no more naive than he was. I mean what was he? He was serving in a record shop. He saw this group of rockers, greasers, playing loud music and a lot of kids paying attention to it. So he thought, Well, this is a business to be in. He liked the look of us, and thought, I'll be a manager, it was as simple as that. We had nobody better and we said, all right, you can do it. Then he went shopping around, getting us work. We were pretty greasy. And outside of Liverpool, when we went down South in the leather outfits, the dancehall promoters didn't really like us; they thought we looked like a gang of thugs. Then he said, 'Look, if you wear this suit . . .' We liked suits. Everybody wanted a nice, black, sharp suit. We liked the leather and the jeans, but everybody wanted a nice suit, even to wear offstage. Yeah man, I'll have a suit. So, if you wear a suit, you get this much money. All right, wear a suit, you get more money, wear a suit, I'll wear a fucking *balloon* if they're going to pay me. Epstein fronted for the Beatles. He played a great part at whatever he did, he was theatrical, that was for sure, and he believed in us. But he certainly didn't package us the way they said [he did]. If he was so clever at packaging products, what happened to Gerry and the Pacemakers and Cilla

Black? Where are those packages? Only one package survived, the original package. We weren't picked up off the street, we *allowed* him to take us. Paul wasn't that keen. He's more conservative in the way he approaches things, and that's all well and good. Maybe he'll end up with more yachts."

I told John there were rumors that he hadn't been able to see George Harrison at George's concert with Ravi Shankar at Madison Square Garden. And I asked about the supposed kerfuffle with lawyers and signing the papers that dissolved the Beatles. "I like George and I love him," John said, "and we're all right, and I saw him and there was no big deal. But the business was always interfering with the pleasure. And it was hard to deal with each other anyway. I've seen a lot of Paul and Ringo over the last two or three years, because they come to town a lot. I see Ringo in L.A., and when Paul is in New York, they always come to see me. George and I were trying to talk to each other after having not talked for three years, except vaguely, through lawyers. Plus he had the pressure of his concert and all the shlack that was going 'round it, so we just tried to communicate in the hotel. I just hung around there for a couple of days, virtually living in the hotel with him. But it's still hard to communicate because he was in the middle or the end of a psychic drama he was going through. And then, I just didn't happen to turn up on the day that they wanted [the papers] signed. But I signed it in the end, in Disneyland. I wanted to go over it one [more] time. I'd already seen [his show] in Long Island, at Nassau Coliseum, so I wasn't going to go to Madison Square Gardens [*sic*] because I don't really enjoy sitting in shows, no matter whose they are. Because you either have to go backstage with all that hassle or you've got to sit in the front. I did that with Elton in Boston, but I got all that, 'Oh look who's there' business. I know they all do it, Mick . . . they're always doing it, but it wears the shred out of me, sitting in concerts. I'd rather hear records anyway. There are very few people I want to see in concerts; I'd only go to friends. I prefer records, I always did. It's like watching a painter paint. Just give me the painting."

"My personal opinion about George," John continued, "and I can't blame him because I understand it, but I think he should have kept Ravi separate. It just doesn't work. Although I'm no one to talk about what works and what doesn't work, but it's easier to see it from a distance. Apparently some shows were all right, the one I saw was a good show. And I don't know whether it was *because* Ravi wasn't there, but that's my opinion. I think Ravi's great and all that, but I'm with the kids; I want to see George do George: George Beatle or George ex-Beatle, whatever it is. I think it's a case of being cut off—either deliberately, or because he's so involved with the Eastern trip. It's easy to get cut off. If you're just surrounded by people who aren't rocking, you forget what it is."

o o o

On November 14, 1976, a little more than a year after that conversation with John, I visited George Harrison in his rented house at the top of Beverly Glen Canyon in Los Angeles. The beard and the mustache were gone, his hair was slightly wavy, and in his own words, George Harrison was "cute" again. He wore a denim jacket trimmed with satin, jeans and a Dark Horse (his record label logo) t-shirt. He smoked Gitanes cigarettes nonstop. He was much smaller and initially, far more amusing than I had expected. Derek Taylor had arranged for us to do an interview to promote George's new solo album, *Thirty Three & 1/3*, because, George said, "I think I needed to come around again. Like another lap—remember me, folks?" There was a press dinner that night at Chasen's, and all of this promotional activity was an attempt to overcome some of the negative press he'd received for dragging Ravi Shankar and all those Indian musicians on tour with him in 1974 to an audience that really just wanted to hear "Here Comes the Sun." George admitted to me that when he sings, he knows he sounds "sad," even though, he said, "I've written a lot of funny lyrics. There are a lot of jokes. But because I sound sad, and because some people just don't *like* Indian musicians, well . . ." he trailed off. "For me," he said, "the problem with [Paul McCartney's] Wings concerts were that there weren't *enough* Indian musicians."

During our very lengthy talk, he had a lot to say. Occasionally, he sounded bitter. He said the Beatles had sold fifty million albums but were treated shoddily by their record company. In fact, he spoke much more about money and record deals and record label executives than I'd ever heard from John Lennon—with whom I'd spent far more time. He talked, as John had, about how he was getting used to lawsuits. He talked about the 1976 plagiarism lawsuit against him for his song "My Sweet Lord" in great—*great*—detail. He had never, he said, thought his song sounded like the Chiffons' "He's So Fine," that the guy who wrote "He's So Fine" had died in the late 1960s and had never even heard "My Sweet Lord." "But," George said, "if he'd been a musician, he probably wouldn't have flinched." How his own inspiration for "My Sweet Lord" had been the Edwin Hawkins Singers' "Oh Happy Day." George told me, "I just loved that song. The chord changes in 'My Sweet Lord' were the same as 'Oh Happy Day,' and I was trying to come up with something like that." He said that the whole thing had made him so paranoid that he was afraid to pick up a guitar. "I suppose if it was the only song I'd ever written I would feel bad, you know? But I feel . . . *annoyed*. Because I know the motives behind that lawsuit weren't very nice. I saw that guy in court and I wouldn't buy a secondhand motorcar off him. It was very emotional to be in court, playing a guitar. And there were all the secretaries from the other courts, everybody coming in, let's see George giving a concert."

He went on and on about Indian music and the Hare Krishnas and Hinduism. He talked about god and Vedic literature and Swami Muktananda. No one who has ever done a proper interview with him would ever describe George Harrison as the "quiet Beatle." At that time, I didn't even bother to transcribe our entire talk. He was very serious and extremely intense. And when I, an atheist, could no longer bear the spiritual path this conversation had taken, I asked him how he balanced a spiritual life and living in a world of drugged-up rock and roll musicians, which can be . . . "Seedy?" he offered. "Yes," he admitted, "that's probably the most difficult of all, because I really relate to these people. I love them, and they're my friends, and from time to time I've really gotten into that—being crazy and boogying . . . parties and whatever all that involves. I go from being completely spiritual and straight. Then, after awhile, I've gone back in with the rockers again. But I've got a good sort of tilt mechanism in me. And when that hasn't worked, I've had hepatitis."

George talked more about how, when he took all these fantastic musicians on the road and "gave people some other experience than just watching Led Zeppelin all their lives, they don't like that. People have a fear of the unknown. They'd rather you just go out and sing 'She Loves You.' So, now I'm just going to be selfish and write my own songs, make my own music, and sing all the nice tunes that people like." I asked, why was that selfish? "It's the glorification of myself," he said. I suggested that, in actual fact, wasn't he really pleasing a paying audience as opposed to trying to ram something down people's throats? He finally admitted yes, okay, a lot of people don't like Indian musicians. I pointed out that a lot of people don't like Yoko's wailing either, but John was intent on including it in his own work. George was silent for awhile, and then said, "Well, I don't like the idea of compromising myself down to the point of like, say, Wings, or

149

Paul. I could sing all the cute songs and everybody would love me. But it's not very . . . creative." He talked about Billy Preston and how great he was, and how he never could do what the Stones did. Which, he said, was to let Billy sing one or two songs and as soon as he got people dancing, just cut him off quickly and then "Mick swings across the audience on a rope. That's disgusting. Billy is such a fine musician. If you're going to have him, let Billy be Billy. Don't have him and then strap him to the back of the stage."

George talked about how difficult it was being an ex-Beatle. "People in America think we got together somewhere around 1964 and split up in 1968. But I went to school with Paul, he was a year elder to me, and we grew up from when I was thirteen and met him, and were together for seventeen years until we split. When you're that close, you just lock each other up in pigeonholes. Musically, Ringo and John and I had no problem. But musically with Paul, I had a terrible problem, because later on I would come to the session, go to get my guitar out of the case, and he'd say, 'No, no, we don't want any guitar yet. Let's do that later.' So over time, it stifled my feelings. And I just had to get out of there." I told George that when I had once asked Paul McCartney about all this, Paul had said that he could see where George would think the way he did, because George had been playing with such [other] "funky" musicians. But Paul disagreed with George's assessment that the Beatles weren't a very good band. "Well," George said, "when you put it all together, it's great. But each piece of it, it's not that good. Ringo's a great rock and roll drummer, but he'd be the first to admit that technically, he's not very good. John was a lousy guitar player, but he played certain things that nobody else could play. He was brilliant and his singing was fantastic. Paul had amazing charm and he could write those sweet melodies. I don't know what I had, but when you put it all together, it was the Beatles."

As day turned into night, George continued talking. "There just was a time," he said, "around 1968, when everybody's egos started going crazy. A lot of feelings got hurt. And then there was the problem, which was the biggest problem of all: there was no way that Yoko Ono and Linda McCartney were going to be in the Beatles. That just helped put the nail in the coffin. *Let It Be* was the final straw for me," George said. "On the very first day, soon as we started playing, it got back to 'you do this, do that, don't do this, do that.' I thought Christ, I'd hoped [Paul] had woken up to that by now. But it was just misery. And with Yoko there, wailing 'John . . . John' on one side, and Paul waving his finger on the other side, I thought, I don't need this." As for Beatles nostalgia, George said (and this was in 1976), "I expected it. Beatles nostalgia was there anyway, it just took Capitol Records to package it. I can see it coming every ten years. Obviously, if you own the Beatles' masters and you can do whatever you like with it, you can create nostalgia every time you have a deficit on your statements."

o o o

On July 27, 1976, at one p.m., on one of the hottest days of that summer, John and Yoko arrived at the Immigration Building in lower Manhattan with lawyer Leon Wildes for the hearing that would end John's four-year struggle to obtain permanent residence in the United States. Security was tight. The tiny courtroom was packed with about fifty people. John had a shorter haircut than the last time I'd seen him. He wore a white shirt, black suit, black tie, and black cowboy boots. He was tan, slim, and appeared healthy. Yoko had her hair pulled back from her face; she wore a long white dress and a serene expression. Peter Boyle and Bob Gruen were there for support. Assembled character witnesses included the aging actress Gloria Swanson—who shared an interest with the Lennons in the evils of eating sugar—Geraldo Rivera, Norman Mailer, and the Japanese de-

signer Isamu Noguchi. The judge actually said to Noguchi: "I've enjoyed your coffee table for years." John muttered to me, "How do you
like this cast Yoko produced for me? It's like *The Gong Show*." Had he
ever even watched *The Gong Show*? "Oh it's wonderful," he said.
"They have all this amateur talent, and people hit a gong when
they're terrible. Eighty-year-old women dancing in men's trousers,
singing 'Goin' Through the Rye.'" The hearing appeared to be a for-
mality; the foregone conclusion was that John would get his green
card, which he did. I asked him, now what about making records?
"It's not just making records or getting musicians together," he said.
"First, I've got to make a bloody *deal*. I can't think about making
music. I just want to clear up all the lawsuits, be with the family, rest
for a while longer, and travel. Then I can think about recording."
John got his green card, which was really pale blue, and he thanked
Yoko: "I've always said there's a great woman behind every idiot."
He told me that now he could go to Japan to "show the baby to rela-
tives." Then he and Yoko went off to the Upper East Side ice cream
parlor Serendipity to celebrate. So much for the evils of sugar.

And then, after that four-year battle to remain in this country, the
Lennons spent the next three and a half years rumored to be holed up
in the Dakota on drugs and turning away old friends. Except that in
fact, they traveled, went to parties and baby showers and Loraine
and Peter Boyle's wedding on October 21, 1977, where John was
Peter's best man. We all went from the four p.m. wedding ceremony
at the UN Chapel, to a dinner at the French restaurant Lutèce, and
then, for some reason, to a party for Rod Stewart at the Regency
Hotel. In 1980, when the Lennons "re-emerged"—which to most people meant they returned to the music scene—it was to record *Double
Fantasy*. The Lennons were paying for the album themselves, then

would sell it to the highest bidder. That turned out to be David Geffen, because he showed respect to Yoko, he spoke to her and not John about business—which both Lennons appreciated. There was a rumor, too, that the couple threw the birthdates of various executives into their son Sean's crib and he picked Geffen's.

In August of 1980, I visited John and Yoko at the Hit Factory studio during the recording sessions for *Double Fantasy*. I found John in the control room, eating custard out of a cannoli. He told me he'd been on a sugar and caffeine binge. There were raisins and nuts in a bowl, and I was offered tea, coffee or Perrier. "If there's anything stronger it's probably going on in the back room," John said. He talked a lot about a boat trip he had taken where he sailed the ocean with a captain and an instructor. "Yoko wouldn't go," he said. "Not unless it was Onassis' yacht." Yoko said, laughing, "I don't like to slum it."

We talked that day for a long time. And then a month later, in September, I went back to see them—this time at the Record Plant, where they were mixing the album. We did a lengthy interview about the album and their life over the past few years. They decided I would interview Yoko first, John second, and then, maybe the two of them together. Yoko started out by talking to me about women—how women were better for their inner wisdom and men were better for their outer wisdom, because the outer world had been structured by men. She talked about how she had been so involved with her work, but John had more experience with the world. About how so many women built their lives around men, but that was not her thing. With her, she said, it was always men building their lives around her. "Because," she actually said, "I was Van Gogh. And whoever was with me was an assistant." Then she said, "I thought men were less intelligent than me, but they could lift heavy things for me. But when I met John, I met another strong character. So, John could not only lift heavy things for me, he also had a sensitive soul. And through him, I learned what it was like to be a guy in this society. It's not all that easy."

At some point during my talk with Yoko, John came in and said that it would be best if he and I talked then, because there was a lull in the control room. We moved into another room and I turned on my tape recorder. I asked John when he decided to return to this rat race. He said he went through every thought you could possibly go through over the last five years. The first eighteen months it was hard for him to stop from jumping onto a piano, he said, because he'd been turning out singles and albums since 1962. So why now? "Because Sean's five, I'm forty, and I've got the songs." He described being a "househusband" in painstaking and lengthy detail. How he took care of Sean and oversaw every morsel of food that went into the child's mouth every day. He described a typical day: he would wake up, oversee breakfast and the play periods, then lunch, then teeth-brushing, then perhaps a foray (a nanny would take Sean to the park while John took a nap), then dinner. He laughingly described himself as a "rich housewife," because in truth, he had assistants, nannies, cooks and housekeepers. Yoko spent her time downstairs in the office, taking care of the family business, buying cattle, and purchasing additional apartments in the Dakota. John said he regretted not having been there for his older son Julian, who was born while John was in the Beatles and constantly on tour. It is possible that this was all a spin on things for my benefit, or for the benefit of the readers of my article. Every marriage has an unspoken—or spoken—deal, arrangement, something, that is known only to the people in it. Was he really happy to be home, safe, besotted by his son? Probably. He said he and Yoko made a conscious decision to live this way, and there can be no question that he was unequivocally present for the first five years of Sean's life.

Backstage at his concert at Nassau Coliseum in the summer of 1973, Eric Clapton actually fell to his knees and kissed my hand. Neither of us remembers it.

Always relieved upon landing, I exit the "Starship" before Mick Jagger, somewhere in America during the Rolling Stones 1975 summer tour.

Somewhere in the U.S. on the Stones' 1975 Tour of the Americas, Mick Jagger and I make some prank phone calls.

At a party in the ballroom of a Milwaukee hotel during the
Stones' 1975 tour, Ian Stewart and I admire his birthday cake.

I listen while Mick makes a long distance call during
the Stones' 1975 summer tour.

Photo © Annie Leibovitz

Mick sidles up to me backstage at Madison Square Garden in the summer of 1975 to tell me what Bob Dylan is wearing.

Photo © Bob Gruen

Photo © Bob Gruen

Keith and I are joined by a buoyant John McEnroe backstage at the Ritz in New York City following a Tina Turner show in the 1980s.

Me, Keith Richards and Jack Daniel's in New York City, sometime in the 20th century.

Jimmy Page and I talk without moving our lips. Led Zeppelin manager Peter Grant *(left)* eavesdrops.

Atlantic Records president Ahmet Ertegun and me on Led Zeppelin's jet en route to Pittsburgh, July 24, 1973.

Did Robert Plant dial a number at random and hand me the phone? At Nirvana restaurant, New York City, January 1976.

In August 1976, Richard Robinson *(center)* tries to leave CBGB's. Owner Hilly Kristal *(right)* urges him to stay.

We'll always have Paris: with the Ramones and their manager Danny Fields at the Café de Flore sometime in the 1970s. *Left to right:* Joey, Johnny, Dee Dee, Tommy, Danny and me.

Patti Smith and I have a chat backstage in 1976 at the Ocean Club.

The original New York Dolls, backstage at the Bottom Line in July 1978: me, David Johansen and Fran Lebowitz.

Smoking inside: Iggy, Cyrinda Foxe, David Bowie and me at the Ocean Club in March 1977.

At a party at Feathers in New York City on November 12, 1976, Lou Reed explains his hat.

Iggy, David Bowie and I take time out to relax after one of David's Thin White Duke shows sometime in the 1970s.

At a Rolling Stones party in New York City in 1983, Andy Warhol and I share a contemplative moment.

At a party in New York City following a Queen show in February 1976, David Johansen, Freddie Mercury and I gossip.

Lou Reed asks me to hide a blank cassette from Television's Tom Verlaine at CBGB, August 1976.

In Bungalow 5 at the Beverly Hills Hotel, David Johansen and I extol the virtues of Bungalow 5 at the Beverly Hills Hotel, September 1973.

Backstage at the Ocean Club in March 1977, Richard Robinson explains to David Bowie why he'll only drink out of a bottle below 14th Street.

My first interview with John and Yoko at their Bank Street apartment, New York City, January 1973.

John Lennon and I look for David Bowie backstage at the Uris Theater in New York City at the Grammy Awards, March 1, 1975.

David Bowie and I look for John Lennon backstage at the Grammy Awards on March 1, 1975.

With Michael Jackson and my Sony cassette recorder at
the Jacksons' house in Encino, California, October 1972.

Family harmony in Encino. The Jackson Five crack me up in this undated photograph.

Sex Pistols lead singer Johnny Rotten in a rare smiling photo   backstage at Manchester's Electric Circus, on the "Anarchy in the U.K." tour.

With ex–New York Doll and Heartbreakers guitarist Johnny Thunders at Manchester's Electric Circus, December 1976, on the "Anarchy" tour.

Then in Public Image Ltd., John (Johnny Rotten) Lydon talks with me and filmmaker and dub tape maestro Don Letts at the Kitchen in New York City in April 1982.

With guitarist Mick Jones while he was still in the Clash.

With Joe Strummer of the Clash —one of my favorite bands— somewhere on their 1980 U.S. tour.

Backstage at *Saturday Night Live* in 1982, Joe Strummer and I have a laugh over my column in the *New York Post*.

Out on the town with Elton in New York City in the 1980s.

Me, Keith Richards and Fran Lebowitz photographed by Jane Rose sometime in the 21st century.

At the Rainbow Room in New York City on April 5, 1976: Mick, me, and Lenny Kaye in a rare portrait.

Dr. Dre, Bono and I talk beats at a Grammy after-party in
2001 at the Cicada Restaurant in Los Angeles.

Jonathan Becker captures the moment while Bono
and I reminisce at the 2003 *Vanity Fair* Oscar party at
Morton's in L.A.

Jonathan Becker took this photo
of me with two of my favorite
musicians—Jay Z and Jon Brion
—at *Vanity Fair's* 2005 Oscar
party in L.A.

Photo © Benjamin Tietge

At his *Vanity Fair* cover shoot in June 2013, Jay Z poses with four chains and me.

Lady Gaga and me in an elevator in 2012. She's wearing twelve-inch heels. I'm not.

Photo © Annie Leibovitz

Smokey Robinson, Berry Gordy and I are all smiles for Annie Leibovitz's camera.

Yeezy's world: backstage at Madison Square Garden in November 2013 with an Apollonian Kanye West.

Photo © Gabe Tesoriero

At the 2001 cover shoot for the *Vanity Fair* music issue. *Left to right:* Jewel, Stevie Wonder, Beck, Joni Mitchell, Gwen Stefani and I take a break.

Paul Rosenberg captured this special moment with me, Eminem and Rick Rubin backstage at *Saturday Night Live* on November 1, 2013.

Then again, there were always rumors that he was, in fact, drugged and depressed, and not making music because Yoko's astrologist decreed that the stars weren't aligned correctly during that five-year period. We will never truly know, because the only people who have written about this are people who were either disgruntled or fired employees, or disreputable authors who never met the couple. Of the two people who were actually there, one is dead and the other still attempts to keep some things private. But John seemed happy on that day we talked, and took great delight in describing having settled in at home. (I remembered how, five years earlier, he had told me he never wanted to settle down. But in the midst of this happy reverie, I chose not to bring that up.) He did admit that baking bread or preparing food for the family wasn't as satisfying an accomplishment as writing and recording a song. "There's nothing to show for it when you're done," he said. "But if you think about it, I've been under pressure since I was twenty-one or twenty-two—that's in public, being very famous. That's a long time to be expected to be churning out thousands upon thousands of things. And even if it was a hit, there came a point where I didn't want to be churning out things anymore. Mal Evans, who worked for us, said he saw Elvis [Presley] recently, but I would never go see him, even though I worshipped him when I was a kid—before he went into the army. I would never go see him in Vegas. And I asked Mal, 'What was he like?' And Mal said, 'Well, if you pretended you were sixteen, then it was all right.' I don't want to be a person that people have to pretend they're sixteen to be able to see." He went on to say that here he was, rocking and rolling, but that if it ceased to be fun, now he knew he could walk away—because he'd done it before. He talked about his new songs and said, "There is no way I could have written 'Starting Over' in 1974. I was a miserable son of a bitch. I'd split from Yoko, I'd been drinking myself nearly dead, making an ass out of myself, being a drunk in public. I'd always been a bit intense, but this was really a miserable period. I count myself lucky to be alive. I could have killed myself, easy. If I get depressed I think I want to jump out of a window. But it usually passes. I mean I was stepping out of moving cars in 1973 in Los Angeles." I pointed out that when we spoke in 1974, he didn't say any of this; that he seemed happy at the time, and had dismissed the craziness of his time in L.A. "Well," he said, "I was pretty out of it. I've always been like that, even as a youngster. But then, I was surrounded by the Beatles and managers and they would protect me and cover for whatever I was doing. Paul or Brian Epstein would shuffle me off into a room before I would go wandering the streets again, looking for action. When I split from Yoko, there was nobody to say 'No.' I would be dead or insane or both if it wasn't for her."

We talked that day for hours. He seemed indignant about people—some critics, some other rock stars—who had publicly criticized him for "hiding" in his house. "People said I went 'underground,'" he laughed. "Underground? I was living *above the park*. Mick [Jagger] was going on and on about me—how 'John never calls and he keeps changing his number all the time and he's hiding behind the kid.' Everybody was trying to get me down to a recording session. They all thought, what John needs is a good *session*. As if they fucking know anything. They don't know me at all; all they've got is their image of a person they've been in a disco with or something. The fact is, I never called Mick once in my life, so I don't know why he's complaining that I don't call him. I never call anybody." (I reminded him that he had, in fact, called me.) "Well," he said, "I never even called the other Beatles, they always called me. I'm self-involved, I'm paranoid and I don't like phones. I didn't *see* a phone until I was about fourteen, we didn't have one in the house. The phone was for emergencies and telegrams. Telegrams still scare me. From where I come from, it means somebody's dead. Why were people angry at me for not calling them? If I was *dead* they wouldn't be angry at me. If I'd conveniently died in the mid-1970s after the *Rock 'n' Roll* album they'd all be saying, 'what a great guy and wasn't he funny with a Tampax on his head.' It's all right when you're dead. But I didn't die, and it infuriated everybody that I would live and do what I wanted to do, which was to hang around the house and be with the family."

He said that Yoko turned him on to Zen and haiku and he turned her on to the heartbeat. He talked about how great David Bowie was in *The Elephant Man* on Broadway. How he thought the funniest remark he had read about himself was that he and Yoko never went out unless they went to Japan. He said they often ordered dinner in from Dial-A-Steak, but that they *did* go out of the house, adding that there were other entrances and exits out of the Dakota besides the front door. And he talked about Beatles nostalgia. "I think it'll go on forever," he said, "like Glenn Miller." He said he wasn't particularly interested in the Beatles, or the Kennedys, or the 1960s. "The adults that were the twenty-year-olds in the '60s have all turned into what we were supposed to be saving ourselves from—asking for the '60s to come back with the Beatles and the Kennedys. They probably even want a war, so we can have an anti-war movement. They're not getting their jocks off with the nuclear thing—it's not big enough to draw a crowd. We don't need the '60s and we don't need the Beatles and we don't need the Kennedys. Let's leave them where they are, in a nice memory."

I asked him if he still believed in peace and love. He said he was always wavering on that subject. "It's hard to be Gandhi or Martin Luther King or to follow them. I don't admire politicians particularly, I think they're showbiz people. But people who put their thing on the line, like Gandhi, who threw the British out by not shooting anybody . . . those are the political people I admire. But I don't want to be shot for it like Gandhi and I don't want to be shot for it like Martin Luther King. I admire their stance, but I don't want to be a martyr."

o o o

Epilogue: Less than a year after John was shot and killed, I got a call from one of her assistants that Yoko was inviting me to the Dakota to see her. I was told that this would not be an interview, I needn't bring a tape recorder. I hadn't spoken to her since John had been murdered, although I had received word in the days after he was killed that it would be all right with her if I went on television, specifically the Tom Snyder show to talk about John. I went to see her at the Dakota. She was in their seventh-floor apartment, propped up on her king-sized bed, with lots of white pillows behind her head. She had tinted glasses on, and she talked very softly about the night of the murder and the days that followed: about all the fans singing in the street and how she could hear them all night long. She talked about John's shattered eyeglasses. About how she had told Sean that John was dead. And she talked about her new album (*Season of Glass*). She said several times that this conversation was not an interview. I listened sympathetically. I expressed the expected condolences. I respected her wishes. I wrote nothing. And then, about a week or two later, I read the exact same conversation, practically word for word, written by someone else, in an interview in *Rolling Stone* magazine.

Five

Long before the disfiguring plastic surgeries, the onstage crotch-grabbing, the bizarre disguises, the over-the-top fantasyland ranch, the friendships with aging showbiz legends, the suspect marriages and subsequent divorces, the mysteriously conceived children, the drug addictions, the hospital stays, the grotesque chotchke hoarding, the child molestation accusations, the child molestation trial, and the involuntary manslaughter trial of "concierge" doctor Conrad Murray, Michael Jackson was one of the most enthusiastic, sweet, inquisitive teenagers I'd ever met.

On October 8, 1972, I went to 4641 Hayvenhurst Drive in Encino, California, to meet the Jackson Five for the first time. I was there to do a big story for a little fan magazine I edited called *Rock & Soul*. We put the Jacksons on the cover as often as possible, because the family group had sold over fourteen million albums, had four Number One singles, and were teen heartthrobs—complete with lunchboxes, posters, a television cartoon show and dolls. Like most of the houses that Michael would live in for the rest of his life, it had a long driveway leading to a locked gate. This gate had a sign on it—"Beware of Guard Dog"—with the phone number of the dog training establishment. ("Promotion," Michael would tell me later.) The family had two dogs: a German shepherd named Heavy, and a Doberman named Hitler. One of the Jackson kids, I don't remember which one, told me that their bodyguard named the dog Hitler but they all officially referred to him in interviews as "Duke." But unlike the other houses that Michael would live in, the house on Hayvenhurst was not crawling with security or cloaked in secrecy. In fact, Michael met me when I arrived, and was friendly, outgoing, curious, fun. For Katherine and Joseph Jackson and their nine children, this Encino house—with its swimming pool, small outdoor basketball court, lemon and orange trees, and room for the family's menagerie (dogs, snakes, llama, giraffe)—was a "mansion." Michael told me that Liberace used to live across the street and the Jacksons would visit him and look at his diamonds. On that day in October, Michael wore a short-sleeved brown shirt, jeans and sneakers. His hair was in an Afro. In his hand was a comb that he used to keep fluffing out his hair. He took me on a tour of the house—showing me the rehearsal room, the pay phone, and his bedroom, which he shared with his younger brother Randy. The bedroom had two beds, a telephone, a clock with time zones from various cities around the world, and a TV set. Michael showed me some dance steps—routines that had been drummed into him by his father, who managed the family group. By the time Michael was six, he had performed with his brothers Jackie, Tito, Jermaine and Marlon in strip clubs. When they performed at the Apollo Theater in Harlem, Michael stood in the wings and watched—no, *studied*— Jackie Wilson and James Brown. Michael was fourteen years old when I met him, but I thought he was twelve, because when the Jacksons were signed to Motown in 1969 and Michael was ten, he was told to say he was eight. Motown owner Berry Gordy thought it would sound "cuter." After spending the day interviewing all of the brothers, but mostly chatting with Michael, I called a friend and said, "This kid is going to be the greatest entertainer ever. Seriously, like Frank Sinatra."

Michael asked me more questions that day than I asked him. He told me he was going to London "to perform for the Queen," and asked if I had seen her palace. He said he wanted to go shopping for souvenirs and antiques. He said the Temptations and the Supremes told him Ringo Starr had taken them shopping when they went to London. I told him about the antiques on Portobello Road, and he asked, "Cheap?" He asked if I had ever heard of Napoleon—he said he "wanted to see him" when he was in Paris. He asked what airline I took to Europe. He asked if I'd heard of the comic actor Marty Feldman. He asked what kind of tape recorder I was using. We talked about how, if tape recorders were made much smaller, people were going to be able to sneak them into concerts and make bootlegs. I asked him the usual fan magazine questions: what did he like to do in his spare time? "Swim . . . play pool," he said. "When we lived in the other house we would go to the park to play basketball, but now we have everything here." There was a discussion about my maroon nail polish. He told me he loved magic tricks. He practiced speaking in French. When I asked him if he ever got scared onstage, he said, "No. If you know what you're doing, you're not scared onstage."

Like *Rock Scene* magazine, *Rock & Soul* was a newsprint fan magazine that featured similar budget ads: "How to Make Others Secretly Do Your Bidding!!!" and ads for wigs, self-defense manuals, and products to help people put "Wate-On." This magazine too, was a family affair: Richard and my sister (and longtime assistant) Deane Zimmerman and a few of our friends did all the so-called editorial.

Mostly, we ran "photo spreads" of Michael with various celebrities—Liza Minnelli, Caroline and John F. Kennedy Jr., and the young actress Stephanie Mills, star of the Broadway version of *The Wiz*. When Michael's black teenage fans got angry because he was photographed with white girls (Brooke Shields, Tatum O'Neal), his publicist decided it would be a good idea for him to be pictured with Stephanie as often as possible. Those photos with Michael and Stephanie littered the pages of *Rock & Soul* until we decided it was just too much of a setup. Even then, it was obvious that Michael was the most charismatic of the brothers, and the star. We got along instantly, and I visited him and his family several times over the course of the next few years. Michael often called me on the telephone. Or a publicist called and put him on the phone. And when he came to New York—to perform at Radio City Music Hall and, later, Madison Square Garden—we would catch up.

On February 5, 1975, we met at the Warwick Hotel in New York City. He was, by then, sixteen, but it's possible I still thought he was fourteen. He was self-conscious about his acne, and admitted that his brothers teased him about it. We talked about *Dancing Machine*, the first album that Motown had allowed the brothers to produce themselves. "I got to sing free," Michael said. "It was the first time I got to do my own thing. Our persistence in continually telling the record company we didn't want other writers, was what finally changed their mind. You've got to remember," he said, "I've been around studios since I was a child, and I just picked it up." He talked about Stevie Wonder; he admired him because he was always able to "sing free" and insisted on recording where he wanted to record, rather than the Motown studios. "Only a producer-singer knows what he's doing," Michael said, "because he sings also. When you're being told what to do, it's not free." What had he previously been told to do?

"Sing this word this way, this line this way, go up and down—like that," he said. "It's not being 'you,' and you're trying to get the 'you' out. Like Gladys Knight; she sings freely and look how great she is." He talked about the Jacksons' concerts and said, "There's no reason why we can't do anything we want to do onstage. We really would like to do something like Emerson, Lake and Palmer or some of those rock groups do—like when the piano turns around in the air. We have lots of ideas like that and we intend to do them in future shows."

Once again I asked him what he did in his "spare" time. He said because they traveled so much for their shows, he liked to stay at home and read. "The dictionary, adventure books, all sorts of things," he said. "I had four weeks off and stayed home." He told me he hated parties, unless it was a party where you could just talk. "And when there are other entertainers there, it's even better." We talked about whether or not he could go out to concerts, and he said whenever he went out, there was always a problem. "But," he added, "that's the only way you can really tell what's happening." He said he always wanted to work with Barbra Streisand, and that he wrote a ballad he thought would be perfect for her. "Ballads are more special," he said. "You can have a pop song that will be known for three weeks and after that you hear nothing about it. But if you do a good ballad, it'll be in the world forever. Like Stevie's 'Living in the City'—it's a great song and I love it, it opens up the minds of a lot of people. But it won't be around as long as a song like 'My Cherie Amour' or 'You Are the Sunshine of My Life.'"

In February 1977, we talked on the phone about interviews. "People talk to you and they want to know about you," he said, "but interviews help entertainers one hundred percent. I don't [only] mean promotion-wise. I mean, when they ask you questions, it helps you to think about your life, to look at your future. It makes you think about what you're going to be doing in the next ten years." I asked him if he ever got bored. Only when he was stuck inside a hotel room with too many fans outside, he said. But, he was quick to add, sticking to the script that demonstrated his early Motown media training, he felt an obligation to his fans. "They made you who you are. They're the ones who buy the records. If an entertainer did a concert and nobody showed up, he wouldn't do the concert. So he owes it to them." I asked if he resented never having had a normal childhood. "No," he said. "There's such a thing as talent, and I was taught that this was given to me. If I didn't like doing it, if it [felt like] work, I don't think I would have lasted this long. I'd probably go crazy." Another time, when we met in New York at the Plaza Hotel, Michael was wearing a blue sweater, blue pants, a white shirt and, for some reason, an Electric Light Orchestra pin. When it was time to take photos, his publicist called him into another room to tell him to take his undershirt off; Michael came back and said he could have told him that in front of me. Michael said he'd seen *The Wiz* on Broadway three times but wanted to stay an extra day so he could see it again. He asked Bob Gruen questions about lighting while Bob took photos. Michael had visited the Bronx Zoo that morning; it was his first time there. He said he liked the exotic birds the best, that they used to have some at the Encino house but the mating calls were so loud it drove the neighbors crazy, so the birds had to go. He asked if Coney Island was still any good. He compared Disneyland to Disney World and said, "Disney World is better; it's more of a world, like they say. It's a resort, it has everything—golf, tennis, hotels. It's all fantasy, all the time."

Michael, along with all of his brothers and his sisters LaToya and Janet, answered a *Rock & Soul* questionnaire when he was eighteen years old. Among Michael's questions and answers: What do you do in your spare time? *Read, think, write songs.* Would you like to get married? *Later in life.* What kind of girl would you like to marry? *Kind.* How many children would you like to have? *20, adopted, all races.* What would you do if someone gave you a million dollars? *Invest.* Of all the places you've been to in America, which one would you like to go back to and why? *Hawaii. Wisconsin. I love it.* What was the biggest thrill of your life? *Finding what I was searching for.* Who has helped you most with your career? *My father. Experience.* Of all the performers you've worked with, who do you admire the most? *Fred Astair [sic]. Stevie Wonder.* What do you like most about your work? *Learning.* What do you dislike about your work? *Arguing.* What is your most prized material possession? *A child. Words of wisdom.* Who is your favorite actor? *Heston, Brando, Bruce Dern.* Who is your favorite actress? *Garland. Bette Davis.* Do you have a nickname? *Nose.* (And then, crossed out, *niger [sic]*). What do you daydream about? *Future.*

o o o

Towards the end of 1977, when I asked Michael if he still liked meeting his fans, for the first time, a more independent, even slightly cynical tone crept into his conversation. No longer spouting the Motown party line, he said, "I enjoy all that sometimes, seeing people who love me, or buy my records. But sometimes, people think you owe your life to them. They have a bad attitude—like 'I made you who you are.' That may be true—but not that *one person.* And, if the music wasn't good, they wouldn't have bought it. Some of them think they actually own you. They'll say, 'Sit down,' 'Sign this,' or 'Can I have your autograph?' and I'll say, 'Yes, do you have a pen?' And they say, 'No, go get one.' Honestly. I'm not exaggerating. But I just try to deal with it."

In October 1977, there was a party for Michael at Studio 54. On hand were the dancers from *The Wiz*, his mother Katherine, sisters Janet and LaToya, and brothers Marlon and Tito. Also present were Epic Records executives, CBS Records president Walter Yetnikoff, and assorted drag queens. Michael and I sat together on one of the sofas on the side of the dance floor. He told me that he loved New York City. "It's the perfect spot for me," he said. "When I'm in New York I get up early and I have a whole schedule. I'm going to see this play, I'm going to have lunch, I'm going to see a movie. I like the energy. Whenever I come back home, I look forward to going back to New York—I love the big stores, I love everything." He said he had the time of his life in New York filming (the flop movie) *The Wiz*, and now, what he really wanted to do, more than anything, was make more movies. "I can go on tour and it's exciting, but when it's done, it'll be lost to the world. If I do a movie, it's a moment captured for eternity. The stars die—like Charlie Chaplin—but his films will be here forever. If he did Broadway and plays while he was alive, he would have been lost to the world." I asked him about working with Diana Ross—who he adored—in *The Wiz*. Michael said, "It was incredible. I learned so much from her. We're like brother and sister. She made sure I was okay on the set; she was very protective. I just loved the world of movie making; I love it more than reality. Sometimes I just wish I could wake up in the morning to a big production dance number."

In 1979, after he recorded his smash solo album *Off the Wall*, he talked about his producer Quincy Jones. He said that Quincy had worked with all the greats—Billie Holiday, Dinah Washington—and, he said "I wanted to watch and learn from a giant. I wanted an album that wouldn't just consist of one kind of music, because I love all kinds of music. I don't like to label music. It's like saying this child is white, this child is black, this child is Japanese—but they're all children. It reminds me of prejudice. If somebody has a wonderful song that's right for me, I'd love to do it. That's what I enjoy most about doing solo albums. With the Jacksons, we were just doing our own thing in our little private world. That's why I didn't want the Jacksons to produce my album. I don't want the same sound. Mine is different."

o o o

Michael and I talked a lot about television, which he referred to as "the biggest audience in the world." In 1969, Diana Ross had "presented" the Jackson Five on the Ed Sullivan show and was forever incorrectly credited with discovering them. But Suzanne de Passe, who was in charge of artist relations at Motown, brought the Jackson Five to Berry Gordy. Suzanne, a friend of mine, told me that in 1983, when she and Berry Gordy wanted Michael to perform on the *Motown 25* TV special, which she produced, the negotiations were intense. Agent Michael Ovitz—who, at that time, reportedly "ran" Hollywood—was involved. He sat at the head of the table during the negotiations, but had to leave the meeting early to go and see Barbra Streisand or someone. Michael felt disrespected and he cried. He wouldn't perform with his brothers on the show unless he was given a solo spot. At first, he refused to allow them to film the number. Then, he insisted on creative control of the final edit. Berry Gordy had to go to the studio where Michael was recording to ask him to do it to get him to do it. Of course, Michael's astonishing solo performance of "Billie Jean" on that show—with the hat and the glove and the moonwalk—sent him into the stratosphere. It was one of those landmark showbiz performances that put him in a category he could never top, and quite possibly, from which he would ultimately never recover.

Suzanne de Passe worked as a vice president at Motown, co-wrote the screenplay for *Lady Sings the Blues*, and produced the *Motown 25* special as well as numerous other TV shows. She recalled the first time she saw the Jackson Five in 1968. "I was in my apartment at 1300 East Lafayette Street in Detroit, where many of the Motown artists lived," she said. "I was home one afternoon and [musician] Bobby Taylor called up and asked if I would come down to his apartment. He said he wanted me to see something, and I said no. I wasn't about to go to some man's apartment. But he said come on, so I did, and he opened the door and there were all these kids sort of strewn across his living room. He clapped his hands and went, 'OK everybody, this is Suzanne de Passe and she works for Berry Gordy and you need to sing for her because she can get you the audition.' So they snapped to—they had their drummer and keyboard player with them—they sang, and I was blown away. Bobby had seen them at the Apollo, possibly on Amateur Night, and had convinced Joseph [Jackson] that if he drove to Detroit, he would get them an audition with Motown. I was wowed. So the next day, I told Mr. Gordy on the phone what I'd seen, and I said, 'I think you should sign these kids.' And he said, '*Kids?* I don't want any kids. You know how much trouble it is with Stevie Wonder and the teachers, and when you're a minor you have to have a special chaperone and court approval of the contract, and it is a *problem*.' He said no. I had to really muster up all my courage and go back to him and say, 'Really, I don't think you can afford not to see these kids.' Finally he agreed to see them." According to Berry Gordy, who I've talked to at length about Motown, "When I first met with Michael, I thought he was a little Frankie Lymon kind of guy. Suzanne brought them to me, and it's true, I didn't want any kids. Stevie Wonder had five people with him, a tutor and this and that . . . but [when] they came in, I had a new video camera, and I said this is special, we should capture this." He also told me, "It hurt when they left Motown—Diana, Marvin, Michael. I look unhappy on *Motown 25*, because my company was losing millions of dollars."

Suzanne was put in charge of the Jackson Five's first tour. "When we started out," she said, "we could go everywhere. We could go shopping, go get hamburgers, go to rehearsal. And within a very short time, we could go nowhere. We would come out of the hotel and 500 kids came storming at us and we had to dive into the car. It was both exhilarating and frightening. And eventually it became just frightening." According to Lionel Richie, who was in the Commodores and opened the Jackson Five's debut tour, "What I learned most on that tour, was whatever you do, if you sing, dance, juggle, whatever it is, you do it in the first song. Because they may not stick around for the second one. This little kid [Michael] did everything in the first song. I kept waiting for Suzanne to tell me that Michael was a midget, because it couldn't be anything else. Then I realized, that's a real ten-year-old kid [except he was twelve]. I would watch him play with water balloons backstage. Then he'd walk onstage and turn into this full grown entertaining monster."

o o o

In my interviews in the 1970s and 1980s with the other Jacksons, I was told that when Michael still lived at home with his family, he only ate fruits and raw vegetables every day. The family didn't drink, except some wine and champagne when guests came over or brandy when someone was sick. Until they were eighteen, their mother Katherine, a devout Jehovah's Witness, took the children to Kingdom Hall and made them go preach from door to door—often wearing disguises. When they came of age, she let them choose their religion. In the 1980s, in a lengthy talk to promote her solo album *Control*, Janet Jackson told me that the nasty tabloid press coverage of Michael was just part of show business. "Michael told me that when you hear bad things about yourself," she said, "just put your energies into something else. Put it into your music—it'll make you stronger." Still, I told Janet, people think he is weird, what with all that plastic surgery, the chimpanzee companion, the hyperbaric chamber and whatnot. Janet defended the facial reconstruction. "So many stars do that, but the press picks on certain people. I think if more people could afford it they'd do it too. I see nothing wrong with it. Aging is a sad thing. I don't see anything wrong with staying young as long as you can." Michael's older brother Marlon, to whom he was closest when growing up, told me, "Sometimes [the stuff they write about Michael] hurts. But the main thing is they're keeping the name going. Regardless if it's good or bad news. If they stop talking about you, then you're in trouble." As for the constant stories about Michael having had no fun as a child while the other brothers participated in sports and dates, Marlon disagreed: "That's not true, he did the same things we all did. But we all rehearsed constantly, we rehearsed together, and that's how we got to where we are today."

o o o

Michael had a completely different voice (the high, whispery one) when talking in public than he did when he was talking to a lawyer or a record company executive (normal, forceful). I heard both. During the 1980s, I was friendly with CBS Records Group president Walter Yetnikoff, who often told me that Michael called him incessantly about his record sales, marketing and promotion. "Possessed" was the word Yetnikoff used to describe Michael's involvement in his day-to-day business. On February 7, 1984, CBS threw a huge party at the Museum of Natural History for 1,200 guests to celebrate the mega-million success of Michael Jackson's *Thriller* (which, at somewhere between 65–110 million worldwide sales, is still the biggest selling album in history). The invitation to the party was printed on a sequined glove. President and Mrs. Reagan sent a telegram. Walter Yetnikoff introduced Michael as the greatest star ever. And a few days later, Walter told me that Michael was conflicted about touring again with his brothers.

In November 1983, boxing promoter Don King had hosted a combination luncheon/press conference at Tavern on the Green in New York City to announce the Jacksons' 1984 "Victory" tour. Don King came out and talked about the Jacksons and himself: how wonderful the tour would be and how fabulous their association was. He introduced the Jackson parents and the celebrities in the room: Dustin Hoffman, Andy Warhol, Roberta Flack, Ossie Davis, Ruby Dee and a few boxers. King went on about how it would be the biggest grossing tour of all time, the biggest this, the biggest that. He quoted Shakespeare. He introduced the Jackson brothers. Michael introduced his sisters and the brothers' wives. It was a cross between a press conference for a heavyweight title fight and a revival meeting.

During the "Victory" tour, Michael traveled separately from his brothers. He sent Don King a letter stating that no one could communicate with anyone on Michael's behalf without prior permission, and that only Michael's personal representatives could collect money paid to him for his participation in the tour. Basically, Don King could not hire anyone to work on that tour without Michael's approval. Michael referred to the "Victory" tour as the "Last Hurrah" and "The Final Curtain" for the family group. There were rumors of brotherly discord. Jermaine did not feel that he, Jermaine, was getting enough attention. Jackie Jackson wasn't on the tour because he broke his leg when his furious wife drove her car into him after discovering his affair with Paula Abdul. But Jackie still got paid a percentage of the tour grosses. On August 4, 1984, I took Van Halen's lead singer David Lee Roth—then at the height of his band's success—to see the Jacksons' show at Madison Square Garden. Before the show, we met Michael in a private area of the Garden's rotunda. I was surprised at how different Michael looked since the last time I had seen him. I was taken aback too, by how much makeup he wore—it rubbed off on my clothing when we hugged hello. But mostly, I was amused by how fully aware he was of just exactly who David Lee Roth was—probably even down to the number of records Van Halen had sold and their chart positions.

Michael had a keen eye on the competition. He'd often pick my brain about other shows I'd seen and the musicians I talked to. When Michael had his own solo success and moved away from the family, he was far more candid about his feelings and our talks became more conspiratorial. If Michael told me his brothers were married but please don't print that, I didn't print that—even though we both agreed that it was ridiculous. I was, after all, initially writing about him for a teenage fan magazine. In 1982, Eddie Van Halen played a guitar solo on "Beat It" on Michael's *Thriller* album. It may have been producer Quincy Jones' idea. Then again, it very easily could have been Michael's. In 1987, Michael used Billy Idol's guitarist Steve Stevens on "Bad." And in 1992 for Michael's *Dangerous* album, Guns N' Roses guitarist Slash did the solo on "Black or White." These were all guitar players I knew well. It showed how much Michael was aware of other scenes—especially rock. In 1987, Steve Stevens told me, "One of the things I stipulated about doing the track with Michael was that he be there in the studio when we did it. The first thing Michael said to me was that he liked my suit. He was really musically literate, down to things that most people might leave to the engineer. He knew exactly what he wanted."

But while many people justifiably felt Michael—and unfortunately, Madonna—were the artists of the 1980s, to me, no one was more talented or important during that decade than Prince. In 1987, Prince released *Sign O' the Times*, a double album that included the incredible title song about AIDS. One night David Lee Roth, the then eighteen-year-old model Christy Turlington and I went to dinner at Indochine. Christy told me she wanted to meet Dave. I told her she really didn't. But she insisted that she had been a Van Halen fan and she wanted to meet him. After an hour or more at dinner, listening to David Lee Roth laugh at his own jokes, we departed for Mick Jagger's house on the Upper West Side. Mick alternately flirted with Christy (who dragged me into a closet, whispering that he was too old for her) and played us the *Sign O' the Times* album. Mick asked me my opinion. I said I thought it was amazing. He agreed, and told me that Rod Stewart or someone had told him if Prince was white, they'd all be in trouble.

There is no question that Michael Jackson was acutely aware of Prince's talent, his sexuality, and his ascent. I am convinced that just the knowledge of Prince had a lot to do with why Michael—who couldn't play guitar himself and wasn't about to enlist one of his brothers for the role—sought out those guitar superstars for his solo albums. And possibly, it had a lot to do with the onset of Michael's onstage crotch-grabbing. While many of us considered this gesture blatant and more than slightly creepy, Michael's fans apparently did not. In addition, shows like *Yo! MTV Raps* and rap music in general undoubtedly influenced Michael to get "edgier" with his music. In September of 1988, Michael performed for three nights at the Meadowlands Arena in New Jersey the same week that Prince did a two-night stint at Madison Square Garden. Whoever booked these shows at the same time must have had a wicked sense of humor. (And, in fact, in 2009, when Michael was planning his fifty shows at London's O2 arena, it was known that he was intent on beating Prince's record at that same venue. Prince, however, only did twenty-one nights there; Michael could have booked a more workable twenty-two shows and still "won.") In 1988, their concerts were totally different: Michael concentrated on his dancing, while Prince, who performed in the round, employed choreography of a different sort. He had several women writhing around him, miming a ménage à trois situation. Prince's lyrics and onstage patter were overtly sexual—until the second half of his show when Prince turned to God, and invoked a lengthy, religious discourse. Michael steered clear of religion. And despite all that slithering around with a female dancer and a "love" ballad with his then-backup singer Sheryl Crow, Michael's image was asexual. Maybe these images were incorrect. I noted at the time that perhaps Prince read the Bible in private and Michael was wild, but I doubted it. Still, both were huge, reclusive, mysterious stars. (And today, Prince is reportedly a devout Jehovah's Witness.)

Michael couldn't have chosen two crazier guitarists to work with than Eddie Van Halen and Slash. When I first met Eddie in 1982, he wouldn't do interviews; he left that to his lead singer, the occasionally amusing blabbermouth David Lee Roth. Because Eddie refused to do interviews, he was the one I wanted to talk to. One night in 1982, I was at the "new" Peppermint Lounge in New York City with Debbie Harry, David Bowie, and Paul Simonon of the Clash. We were there to see Iggy. David Lee Roth walked in—all flowing blonde hair and leather chaps and a shirt opened down to his waist. He flaunted masculine confidence and a king of the jungle persona—until he walked over to Bowie and Paul Simonon to tell them how much he admired them. I might have been the only person at our table who actually knew who David Lee Roth was, and, as he babbled on, everyone just stared at him and said nothing. Embarrassed, he eventually skulked away. The next day, his publicist phoned repeatedly, asking me why I wouldn't interview Dave. Because, I said, I wanted to talk to Eddie. Finally I agreed to go to dinner with Dave if later, I could interview Eddie. We went out at midnight one night—to a variety of New York "nightclubs" (Danceteria, the Mudd Club) and seedy spots (Hellfire, Diamond Lil's) that I thought might shock him. Everywhere we went, he was greeted effusively by the patrons. I was surprised that he was so much more famous than I had previously thought. He dared me to accompany Van Halen on their tour bus through the South. And so, in November 1982, I found myself in Huntsville, Alabama, on a day off with Eddie's then-wife, actress Valerie Bertinelli, at a mall, purchasing wooden Christmas tree ornaments. I started to enjoy Van Halen's show, although, after years of observing Jimmy Page and Keith Richards up close, I wasn't all that impressed with Eddie's over-the-top guitar histrionics and onstage knee slides. Dave was smart and he often could be amusing. But it was off-putting to witness all those nights when the roadies went into the audience to pick out girls to "meet" Dave after the show. I have hours and hours of tape from that tour of a very coked-up Dave and an equally "inspired" Eddie; at one point they asked me to co-write their autobiography. There was many a night, at many a truck stop, when Eddie and Dave would be hopped up out of their minds, screaming at each other in some parking lot about something or other while the rest of us—the other members of the band, tour managers, crew—would have to sit and wait on the bus for hours. *Hours.* Then, in 1985, they broke up. And, more than twenty-five years later, they briefly reunited. And there's not a shred of doubt in my mind that even if sober, they had the same problems with each other in the 21st century that they had with each other then.

As for Slash, in 1988, after Guns N' Roses first hit big, they came to New York City for a show at the Felt Forum. On an off night, I took Slash down to Phebe's on the Bowery for some drinks and a chat. Thirty or forty shots of Scotch later (him, not me), I had to have someone help me and his then-girlfriend carry him into a taxi for the return trip to the midtown Rihga Royal Hotel. I remember asking him how old he was—he mumbled twenty-three. I told him that if he wanted to make it to twenty-four, he needed to cut back on the drinks. Guns N' Roses and Slash and drugs and drinking have been well chronicled elsewhere, and I digress. The point: Michael always knew who the hot guitarists were, he employed them, and the results were some memorable—albeit the wild, noodling type—guitar solos. All of which made Michael's songs sound more modern.

On February 15, 1985, in a phone interview from Los Angeles, Michael asked me why I didn't come to L.A. more often. I told him it was too bright, that I wore black clothes and the lint became too noticeable. He was surprisingly candid about his dissatisfaction with many aspects of the Jacksons' "Victory" tour. I asked him if, especially after his massive solo success, working with his family again had been a problem. "Well . . . it depends," he said. "I never really wanted to use a lot of the people we had, but it became a voting thing. It was unfair to me, you know? I was outvoted a lot of times. I always like using A-1 people who are considered the best in their field, I've always tried to do everything first class. But it was a different story with the family. And the fact that it was the biggest tour that ever happened, and my success has been so overwhelming, it's as if they're waiting to throw darts at you. You know [Barbra] Streisand once said—I taped it, on *20/20*—she said when she first came out, she was new and fresh, and everybody loved her. They built her up and then . . . they knocked her down. And she felt, 'Oh, is that it?' You know, she's human, she can't take it, she can't just forget about it." I said that backlash often follows success. "Yes," he said, "and Steven Spielberg's going through that. . . . But I'm a strong person. I don't let any of it bother me. I love doing what I do." I mentioned that some of his fans were upset because the ticket prices on the "Victory" tour were high. "You know, none of that was my idea," Michael said, exasperated. "I was outvoted. I mean, mail order tickets—I didn't want that. Our production was so big it had to pay for itself, but still, even then, I didn't want the ticket price so high. But I was outvoted. Don King . . . all of it. It's tough, especially when it's your family. It's hard to see your brothers and look in their eyes and see they're upset with something. Or they won't talk to you. But I'm going to do bigger and better things in the future. I'm compelled to do what I'm doing and I can't help it, I love performing. I love creating and coming up with unusual new things. To be a kind of pioneer. You know, innovative. I get excited about ideas, not about money. Ideas is what excites me."

I asked Michael if he was as insulated and isolated as people thought. "Well, a lot of that is true," he said, "but I get a chance to have fun. I show films and I play games and have friends over sometimes. I love children and stuff. I get to play with them—that's one of my favorite things to do. Performing is fun, I miss that, but I've been writing a lot of good stuff lately and I'm excited about the songs I'm coming up with. I put my soul, my blood, sweat and tears into *Thriller*. I really did. And not only *Thriller*, I was doing the *E.T.* [soundtrack] album at the same time. That was a lot of stress. And [when we first] mixed the *Thriller* album, it sounded like crap. It was terrible. I cried at the listening party. I said, 'I'm sorry, we can't release this.' I called a meeting with Quincy, and everybody at the [record] company was screaming that we had to have it out and there was a deadline, but I said, 'I'm sorry, I'm not releasing it.' I said, 'It's terrible.' So we redid a mix a day, we rested two days, then we did a mixing. We were overworked. But it all came out okay."

o o o

By the early 1980s, in addition to my various print outlets, I had a syndicated radio show called *The Inside Track* and was the host and interviewer on two cable television shows: *Radio 1990* and *Nightflight*. At this time MTV had just started but wasn't available on cable everywhere in the U.S. (thus, the "I Want My MTV" campaign). But the USA Network carried the two shows I was on and I interviewed so many people for both the radio and the cable TV shows that I've lost count. I talked to, among many others, Mick Jagger, David Bowie, Robert Plant, Chrissie Hynde, Pete Townshend, Steven Tyler, Joan Jett, Joe Strummer and Mick Jones from the Clash, Sting and the other two from the Police, Keith Richards, Billy Idol, Billy Joel, Bruce Springsteen, Boy George, Marianne Faithfull and everyone else who passed through New York City. One of the people I talked to and became friends with was Freddie Mercury. I don't remember this, but my husband Richard recalls that when we were in London in 1972 with Lou Reed and David Bowie at the gay club El Sombrero, Freddie Mercury, who at that time was selling secondhand clothes in a stall at the Kensington Market, joined us and told us he was starting a band called Queen. I eventually got to know Freddie through Tony King, or Elton John, or Elton and Queen's manager, John Reid, or Linda Stein (who co-managed the Ramones with Danny Fields). I wasn't really a fan of Queen's music, but I loved Freddie. I especially thought it was hilarious when he performed Liza Minnelli's "Big Spender" onstage. One night in 1984, after Freddie and I had done an interview for *Radio 1990*, he invited me to a party at his New York apartment at 425 East 58th Street. I arrived with Fran Lebowitz, we walked in, and immediately saw that we were the only women in a roomful of young gay men—all of whom were watching slides of their Provincetown vacations.

Michael Jackson and Freddie Mercury eventually became friends. Michael visited Freddie backstage at Queen's L.A. Forum shows, and they recorded some songs together. One of them—"State of Shock"—wound up on the Jacksons' *Victory* album with Mick Jagger singing on it instead of Freddie. Another never-released demo was called "There Must Be More to Life." That song is complete with strings and shmaltzy lyrics. While it's hard to imagine Freddie, who once reportedly celebrated a birthday hanging naked from a chandelier, having much in common with Michael, there is no question that they had a real mutual affection. Freddie smoked. Michael didn't. Freddie slept with boys. Michael, supposedly, did not. (Once, when I asked Michael if he was dating anyone, he said no. He said he liked girls, but that he wasn't interested. I expressed some mild surprise, and he said, "Oh, you think I'm one of those? No, I'm not.") Michael and Freddie respected each other's talent and theatricality. Michael loved "Another One Bites the Dust," and told Freddie it had to be the single from Queen's *The Game* album. In 1984, in one of my talks with Freddie, he was wearing red and black satin boxer shorts and a black embroidered kimono, and was smoothing avocado skin cream on his legs. He told me he didn't consider himself a prima donna. But, he said, he did have tantrums. After all, he said, "I'm a musician"—as if that explained everything. Which, of course, it did. He said that if something wasn't right, he'd throw things, and was capable of destroying a hotel room in about three seconds. "Sometimes, even my own apartment," he told me. "But it got to be a bit expensive; all those Lalique glasses being thrown about." He said he didn't think rock and roll was limited, that he could do anything he wanted. (Today, I think how amused he'd be to hear Queen's "We Will Rock You" or "We Are the Champions" played as anthems at sporting events.) "I'm a trouper, honey," Freddie told me. "Underneath all this drag is a business brain." He had that in common with Michael. Talking about their friendship, Freddie said, "Three or four years ago Michael used to come and see our shows at the L.A. Forum. I guess he liked us and he kept coming to see us and then we started talking and we used to go out and have dinners. Now, I think he just stays home and doesn't like coming out at all. At least that's what he says. He tells me whatever he wants, he can get at home. Anything he wants, he just buys it." I said I thought that kind of isolation was scary. "I know," Freddie said, "and that's not me. But that's his bag. I'd be bored to death. I have to go out every night. I hate staying in one room for too long anyway, I just like to keep moving. Maybe it's because he started very young. I mean sometimes when I'm talking to him I think, my god, he's only twenty-five and I'm thirty-seven, but he's been in the business longer than I have, because he started so young. So, we can talk to each other on a very good parallel, because he has the same sort of experiences that I have."

o o o

On February 23, 1988, I went to Kansas City for the opening night of Michael's "Bad" tour. His manager Frank DiLeo arranged for me to visit Michael's suite at the Westin Crowne Hotel after the show. Alone. There were no handlers present, no family members, no animal companions, no child companions, no bodyguards—unusual for a Jackson visitation. For Kansas City, his suite was lavish, the size of a small apartment. But as I entered, let in by a security guard who waited outside the door, Michael was nowhere to be seen. "Michael?" I called, as I walked around. After a few minutes, I heard giggling from behind a door. The twenty-nine-year-old Michael Jackson was playing hide-and-seek. Finally, he appeared, wearing black trousers and a bright red shirt, his semi-straightened hair pulled back into a loose ponytail with a few strands falling over his face. He hugged me. He was taller than I'd remembered, taller than he appeared in photos. And while his giggling continued, I remember thinking at the time that his hug was a hug from a man—not a boy. There was nothing sexual about it, it was just strong. Then he pulled back, looked at me and said, in the lower and more "normal" of the two voices he could produce at will, "What's that smell? What's that perfume? I know that smell." I laughed and said, "Oh Michael, you don't know this perfume. It's an old drag queen perfume from the 1950s." At the words "drag queen" he started giggling and repeated it: "Drag queen . . . hahahahahaha!!! No, I know it. It's 'Jungle Gardenia,' right?" I was taken aback. How did he know that? I told him that the only people who ever recognized this perfume were Bryan Ferry and Duran Duran's Nick Rhodes. Well, I said, I guess you're not as la-la as they say you are. The words "la-la" cracked him up and he repeated it . . . "La-la . . . hahahahaha!" A week later I sent a case of twenty-four bottles of "Jungle Gardenia" to his hotel suite at New York City's Helmsley Palace. And on March 2nd, I stood backstage in the wings at the Grammy Awards live telecast in Radio City Music Hall, while Michael waited with a gospel group, about to perform "Man in the Mirror." Looking at me he whispered, "Thanks for the smells. . . . I'm wearing it now."

o o o

At some point in the 1990s, either Michael himself, or Elizabeth Taylor, anointed him with that ridiculous title, the "King of Pop." In 2009, before the writer Dominick Dunne died, he told me that he once went to Elizabeth Taylor's house for lunch and Michael came, bringing Elizabeth a huge sapphire ring as a luncheon gift. From the 1990s on, Michael's life had more Marlon Brando and Elizabeth Taylor in it and less Stevie Wonder and Freddie Mercury. Then, probably around the time of the child molestation charges or possibly before, Michael stopped talking to the press altogether—except for one time to Oprah Winfrey, and another ill-advised TV special where he went shopping like a maniac in some tacky Las Vegas mall. (Watching that on TV, I remembered how, over twenty years earlier, Michael had told me he purchased a Silver Shadow Rolls-Royce. He knew how to drive it, he said, but he didn't like to be photographed in it because, he told me, "It's too show-offy. I'm not like that.") Both of those TV interviews were attempts to rehabilitate his image. Neither worked. The phone calls to me stopped, probably because I wrote for the *New York Post*, the first publication to call him "Wacko Jacko." Even those he had once trusted he felt he could trust no more. He was paranoid. Rumors had him hooked on painkillers because of burns suffered from a pyrotechnic misfire during the filming of a Pepsi commercial. He was reportedly holed up at Neverland—his combination home/amusement park. In July 1995, he emerged and attended a press conference in New York's Bryant Park to announce the nominations for the MTV Awards. Michael was nearly an hour late, stayed for two minutes, wore lipstick and pancake makeup, and appeared nervous. It seemed to me that his confidence was gone. In his high, breathy, "public" voice, he announced the winner of the Michael Jackson Video Vanguard award—R.E.M.—said he was honored by his own eleven nominations, thanked "Mayor Giuliano," murmured that he loved New York, posed for photos, refused to answer questions, and fled through the back door. At the actual award show that September, people felt sorry for the technicians because Michael had 140 inputs going into the boards (most bands used 30) to get the sound he wanted before it was mixed down into what was heard on TV. He tied up the Sony Studios for two weeks of rehearsals, reportedly never showed up, but continued to pay his dancers and choir members. He sealed off Radio City Music Hall to rehearse. His performance on the award show was replete with the wind machines, chest-baring and constant crotch-grabbing and crotch-thrusting that marked much of his 1990s stage work. It became fashionable to slam him; his bad press was constant and relentless. It was possible he was a drug addict. Then he admitted he was a drug addict. But many felt that he made that up—and even made a brief visit to some phony European rehab facility—to get out of a grueling concert tour. He was accused of being a pedophile. He insisted he was a victim of extortion. It was possible he was sexually attracted to young boys. It was possible too, that it wasn't sexual at all, that he really just enjoyed eating candy and playing with water balloons. Or, that he wanted a family he *wanted*, as opposed to the one he fled from but could never totally shed. In 1996, Diana Ross told me, "I haven't seen Michael or spent any time with him in years and I know nothing of who he is anymore. I know the little boy that I introduced on the Ed Sullivan show, so [to talk about him now] is hard. Careers can just be devastating for young people. They're forced to live with security around them all the time. If you look back at child stars, well, it takes its toll."

On March 19, 2001, at New York City's Waldorf Astoria Hotel, Michael Jackson was inducted into the Rock and Roll Hall of Fame. The Jacksons had been inducted in 1997; now Michael was getting in for his solo work. Wearing tinted glasses, a long white jacket with gold embroidery on the pocket and a black wig, he carried a cane (he had broken his foot, he said, dancing down some stairs). He was heavily made up. Waiting to go onstage, leaning against the wall in the kitchen of the Grand Ballroom—which serves as the "backstage" for this event—Michael was surrounded by huge bodyguards as well as

Rabbi Shmuley Boteach who, at that time was, for lack of a better word, his "spiritual" advisor. I caught his eye. "Lisa?" he said. We started to move towards each other and his bodyguards put their hands on my shoulders to start to push me back. "NO! It's okay," he said to them forcibly—in that other voice, not the whispered one, not the public one, but rather the one reserved for the lawyers or the record company executives. "I know her. She's my friend." It was the last time I ever saw him.

o o o

In 2002, the MTV Awards were held on August 29th, Michael's birthday. Britney Spears was going to give Michael a cake onstage. In her speech, she called him the "artist of the millennium." Then Michael came onstage, appeared confused, and "accepted" the nonexistent "Artist of the Millennium Award." It was embarrassing. But I knew that no matter how whispery and out of it he seemed—or was—he also was totally capable of segueing immediately back into that other voice—the one that belonged to the control freak, the perfectionist.

On December 30, 2006, Michael Jackson was the only star of any magnitude to show up in an Atlanta church for James Brown's funeral. And, no matter what was going on in his life—the child molestation allegations, the child molestation trial, the plastic surgery, the drugs, the bizarre public persona, the dangling his baby over a hotel balcony—musicians loved him. From Beyoncé to Justin Bieber, they've all asked me what he was like. Athletes loved him. Charles Barkley said that when Michael Jackson died, it was like a death in his family. At every photo shoot with a musician that we did over the last decade at *Vanity Fair*, we played "Don't Stop Til You Get Enough" (still my favorite Michael Jackson song). It always put people in a good mood. Black musicians especially, most of whom grew up with Michael's music (or their parents did), refused to believe the child molestation allegations. He was theirs. When he and his brothers—and the Supremes—were on the Ed Sullivan TV show in the 1960s, as Oprah Winfrey has said, all across America, in black households, families would crowd around their TV sets, call their friends and yell, "Colored on TV!"

In 2008, Suzanne de Passe and I came up with the idea of doing a *Vanity Fair* tribute for Motown's 50th anniversary. We weren't sure exactly which year was the 50th—it could have been fifty years after Berry Gordy first borrowed money from his family to start the company, or it could have been fifty years after he released the first record on Motown. Basically, it was whenever Berry Gordy decided it was. *Vanity Fair*'s editor in chief Graydon Carter wanted me to do an Oral History of Motown. So I went to Los Angeles many times to convince Berry Gordy it was a good idea and, basically, to kiss the ring. Born in 1929, Berry Gordy Jr. has been described as brilliant, charismatic, a genius, mentor, gambler, philosopher, gangster, ladies' man and father figure. In the mid- to late 1950s he was a young songwriter who wrote hits for Barrett Strong ("Money") and Jackie Wilson ("Lonely Teardrops"). At the age of five, Berry, the second youngest of eight children, took classical piano lessons. Later on, he worked in his father's plastering business, sold cookware, served in the Korean War, worked at the Lincoln-Mercury plant, opened and closed an unsuccessful jazz record store, and tried to sell his songs. In the Detroit of the 1950s, Berry went to nightclubs to see Oscar Peterson and Charlie Parker and once met Billie Holiday. Motown had been the only black-owned music company in the 1960s, in a business dominated by white-owned record and distribution companies. In the 1960s, Motown had more than one hundred Number One hits and revolutionized American popular music. When people who know him talk about him, Berry Gordy is referred to either as "The Chairman" or "Mr. Gordy." When I talked to him, I always called him—and still do—Mr. Gordy. I told Mr. Gordy that I thought his music did as much to bring the races together as the civil rights marches did. In the early 1960s, when the Temptations toured the southern U.S., a rope down the middle of the audience separated blacks from whites. By the time the group returned in 1968, after Dr. Martin Luther King had recorded his "I Have a Dream" speech for Motown's Black Forum label, that rope was gone.

When I first met with him about the *Vanity Fair* piece, I told Mr. Gordy that when I was a teenager, I snuck out of my house to go see Thelonious Monk. He asked me to name a Thelonious Monk recording other than "Round Midnight." I said "Blue Monk," "Misterioso," and "Crepuscule with Nellie," and I guess I passed his test. After much discussion, Mr. Gordy agreed that he would cooperate with a Motown Oral History for *Vanity Fair*. He said he would talk to the artists to insure their co-operation. We knew Stevie Wonder would be difficult to pin down—he always was. Diana Ross seemed to be MIA. We agreed that it probably would be futile to try to get Michael. Then, as I moved forward with the project, I was handed a contract that basically stated Mr. Gordy would own the quotes and have approval of the finished piece. This, of course, was unacceptable to *Vanity Fair*, Graydon Carter, and me. I went back to Mr. Gordy's house with Suzanne at eight in the morning on Mother's Day, 2008 (only for him would I get up at that hour), and we went through it all again. I explained that journalism didn't work that way, this was publicity, he would not own the quotes. Finally, he agreed—again—to participate. When I returned to my room at the Beverly Hills Hotel, I got a phone call from one of his lawyers, stipulating that there was just one little piece of paper I would need to sign before we could go ahead with this story. I refused. I called Suzanne and told her the story was cancelled. I called Annie Leibovitz and told her not to bother to fly out to L.A. to take photos. I went down to the desk to pay the bill. When I got upstairs, my phone was ringing. Mr. Gordy was on the line. He said he was sorry to hear that I had cancelled the story. But, he said, he paid people to protect him. No, I told him, you pay people who rip you off and appeal to your paranoia. Dead silence. Well, he said, he was sorry to hear that I felt that way. I said I was sorry too, that we could have had fun doing this story and I was sorry he didn't trust me. He replied that it wasn't that he didn't trust me . . . at which point I interjected: Well, Mr. Gordy, I said, here's the problem—I no longer trust you. *Dead silence.* I was certain that very few people, if any, had ever talked to him this way. But I had been to L.A. at least three times to see him, the magazine had already spent a fortune sending me out there, and I had nothing to lose. After a minute or two of silence, he said, OK, let's do it. I insisted that I would sign no papers. He agreed there would be no papers. And so, we proceeded, over the next few months, to talk for many, *many* hours on tape about his, and Motown's, history. He is a charming, delightful man. We became friends. And on my birthday, he came into his library carrying a cake, singing "Happy Birthday." (And I didn't even have a camera.) Berry Gordy was reluctant to say too much about Michael; by that point Michael was probably as much of a mystery to him as he was to everyone else. But Smokey Robinson told me, "I've known Michael since he was ten or eleven. He is the best who ever did it. The singing and the dancing and the records, the whole package. But somewhere . . . he just got lost. It's easy to do." Jermaine Jackson wanted the Jacksons to be included in the *Vanity Fair* piece, but Annie Leibovitz and I didn't want to photograph or interview the brothers without Michael. We got a message from Jermaine that we needed to contact Michael's "spokesman," a Dr. Tohme Tohme, who only had a P.O. box address somewhere in California. I wrote a letter requesting Michael's participation. We never heard back.

o o o

On June 18, 2009, I met Mr. Gordy for lunch at the Mandarin Oriental Hotel in New York. We agreed that Michael wouldn't make those fifty shows at London's O2 Arena—the ones he announced (shades of the 1984 "Victory" tour) as "The Last Hurrah" and "The Final Curtain." We didn't spell it out, we didn't have to. And we didn't specify how, but we concurred that somehow, some way, he wouldn't be able to fulfill that obligation. There had been rumors rampant in the press and online for months that Michael, even while rehearsing for those shows, was frail, over-medicated, and in a weakened state. Seven days later, Michael was dead. (And later, he was reportedly interred in Berry Gordy's family mausoleum at L.A.'s Forest Lawn cemetery.) To prepare for the tour, Michael had brought some real music business people back into his life, including AEG promoter Randy Phillips (who, when asked at the Dr. Conrad Murray manslaughter trial how long he'd been in the music business, replied, "Too long") and Michael's former manager Frank DiLeo. But Michael, undoubtedly, was still surrounded by leeches and yes men. And reportedly too far gone to perform ten concerts, much less fifty. But even after all the over-the-top hoopla surrounding his death—the attempts by his brothers (Jermaine in particular) to cash in on his death with TV reality shows and lame tribute concerts, his father's inappropriate appearances, the tabloid photos of his bedroom, the coverage of the

Conrad Murray trial—after all that, there is the music. And when I hear the swirling, opening bars of "Don't Stop Til You Get Enough," I want to dance.

o o o

Michael Jackson's life, and death, was bound to wind up in a courtroom. Inevitable too, was the secrecy that surrounded it, as were the lies. After all, Michael's entire life in show business had started out with a lie: he was ten, not eight, when he signed with Motown. The trial of the "concierge" doctor, Conrad Murray, was just another sad chapter in a life that went very wrong. The scene outside that courtroom featured fans holding placards that proclaimed "Justice for Michael" and "Jesus Loves Michael." There were a few bedraggled bystanders who held signs "supporting" Dr. Murray, and some who even testified in court that he was a kind, compassionate man who helped the poor in his hometown of Las Vegas. The trial was less sensational than Michael's child molestation trial; Michael wasn't there to dance on top of a car. But as usual with any Jackson family gathering, it was a sorry lot: his beloved mother Katherine, who, according to some who know the family well, was an enabler who, by her silence, let her husband Joseph get away with whatever he could get away with. And that father, Joseph Jackson, got away with plenty. There were longtime rumors of physical abuse to his children and marital infidelity to his wife. The night after Michael died, Joseph showed up on the red carpet at the BET Awards with a young woman he introduced as his "new act." Someone close to the family told me that he once made a deal with a soda company for a Jacksons soft drink, but turned it into "Joe Cola." He thought he could be Berry Gordy. He couldn't. On hand at the trial too, were some of Michael's deadbeat siblings, to whom he was, and still is, the perennial meal ticket. Naturally Jermaine was there, hawking a new book he had written about Michael.

Michael was in that courtroom too: heard on the slurred tape recordings surreptitiously and suspiciously made by Dr. Murray. On display were photos of Michael's messy bedroom in his rented "mansion" at 100 North Carolwood Drive in L.A. Photos of his slovenly bathroom. A baby doll on the bed. Cannisters of oxygen. And on his bedside table, vials of Lidocaine, lorazepam, diazepam, midazolam—there were enough medications on that bedside table alone to keep even the most doped-up rock band on tour in the 1970s. There was testimony about 250 vials of propofol having been ordered, and there was enough Benoquin cream in that bedroom to bleach a whale. Michael would have died all over again at this invasion of his privacy—no, of the *secrecy*—which had become his way of life.

Watching *This Is It*, the hastily thrown together film of the rehearsals for the tour Michael never did—even with all of the obvious flaws and trickeration—you still see a glimpse of the entertainer that was Michael Jackson. He knew if a note was a millisecond off. His head movements, his rhythm, his directions to the band—"You've got to let it simmer"—here was a man who still had this . . . *thing* inside. "I want it the way I wrote it," he instructed the keyboard player. "It's talent," he once told me. And no matter how hard Chris Brown or Usher or Britney Spears or Madonna or any of them tried—they don't have that talent. Don't even come close. He just couldn't help it. He was a natural. There are certain people you can never imagine getting really old: John F. Kennedy Jr. will live forever in our minds as the three-year-old boy saluting his father's coffin. Michael was almost fifty-one when he died, but still retained the aura of that kid on the Ed Sullivan show who sang "ABC" and "I Want You Back." The young man who did the hysteria-inducing performance of "Billie Jean" on the *Motown 25* TV special. Some people, far more religious than I, felt that Michael was an angel sent to earth who, like Marvin

Gaye, was vulnerable, couldn't last, did what he was supposed to do and left. Quincy Jones told me that he thought Michael had "been here before." Those close to the family have told me that Michael was the most misunderstood person on earth.

Epilogue: On November 7, 2011, Dr. Conrad Murray was found guilty of involuntary manslaughter in the death of Michael Jackson. That night, I was in Kanye West's dressing room at Madison Square Garden for the first of two sold-out "Watch the Throne" shows he would perform with Jay Z. Jay came into the room to go over the set list with Kanye. Over the past six years, I've known both of them fairly well. Kanye, who at first I thought was obnoxious, won me over when I saw him one night in 2005 at the Largo in L.A. He had come to see Jon Brion's unique one-man show; he had hired Jon, a friend of mine and perhaps the most talented musician on the planet, to produce his amazing album *Late Registration*. At a listening party for that album in 2005, Kanye played "We Major," one of the album's longest and greatest tracks. It was sonically akin to a Phil Spector production, with the lyrical urgency that marked the best of hip hop. Jay Z was in the crowd, and I watched him listening, moving his mouth, making up his own words as he listened to Kanye's lyrics. After we heard the entire album, there was a question and answer period. I raised my hand. How many tracks were on "We Major," I asked. Kanye didn't know the answer. Jay laughed and called me "the stumper." Later, I called Jon Brion, who told me that it was a loop some guy had made in his garage. But that album, that song, and the fact that on the Hurricane Katrina telethon Kanye said George Bush didn't care about black people, put Kanye in my heart for life. When he stormed the stage and grabbed the microphone out of Taylor Swift's hands during the 2009 MTV Awards I emailed him to say it was very punk rock. But no one else shared my appreciation. He was vilified;

the *President* called him a jackass. He left the country for a year. But after all of the hatred and the lunacy that came at Kanye, his own tirades and unpredictable antics, he once again made magnificent work.

That night at the Garden, as he and Jay went over the set list in Kanye's dressing room, I heard snippets of the Jackson Five's "I Want You Back"—which Jay sampled on his 2001 song "Izzo (H.O.V.A.)"—and an Otis Redding sample they used on "Otis," the first single from their collaborative *Watch the Throne* album. I told Jay and Kanye that I probably was the only person in that room who had seen Otis Redding—at a concert in Central Park in the 1960s (to this day one of the best live shows I've ever seen)—the Jackson Five, and these two guys about to go onstage.

Eric Clapton and Keith Richards have always talked about the blues, and how they were just "passing it on." They passed on to new generations the things they learned listening to Robert Johnson and Muddy Waters and Howlin' Wolf. That night, sitting in that Madison Square Garden dressing room, I thought, here it was again. Full circle. Michael was dead. But his twelve-year-old voice would be heard by 20,000 hip hop fans in Madison Square Garden. And whether they even knew who it was or why or how it all came about, or what the song was or any of it—Michael Jackson was in the building.

Six

In 1976, the New York rock and punk scene was made up of the CBGB's bands and the few music writers who loved them. In total, this may have consisted of about sixty people. Today, dozens of books have been written about all this, many by people who never set foot in CBGB's. But this needs to be said: the 1970s in New York City was not necessarily the glowing musical renaissance that it has come to represent. It is true that a lot of the music that came from this scene was better than what came later. More to the point: a lot of us were young, there was a lot happening, and the city was a lot more fun. Eventually, there were many bands. Ten were good. Three were great. This small scene did have great influence, but, like any scene, it just sort of happened. A bunch of people formed bands and had nowhere to play. They found a stage. Another bunch of people heard about those bands and went to see them play. Every night. It was similar to when Max's Kansas City had its moment: if you skipped one night, you might have missed something. At CBGB's, there was no velvet rope at the entrance. There was no big deal about "getting in." There was no "list." The same people who went all the time, went all the time. Since we edited *Rock Scene*—which became a kind of house fanzine for CBGB's—Richard, Lenny Kaye and I were among those who just went all the time. I didn't have to call a publicist or get a laminated all-access pass or a wristband to go "backstage." We didn't have to wait for the lead singer to towel off after the performance and receive people. At CBGB's, there was no towelling off— there were no towels. To get backstage, all you had to do was walk a few feet past the stage to the back hallway, to one of the crummy rooms on the right where Patti Smith or Joey Ramone would be sitting on the lumpy sofa. We'd all sit around with a few bottles of beer and just hang out. It was easy then to just hang out. It still was possible to discover something—either hearing about it from your friends, or stumbling across it yourself. It wasn't already written about in *New York* magazine before it had a chance to breathe.

Fueled by what was happening in New York, a similar scene started in London. Malcolm McLaren—with his partner Vivienne Westwood—had a fashionable punk and bondage clothing shop in London at the far end of the King's Road. In 1975, Malcolm came to New York City, saw the Dolls, gave them a spiel that may have involved Communism, and wound up managing them for a brief time. "During one of our particularly uncreative periods, Malcolm came over," David Johansen recalled in 1980. "He had clothes. He hung around us. We had no manager and we needed someone to go around with us and collect money from the promoters. So, he did that for three or four months. We wrote a song called 'Red Patent Leather' about a physical relationship where people wound up with marks all over them. A real rocker. So Malcolm made all these beautiful red vinyl clothes, but they looked like red patent leather. We decided to have a Red Guard flag as a backdrop onstage because it went beautifully with the motif. It was not a conscious overture to Chinese Communism; it was supposed to be *funny*. It was misunderstood, as most everything we did was. But Malcolm wasn't really our manager. He was our *haberdasher*. Then he took off with half our equipment, the bum."

Years later, Malcolm would tell me that he came from art school and never really cared about rock and roll. He started the Sex Pistols because he honestly thought it would help him sell a lot more trousers. "It was a seasonal thing for me," he said. But of course, he was plotting all along to form a British band that would sound like the Dolls. On July 4, 1976, the day of the American Bicentennial, the newly formed Sex Pistols and the Clash snuck in a back door at the Roundhouse in London to see the Ramones' show. According to Ramones manager Danny Fields, Clash bassist Paul Simonon had told Johnny Ramone, "We don't think we're good enough to go and play yet." To which Johnny replied, "Wait until you see us. We stink." The consensus was that the Clash stole from the Ramones and the Pistols ripped off the Dolls. In this very small circle, Malcolm got a bad rap for ripping off the Dolls when "he" "formed" the Pistols. He talked about how inspired he was by Richard Hell's song "Blank Generation." He extolled the virtues of Richard Hell's "Please Kill Me" ripped t-shirt. Malcolm claimed it inspired a movement. The truth is that the truth is never that simple. For a start, no one remembers any of this the same way. Some say Sex Pistols guitarist Steve Jones had a life-changing moment when he saw Iggy perform in London in 1972. Others say it was Johnny Rotten who was there. British music writer Nick Kent proclaimed that Steve Jones—not singer Johnny Rotten—was the real leader of the Pistols, and the band had nothing whatsoever to do with Malcolm McLaren's "crackpot art college concepts." Nick Kent took credit for turning the Sex Pistols on to the Stooges. What really happened was that there was an emerging music scene in London with bands that knew and loved "underground" American bands like the Dolls, the Flamin' Groovies, the Patti Smith Group, the Stooges and the MC5. Richard Robinson had produced the Flamin' Groovies. Lenny Kaye was the guitarist for the Patti Smith Group. I wrote constantly in the *New Musical Express* about the Dolls, Iggy and Patti. So when the "punk" scene started in London, which let's face it, is a small town compared to New York City, it was not exactly a hard world to crack.

In December of 1976, the Sex Pistols said "fuck" numerous times on a live talk show on British TV. This created a scandal. The Fleet Street tabloids proclaimed outrage with such headlines as "The Filth and the Fury!" The Pistols' single "Anarchy in the U.K." was banned from the radio. Stores refused to stock it. Women in factories wouldn't put labels on the records. The band's "Anarchy in the U.K." tour was reduced to ruins when local town councils in Newcastle, Liverpool, Bristol, Glasgow, Cardiff, Bournemouth, Guilford, Derby and Sheffield cancelled the band's shows. In the towns where the concerts were allowed to go on, the venues were moved from civic halls to colleges.

On December 8, 1976, I went to London on a press junket to see a band called Steve Harley's Cockney Rebel. I had no interest whatsoever in Steve Harley's Cockney Rebel. I wanted to see the Sex Pistols. And I wanted to see the opening acts on the "Anarchy" tour: the Buzzcocks, Johnny Thunders' Heartbreakers, and the Clash—whose bass player, Paul Simonon, was "dating" Patti Smith. New York bands—like former Dolls guitarist Johnny Thunders' Heartbreakers—and the British bands like the Pistols and the Clash, were all connected. The music writers in New York and London who wrote about these bands all knew each other. There were only about ten to twenty of us at the time—along with the other six or so serious critics who may or may not have been too principled to take free trips. No one took rock journalism seriously. Except for the six people who took it seriously. But even some who are now considered legends, who took it seriously, were, at the time, the first in line at the bar for the free drinks.

On December 9th, the "Anarchy" tour was set to go on as planned at Manchester's Electric Circus—a large, ballroom type venue that years later would be prominently featured in the movie *24 Hour Party People*. The British press descended on the place en masse. None of them were allowed inside. But because of my relationships with former New York Dolls guitarist Johnny Thunders, Leee Black Childers—the Heartbreakers' manager—and Pistols manager Malcolm McLaren, I had complete access to the show, the bands, the backstage. I fled the Steve Harley junket and got on a train from London to Manchester. That afternoon, in the cold, damp, Electric Circus, I hung out with the bands. I watched what passed for a sound check. The musicians in the Buzzcocks, Clash, Sex Pistols, and Heartbreakers were a scruffy, even slightly menacing bunch. If you saw them all walking towards you, you probably would have crossed the street. They were dressed in various stages of meticulously arranged disarray. The goal was to look like they were not "performers" getting ready for a "show." Except, of course, they were performers getting ready for a show. The image had been carefully worked out: leather motorcycle jackets, ripped jeans or bondage trousers, heavy boots and short, spikey hair. Compared to the glamrock of the day, these bands looked fresh, different, new. The punk bands had attitude. They all looked like members of the same gang.

At the Electric Circus that afternoon, Malcolm McLaren told me that the EMI Records shareholders had held a special meeting that week to decide whether or not to drop the Sex Pistols. I told Johnny Rotten that the headline in that day's paper was "Rotten insults Queen!" What, he asked, "The group? Or her Royal Majesty?" We talked for awhile and he said, "I don't have any rock and roll heroes; they're all useless. The Stones and the Who don't mean anything anymore—they're established. The Stones are more of a business than a band. I don't need a Rolls-Royce. I don't need a house in the country. I don't want to have to live in France. The people who come to see us are bored out of their brains. They're bored with hippies. Hippies are complacent." Later, reading back my notes, I thought, hippies? In 1976? And I remember thinking that Johnny Rotten could well afford to be "working class" and "rebellious" because his then-girlfriend, who would later be his wife, was the German publishing heiress Nora Forster. During one of the "rehearsals," a fifteen-year-old kid with a safety pin stuck through his hand and a paper clip pierced in his earlobe stood near the stage. "My girlfriend hates the Pistols," he told me. "She hates me for this. She likes the Ramones."

Despite some really bad front teeth, Paul Simonon was incredibly handsome. Patti had told me to make sure I checked out his Jackson Pollocked paint-splattered clothing. In Manchester, Paul had a silk-screened image of Patti on his shirt. He told me that there were so many Fleet Street journalists at their hotels he could never go down to the bar. The Clash had been put together by Bernard Rhodes, who thought Joe Strummer would be a good lead singer for Paul and guitarist Mick Jones (drummer Topper Headon would join later). Joe Strummer was born John Graham Mellor in 1952 in Turkey. His father was in the British diplomatic service. By the time he was fourteen, Joe had lived in thirty-four countries. He went to an English boarding school, hated it, went to art college, lived in a London squat, busked on the streets, re-named himself "Woody" and played in a rockabilly band called the 101ers. When he joined up with Mick and Paul to form the Clash, he wanted, he later said, "To change things. To play the unplayable, say the unsayable. Authority was to be avoided—attacked, actually. We conspired together to make noise." Later in his life, Strummer would credit the Ramones with showing him not to "muck about a stage, not spend hours shambling around." But egged on by their manager Bernie Rhodes, the Clash initially adopted a more socio-political point of view. And like the CBGB's bands, none of the British punk bands sounded the same. The Clash had a variety of musical influences: they were turned on to reggae by Don Letts, who sold clothes in a stall in the Chelsea Market and made Jamaican dub tapes that Patti Smith played before her shows. Clash guitarist Mick Jones had been a former Mott the Hoople groupie; he had literally followed them around on tour. At the Electric Circus, the music playing over the sound system before the show was Patti Smith's "Ask the Angels," the Modern Lovers' "Roadrunner," the Dolls' "Personality Crisis" and the Stooges' "No Fun." When I first saw Iggy perform at Ungano's on West 70th Street in New York City in the early 1970s, he was shirtless, bleeding, wearing a dog collar and dragging spectators across the floor. The Stooges, led by Iggy, were dangerous. To put it in perspective, the Doors, by comparison, led by Jim Morrison, were a pretentious college band. The Stooges' Ann Arbor colleagues, the MC5, caused riots in New York City in 1969 when they came to blows with an East Village "community" group called the "Motherfuckers," who threatened to close down Bill Graham's Fillmore East. Whether they acknowledged these influences or not, here's the truth—without the Dolls, no Sex Pistols. Without the Stooges and the MC5, no Ramones, no Clash. And without the Ramones and the Clash, no U2.

I had my small Sony cassette recorder with me at the Electric Circus and was excited enough by the first opening act, the Buzzcocks, to tape the show. Then the Clash went onstage. They performed for about twenty minutes. They only had twenty minutes' worth of material. I stood right up front with people pushing and shoving into me. I taped their set. Thirty-six years later, that tape (which has the Pistols on it too) is rough; it sounds like a lot of noise. But it still sounds great. Paul didn't really know how to play bass yet, but he knew enough to wear it very, very low. Nothing reveals the personality of a bass player as much as where he wears his bass.

To me, the mark of a very good bass player is to wear the instrument low; it's much sexier. Paul McCartney, without question, wears it too high. The Clash's set—such as it was—included "White Riot" played at breakneck speed. The Ramones played at what I had formerly thought of as breakneck speed, but next to the Clash, the Ramones sounded more melodic and tame. The Clash were urgent, intense, furious. After their set, I raced back to their dressing room to tell the band how they literally took my breath away. I was excited. They seemed pleased. I was a journalist from America who had traveled with Led Zeppelin and the Rolling Stones and wrote for the *NME* and was enthusiastic about their set. Despite the fact that I had traveled with "dinosaur" bands, that I was (just) a woman, and I was not a "critic," there was enough of a credibility factor here for them to feel encouraged about their future.

The Clash came along and musically smacked me in the face. Joe Strummer was the most exciting live performer I'd seen in ages. He was manic, hoarse, angry. I loved the Rolling Stones. I loved Led Zeppelin. I'd been turned on by the Ramones. David Johansen was the wittiest, and certainly one of the best live rock and roll performers ever. Tom Verlaine's guitar playing was transcendent. Patti Smith was unique. But the Clash, at that moment, made everything that came before it seem obsolete. This band mattered. And, as is always the case with any new music, it fulfilled a need that no one even realized was there until it was there, in front of them. Right band, right place, right time.

That night, I took the train back to London to my room at the Montcalm Hotel. I couldn't sleep. When it was morning in New York and an ungodly hour in Los Angeles, I called every record company president I knew to tell them they had to immediately sign the Clash and the Sex Pistols. My friend Ahmet Ertegun, the president of Atlantic Records, told me that he'd been told they sounded like noise. I told him that thirteen years earlier, he might have said the same thing about the Rolling Stones. Casablanca's Neil Bogart was worried they would say "fuck" onstage. Arista Records president Clive Davis told me he'd signed Patti Smith already so he felt he'd done his part. And he added, "Lisa, I'm telling you as a friend, you shouldn't become too closely identified with punk rock." Elektra's Joe Smith and Warner Brothers' Mo Ostin both chided me: "Oh Lisa, you and your punk rock." It wasn't hard to get to know a president of a record company then. I knew these men from traveling with the Stones and Zeppelin (Ahmet). Or when they made an occasional foray to check out a band at a club (Clive). Or through Richard's work at various labels (Neil, Clive). Or seeing them at press parties. Or just because I had a byline. But only CBS Records president Walter Yetnikoff said, "Okay, fine, I'll sign them. Tell their managers to call me." They did. He eventually signed the Clash. And I stupidly never even asked for a finder's fee.

Of course the Clash, when they did sign to CBS, had no idea what label they were signing with. They thought they were signing to Polydor. They also thought they were being signed by Columbia Records' UK chief, Maurice Oberstein, who everyone said was taking a big "risk." Certainly, the band's manager, Bernie Rhodes, took all the credit for the predictably lousy, standard record deal. The band probably had no idea who Walter Yetnikoff was. A year later, I was at the CBS Records convention in London when one night, I saw a young singer named Elvis Costello at the tiny Hope and Anchor pub. The next day, Elvis' manager cooked up a scheme for Elvis to "petition" the CBS Records convention by singing on a flatbed truck in front of the Intercontinental Hotel. I badgered Walter Yetnikoff to go downstairs; you have to see this kid, I said. He's really talented, I said, you should sign him. Walter, who was eating breakfast in his suite, wouldn't budge. I kept at it until he finally agreed to go downstairs for a minute. We went downstairs to the street, he saw Elvis sing for about a minute, turned to me and said, "Okay, I'll sign him. Can I go upstairs and finish my breakfast now?" Again, I never thought to ask for a finder's fee. Thinking back, I realize I wasn't thinking ahead.

o o o

In late 1977, when the Pistols planned their first (and last) tour of the U.S., Malcolm McLaren told me they would only play the New York area if they could do a show in Harlem—presumably for the many black fans of the group. I pointed out to him that the residents of Harlem could care less if Johnny Rotten hated the Queen of England. But Malcolm was insistent on having the Pistols play for "the people," to identify with the downtrodden. Then, the band refused to do interviews except with *Time* and *Newsweek*—which at that time were the two most important American weekly magazines. In early 1978, the Pistols performed eight shows only in mostly secondary and tertiary markets: Atlanta, Memphis, Baton Rouge, San Antonio, Dallas, Tulsa and San Francisco—where the band famously broke up after Johnny Rotten's parting line: "Ever get the feeling you've been cheated?" It summed up his contempt for the audience, his contempt for the band, the audience's contempt for the band, or perhaps all of the above. The Clash, by comparison, were the Rolling Stones. They took their time getting to the U.S. They released six albums—five of which were great. They performed incredibly exciting shows. They played bigger venues over the course of the next six years. And then they broke up.

o o o

Between 1977 and 1983, I talked to the Clash a lot. While I've carefully kept all of my interview tapes all of these years, a few of the thousands of cassettes are haphazardly labeled. Sometimes, it's not clear who said what, when, or where. But Joe Strummer's voice was unmistakable. He was the one I talked to the most. For me, the most compelling member of the Clash was always Joe. He was the one I couldn't take my eyes off of onstage. On our interview tapes, his voice is hoarse and raspy. You can hear him inhale on the cigarette he always had in his hand. (In Julien Temple's 2007 documentary *The Future Is Unwritten*, Joe would protest the anti-smoking movement: "If you took cigarettes away from the 20th century," he said, "we wouldn't have any of the writers [you] go on about or anybody worships. This wouldn't exist. And I want this acknowledged. Nonsmokers should be barred from buying any product that a smoker created.")

In 1978, I talked to the band in London. They were a big deal in the British press but had not yet done a show in the U.S. I asked Joe if the same jealousy that existed at CBGB's was true of the British punk bands. He told me that there had been camaraderie in the London punk scene for about a week. "Everybody's jealous as hell in this business, and if they don't admit it, they're just lying," he said. "Of course I'm jealous of everybody. Anybody who's successful, for a start. Everybody's like that—they just don't admit it. If Elvis Costello brings out a record, I'll go 'bloody rubbish,' and I don't even bother to listen to it. And I can't stand all that hard driving rock, all those butch singers, screaming. I'd rather be a wimp than that. I hate them all." Paul Simonon told me that when they first started to play with bands like the Pistols, there was a big rush to see who could get a single out first, who could get an album out first, and then—who could get to America first. "People get obsessed with 'breaking America,'" Joe said. "So they bash out a decent tune and then the album sounds like something's gone wrong somewhere. I don't know— look at Slade. I can remember [manager] Chas Chandler saying, 'Slade is going to be the biggest band in America—headlines like *that*.' And well, I mean, what's the *hurry*?"

On February 17, 1979, the Clash played their first show in New York City. Backstage well wishers at the Palladium on East 14th Street included Martin Scorsese, Robert De Niro, Bruce Springsteen, Debbie Harry, Nico, Andy Warhol, John Cale and Paul Simon with his then-wife Carrie Fisher. In the band's small dressing room after the show, Mick Jones was clearly upset with the ads that CBS Records had taken for them in the U.S., ads that read: "The Clash claim they're the only band that matters." Mick said, "This wouldn't happen in England. We'd die of shame under the sofa." He talked about how he couldn't believe it when he saw his name above Keith Richards and Eric Clapton in some magazine's Best Guitarists poll: "I was twelve years old when I saw the Stones in Hyde Park," Mick said, "when they tossed out all those butterflies. I'll never forget how I pushed my way up to the front of 100,000 people to get up there. I love the Stones, it's the music I grew up with, and I have no quarrel with them. I don't know how I see [our] scenario ending, but we really are determined not to follow all that rockstar biopic. I find it disgusting." Paul said he didn't feel like a rock star: "I feel like an ordinary geezer. We don't ride around in limousines, drinking champagne—all of that makes me sick. We've always been a punk band and always will be. I don't care what the term means in America, I'm proud of it." The night after that Palladium show, I went with the band to Bob Gruen's studio to take pictures for *Rock Scene*. By then, the Clash was used to posing for photos. They had never *not* been comfortable posing for photos: their collars were turned up, their jeans were rolled up just enough to reveal heavy boots. They were a cool looking band and they worked it. Mick told me that he couldn't imagine what he'd be doing in ten years time. Maybe, he said, he'd go back to painting, which is what he started out to do. "Or maybe I'll be standing here telling you I don't think we're too old to rock and roll." After the photo session, we went out in the snowy night to the Brasserie restaurant on East 53rd Street. In those days, the Brasserie was open all night. Many restaurants were open all night. You could go there and have hamburgers, or eggs. And you could smoke. Then, at around two in the morning, we went to Studio 54. Proprietor Steve Rubell, wearing his trademark, Norma Kamali–designed puffy, down coat, greeted us at the front door. The velvet rope was pulled back to let us in. Joe had been there earlier that week and (shades of Mick Jagger) wanted the band and their crew to see the lights and hear the sound system.

o o o

For a very long time, longer than anyone usually did, until it became impossible, the Clash met fans after their shows. The band just wandered into the crowd and hung out. In 1980, after the release of the Clash's *London Calling* album, we ran a photo spread of the band in *Rock Scene* titled "The Clash Call Collect." The Clash—much like the Stones—invited black acts like Sam and Dave, Screamin' Jay Hawkins, Lee Dorsey, Grandmaster Flash (who got booed off the stage at Bonds in 1981 when he opened for the Clash) and Bo Diddley to open their shows. Years later, Bo Diddley said that his ears were still hurting from "that crap." Joe told me that growing up, he'd been inspired by Jackie Wilson and black music. "If you didn't know who Howlin' Wolf was," he said, "you were square. We used to buy those Chess records. Blues was hip. But the cliché was that the Rolling Stones discovered Chuck Berry, copied the music and re-sold it to the white American kids who never heard it before."

In March 1980, the Clash were back in New York City for another show at the Palladium and some recording at Electric Lady Studios in Greenwich Village. I went with Joe, Mick and Paul to the Minskoff Theatre on Broadway to see the (first) revival of *West Side Story*. They arrived at the theater in a limousine. Wearing leather jackets, Doc Martens and tight jeans, Joe, Mick and Paul looked like they could be in the cast of the show. Their vivacious record company publicist Susan Blond was with us and muttered that while we usually sat in the orchestra, we were sitting in the balcony this time because she was sure the band wouldn't want to sit in the "elitist" seats. The band's ever-present aide-de-camp and tour manager Kosmo Vinyl said that as a child, he listened to the original cast album of *West Side Story* every day. We talked, as we always did, about music. I asked Mick Jones if he'd ever heard of Thelonious Monk. He said no, but he was just starting to get into John Coltrane and Sonny Rollins. I told him I'd send him some Monk tapes. "OH NO!" shrieked Susan Blond. "Don't let them listen to *jazz*!! You'll *ruin* their music!" I was surprised to hear both Joe and Mick say that one day they wanted to try to write a Broadway musical: "Perhaps when my stomach gets too full to fit into these tight trousers," Joe said. After the show, we went to the "trendy" French "bistro" Un Deux Trois in the theater district. Susan Blond pointed out the fashionable stylist Marina Schiano: "She does all the stuff for Yves Saint Laurent," Susan said, to an unimpressed Joe Strummer. Mick said he always ate too many eggs, and proceeded to order an omelette. Joe ordered a steak and french fries. We had many cocktails. Afterwards, we went to the funky Mudd Club on White Street—which today is Tribeca but then was considered *all the way* downtown—to see art-rocker Lene Lovich. On another night that same week, I met the band at Studio 54 to see a performance by James Brown. Later that week, I stopped by Electric Lady where the band was recording. Upstairs, in a different studio, Mick Jagger was re-mixing one of the tracks for the Stones album *Emotional Rescue*.

At that time, I was still a regular at Studio 54—which I always called "54," although many people referred to it as "Studio." Often, I went back and forth in the same night to Chin Ya—a Japanese restaurant in the basement of the funky Hotel Woodward in the West 50s—then on to Studio 54, the Mudd Club and CBGB's. Cabs were cheaper then. Or I'd go to the newly opened, multi-floor Danceteria—which drew both a punk rock and the new rap crowd. It wasn't at all disconcerting to dance to Alicia Bridge's "I Love the Nightlife" at 54, then go to a performance of Don Letts' dub tapes at the Mudd Club. It was normal to come home at three or four a.m. To sleep until noon. Being married to someone who was involved in the same life, and thankfully, not having children made this life possible. (Not having children wasn't ever a "decision"; I never wanted any. This was neither the 1950s nor the 2000s—no one I knew had, or was having, children.) This wasn't social life, it wasn't work life, it was just life. Writing about bands, or going with them to parties or the recording studio, with or without a tape recorder, didn't feel like work. It wasn't as if these people were friends exactly—although Pretenders leader Chrissie Hynde was, Patti Smith was, and Lou Reed had spent a lot of time at our house. For a while, we just were all in this together. Until we weren't. It never felt like a job; it was fun, it was new, it felt like a "calling." Whether I was in a private plane with Led Zeppelin or the Rolling Stones or at a ballroom in Manchester or standing in two inches of beer on the floor at CBGB's—it was exactly where I wanted to be.

o o o

In the late 1970s, I became friendly with Chrissie Hynde, who formed the Pretenders in 1978. In 1980, I introduced her to the Kinks' Ray Davies, also a friend. She had wanted to meet him. I told her it would be a mistake; he would break her heart. She said she just wanted to thank him for the Number One hit the Pretenders had with a Kinks song that Ray wrote called "Stop Your Sobbing." The night I introduced them, Chrissie, who usually dressed in black leather pants and motorcycle jackets, showed up at a New York City club called Trax wearing a dress. She was acting all flirty. The two of them disappeared into the night, had a stormy relationship for years, had a child together, then broke up.

In the mid-1970s, Chrissie had moved to London from her native Akron, Ohio, and hung out with all the musicians who would start the punk bands. She told me that the scene was ruined when the Heartbreakers came over to London from New York with their drugs. "The Heartbreakers already had respect because of the Dolls," she told me. "No one gave a shit about any of the other New York bands. The Heartbreakers were the first young rock and roll band we saw that played twelve-bar blues progressions. So even though it was a little old fashioned, the musicians were impressed. Johnny Thunders was a big inspiration. He was a great guitar player. Plus, he was really New York street, and cool. No one had seen anything like this. And the Heartbreakers were all stoned on smack. They brought Nancy Spungen, who had been a junkie since her schoolgirl days, to

London with them. She wanted to find someone to marry so she could stay in London. Sid [Vicious] was basically a lovely guy whose heart was in the right place, but when he got drunk, he got violent. When Nancy got together with Sid, everyone told him, 'get rid of her, man, she's fucked.' But that's like telling a kid not to put his hand on the stove. And Sid was a kid. A whole string of casualties came after the Heartbreakers arrived on the scene." Talking about the Clash, Chrissie said, "I tried to work with Mick for a long time, and he was great, super enthusiastic. But we couldn't meet on a musical ground. I'd bring over a Mitch Ryder and the Detroit Wheels album or an R&B record from Bobby Womack and Mick would just be listening to Mott the Hoople. And Joe's no spring chicken. He'd be listening to Cajun and country and western music. I'd say, why don't you try to play music that you'd listen to?"

o o o

Scenes aren't meant to last. The best of them sneak or burst into the consciousness of a few. They blow up into something they weren't to begin with. And then, they eventually burn out. Discussing the Laurel Canyon music scene in California in the early 1970s, Stephen Stills told me, "It wasn't Paris in the '20s, but it was a vibrant scene." Until it wasn't. By the end of the 1970s, "punk" had become a category, a "genre." It attracted an audience and a notoriety that had nothing to do with its original intention or love of "underground" music. Disco doyenne Regine threw a "punk party" at her Paris nightclub New Jimmy's and served beef stew in dog dishes and chocolate mousse in a toilet bowl. At that time, writer Bob Colacello told me that Regine was "thrilled" when some "real punks" crashed, started fighting with the "fake punks" hired to loiter around the place, and she had to call the real police. Yves Saint Laurent's "muse" Loulou de la Falaise had a punk band at her wedding. TV specials on punk featured narratives similar to those in the old 1950s, black and white "Rock Around the Clock" movies: "loud, violent, filthy music." The English punks on those shows were pictured strangling each other as they leaped around London clubs. Zandra Rhodes charged a then-unheard-of, obscene $600 for ripped up "punk" dresses. Punk boutiques appeared in Bloomingdale's and Macy's. *Time* magazine did a cover story on the "punk phenomenon." As usual, they got it all wrong.

Pressed by my editors, I wrote columns with comments about punk from more established musicians. Eric Burdon of the Animals said, "Anything that publicizes hot rock or more sex is all right with me." The Who's Roger Daltrey said, "This is good old rock and roll hype. It's not that original. It's like reading about the Who smashing up hotel rooms." Bette Midler asked me, "So, tell me about these English punk bands. Is the *music* any good?" Mick Jagger told me, "Punk rock? Oh, I've been into it for years, dear. Actually, I saw the Sex Pistols at the 100 Club [in London] and thought they were pretty good. Well, not *good*, really, but they could be. This scene has been going on in the streets for three years. The press just picked up on it now." Ray Davies told me, "I like the music, but already, it's a business. It's like what [playwright] John Osborne said: that now he's part of all the things he rebelled against years ago. In the end, you become a part of everything you hate, basically, if you mean it. Because if you become successful, you use the same machinery to do it. I think if you really want to do it, you have to create a new form. Unless you decide that all the money you make, you'll give away."

o o o

In 1981, I asked Joe Strummer what his hopes were for the Clash. "Making good music is my priority," he said. "If you can write a song in twelve lines that ain't rubbish and tells the truth, I think it's the highest form of writing prose. In most prose, you can get away with one or two daft lines, but with a song, you can't. You boil it down to its purest form. If we make good music, then it'll go somewhere. Something you can listen to in fifty years." I asked if he thought we'd all be around in fifty years. "Yeah," he said. "Boring isn't it?" Optimistic, I said, given the state of the world. "Well," he replied, "I remain optimistic. You can't blow the world up. There's no money in it."

At the end of May 1981, the Clash caused riots when they put tickets on sale for a week's worth of shows at Bonds International Casino in Times Square. The gigantic venue, a former menswear store and later, a discotheque, was overbooked. The fire department threatened to close it down for faulty sprinkler systems, too few fire exits and whatnot. The shows were quickly re-scheduled and during that time, the band stayed at the nearby, crummy Iroquois Hotel. Joe and Paul liked it because James Dean had stayed there. Joe and I did a lengthy interview and we talked about James Dean and Montgomery Clift. Joe said he recognized a tendency he had for self-destruction but, he said, "I don't want to drink myself into a fat slob and keel over and die on the floor. It doesn't have any dignity in it. I have a drinking personality, probably a fatal attraction to it; but I could never go out drinking every night; I'd never get any work done." I asked him about the word "punk" and he said, "Punk music was more desperate, more paranoid, more schizophrenic, more sick, more demented. It just reflected the times. I believe that talking fast is one of the finest things America has ever invented. Fast talking. It's like if you go into a shop, you can make your deal in ten seconds flat. So I think that 'punk' is a good handle, because you know what I mean, right? Otherwise, you'd have to say 'loud, thumping music with people shouting' . . . blah blah . . . long sentence. This way, you've got the idea already. To me, punk is a good way of looking at the world I want to maintain at all costs." We talked about early punk days in London and Johnny Rotten in particular. "It was a game of tennis," Joe said. "He serves well, but he's got a weak backhand."

o o o

In 1982, the Clash had an actual Top 40 hit with "Should I Stay or Should I Go" (which was, as I pointed out to the band on numerous occasions, a dead ringer for the old Righteous Brothers song "Little Latin Lupe Lu"). By October 1982, they received a gold record for their album *Combat Rock*. Their video for "Rock the Casbah" was played constantly on MTV. And on October 9th, they were on *Saturday Night Live* with host Ron Howard. There was some fuss about what songs they would and wouldn't play on the show. They refused to play their hits, opting instead for some quasi-political song unfamiliar to the network TV audience. That week, the band went to Harlem to buy records (they went without a film crew—unlike U2, who years later, took one with them for an "impromptu" scene in their movie *Rattle and Hum*). Clash fans now included Jim Jarmusch, John Cusack, Johnny Depp and Matt Dillon. The band made an extremely brief appearance in Martin Scorsese's underrated masterpiece *The King of Comedy*. Despite their initial intentions, the Clash—what with the hits and the *SNL* appearance and the heavy MTV rotation—were now mainstream.

When the Clash opened for the Who in stadiums in 1982, Joe had mixed emotions. On the one hand, he was pleased that so many people were getting a chance to see the Clash. On the other hand, he knew damn well that people weren't getting to see *the Clash*. The band had to perform "Should I Stay or Should I Go" and "Rock the Casbah"— and forgo "White Man in Hammersmith Palais." Of course, when they did "I'm So Bored with the U.S.A.," it got massive cheers. But it no longer meant what it meant when they wrote it in 1976; now it was just ironic. On September 25th, at Philadelphia's JFK Stadium, Joe told me, "I'm of two minds sometimes about the Clash getting bigger. It's like having a split personality. Of course you want to get bigger so that people can hear your songs and all that. On the other hand, I'm a bit wary of it getting too big to handle. You know, you always think you can handle it, but you never know." (That show was attended by Mick Jagger, who, accompanied by his eleven-year-old daughter Jade, arrived by helicopter and posed for photos with the Clash.) Joe told me he thought rock and roll was best in venues of 3,000 people: "With the pit for the energetic people and the back for the geriatrics." At that time, the band was selling 500,000 records, but Joe said, "It still isn't on the level of, say, Barbra Streisand. She gets the Top 10 hits with those ghastly ballads that go on for ten minutes." After their set at JFK Stadium, I asked Joe how he felt. "Awful," he said.

In 1983, I went with the Clash from Los Angeles to San Bernardino by helicopter to the US Festival. They were on the bill for "New Wave Day." All I recall about that ride was that there were far too many people in that helicopter, and some people had to stand during the short flight. I've never liked flying. I especially hate helicopters. I was terrified. Promoter Bill Graham (a friend of mine who would later die in a helicopter crash) was at the site. He had promoted the festival the year before along with Apple's Steve Wozniak, and Bill was alternately hilarious and scathing about the whole punk scene. The band's manager Bernie Rhodes insisted that the Clash hold a press conference before the show to denounce something or other about slum conditions in Los Angeles. No one remembers this the same way, but my notes from that day read that after the Clash's set, but before an encore, the stage crew thought the band was done and shut off the amps. A furious Mick Jones kicked someone, and a full-scale fistfight ensued onstage. I watched all this from the side of the stage. Drummer Topper Headon had already left the band a year or so earlier because of his drug problems, and Joe and Mick, and Mick and Paul, were barely speaking to each other. That day marked Mick's last performance with the Clash.

The following day, U2 did a set complete with Bono leading the crowd in a singalong of John Lennon's "Imagine." He waved a massive white flag as he danced along the stage scaffolding—as was his habit during U2's early days. After U2's set, a hoarse and exhausted Bono sat and talked with me backstage. "Tell Joe Strummer that I'm the biggest Clash fan in the world," he said, "but I will never buy another Clash album again if they don't apologize to that stage crew. It was disgraceful. These are *working* people; they're the very people the band claims to care about."

In 1984, I was staying at Claridge's Hotel in London. I set up an interview with Joe to talk about the post–Mick Jones incarnation of the Clash. I felt it necessary to warn the snobby doorman and the staff at the front desk that "a very famous rock star" who "looked like a ruffian" was coming to do an interview with me. I asked if we could borrow a suite for a few hours. My room—which was then $90 a night—wasn't appropriate. When Joe arrived, accompanied by his road manager Kosmo Vinyl, the concierge called and said somewhat stiffly, "Madam, a Mr. Kosmo is here." The hotel set us up in the massive presidential suite, where previous guests had included Franklin D. Roosevelt and John F. Kennedy. At the time, I thought, how fabulous, they're aware of the Clash, they're making a lovely accommodation available. Later I realized that they probably just didn't want Joe Strummer seen in the bar.

In 1984, in that luxurious presidential suite at Claridge's, with its extremely high ceilings, tapestries, marble tables and huge, glass chandeliers, I reminded Joe that three years earlier, he had told me, "You've got to stick at it. Many groups break up on the spur of the moment, in the middle of a fight. Sometimes the next day you don't even remember what you were fighting about." Now, I asked Joe why he kicked Mick out of the band. "I thought I'd rather dig a ditch than put up with the behavior I had to put up with," Joe said. "He had no enthusiasm whatsoever. He was sarcastic about everything. He wouldn't turn up at recording sessions. We wasted our energy arguing with each other for three or four years. I tried to get him to snap out of it, but in the end, I just couldn't see how you could make music together with all that gloom and doom. That's what drove me to the end of my tether. Groups have an atmosphere. At first it's all enthusiasm and idealism. It's fun to play music. And then one day you turn around and realize you can cut the atmosphere in the room with a knife. So I thought, well, you can shove off. While we've been arguing, people like Mick Jagger and Sting have been having a field day."

o o o

The Clash fumfered on for a year or so with two new guitarists and the drummer they hired after Topper left. But it wasn't the same, and it wasn't very good. For years after Joe broke up the second incarnation of the Clash in 1986, and Mick Jones was touring with his band Big Audio Dynamite, there were persistent rumors of an original Clash reunion. Those who knew them well knew they would never do it without Topper, who still wasn't healthy. In 1996, Kosmo Vinyl sneered when he heard about a Sex Pistols reunion. He told me that the former members of the Clash had all gone to see the Velvet Underground reunion, which they thought was terrible, and it put them off doing one. He added that there was no real need for Johnny Rotten to do a Pistols reunion. "[His wife] Nora's got money," Kosmo said, "and John isn't that interested in helping the others. In fact, he was only in the band for two years, twenty years ago. Can you imagine John onstage screaming at the kids? At his age? He's older than their parents. It would be like your crazy art teacher." When I brought up a possible Clash reunion to Joe, he said, "I'd be busy that day."

In 1998, producer Rick Rubin recorded a song with Joe and Rage Against the Machine guitarist Tom Morello for the *South Park* soundtrack. Rick and Joe were friends, and whenever Joe would go to Los Angeles, he'd drop by Rick's house on Miller Drive. "I'd come home and Joe would be swimming in my pool," Rick recalled. "One of those days in 2002 when Joe was in the pool, I was in the studio with Johnny Cash. I invited Joe to come in and watch. He was so excited. He was supposed to go back home to England the next day, but I remember he stayed an extra week. He would just come in and lie on the floor in the corner of the control room and look through the glass and watch Johnny sing. Joe was obsessed with Johnny, but Johnny had no idea who Joe was. And every day we'd leave the studio and Joe would say, 'Okay, what time are we starting tomorrow?' One day I suggested they do a song together. Joe said, 'I'll do anything. What should it be?' We thought a Bob Marley song would be a good idea; Johnny had always wanted to do a Bob Marley song and Joe had never done one. We picked 'Redemption Song,' and we did a version where Johnny sang the whole thing and one where Joe did the whole thing." I asked Rick if it was magical, and he said no. Neither of them really knew the song, Rick said, both of them had trouble singing the song, it was more like a lot of work. "This was just cool guys who I liked and got to spend a lot of time with," Rick said. "What was cool about it was the different eras, and trying to explain to Johnny who Joe was. What finally got through to Johnny was when I played him Joe's version of 'I Fought the Law' [which many people thought Joe actually wrote] because Johnny knew the original [Bobby Fuller] version. Johnny was old, and ill. If you were in the room with these people, you would think that Johnny was the one who was going to die. The fact that Joe died before Johnny was *shocking*."

o o o

On December 22, 2002, while taking a walk outside his home in Somerset, England, Joe Strummer died at the age of fifty of an undiagnosed congenital heart defect. By 2004, Joey, Dee Dee and Johnny Ramone were all dead. Two bands that thought they would change the world—the Ramones and the Clash—were over. Today, there are books exclusively devoted to the Clash. Epic Records has released Clash boxed sets and DVDs. And U2, a band who went from a "new wave" band to, in Bono's mind, a "punk" band after hearing the Ramones and the Clash, may have raked in the cash as the writers of the critically panned—albeit initially successful—Broadway show *Spider-Man*. Green Day, the cartoon version of punk, also had a huge Broadway hit—*American Idiot*. And I can't help but remember that night thirty-three years ago at the Minskoff Theatre at *West Side Story*, when Joe and Mick told me that one day, they'd love to do a Broadway musical. So much of what you remember about bands, and music, has to do with your age, where you lived and when you lived there. Where you were when you first heard a particular band. For me, the Clash were more important than the Ramones. Maybe I knew the Ramones too well, saw them too often at CBGB's, couldn't get past Johnny Ramone's demeanor, his rudeness, his . . . Republicanism. Growing up in my liberal family, to be a Republican was something akin to being a fascist. For me, the Clash songs are more sophisticated, more complex, more intense, more urgent. Because Joe Strummer was more sophisticated, more complex, more intense, more urgent. Today, "London Calling" is played on TV during Wimbledon. It's also referenced in an iPhone ad. It's hard to know, but I'm not sure if Joe would be pleased.

Seven

The first person who told me about U2 was a gay makeup artist who would ultimately die of AIDS or a drug overdose, or both. He was not the typical U2 fan. It was 1982, and MTV was pushing "new wave" bands who were considered the latter day versions of "glam." These supposed descendants of David Bowie and Roxy Music had, for the most part, one hit song. They had the hair and makeup but none of the talent of their predecessors. Exceptions were Boy George (Culture Club), and perhaps Duran Duran, who had some good songs accompanied by over-the-top videos featuring yachts and models. They also wore suits made by Antony Price, Bryan Ferry's tailor. Later on in the decade, there was an onslaught of "hair bands" who wore spandex and screeched. U2 was not in either of these categories. U2 was, as Bono told me early on, "plain." U2 was very straight—even slightly butch. Their music wasn't funky—they didn't have blues references or R&B influenced bass lines. No four on the floor dance beats. No Motown inspired drumming. Their music was very white. There was more rock, less roll. Bono initially had a really unfortunate hairdo that was half mullet, half Flock of Seagulls.

He wore black jeans that were too tight for his stocky frame, and boots outside those jeans. He wore sleeveless denim shirt vests. His whole look was somewhat . . . off, but girls thought he was sexy. The Edge had hair. The bass player, Adam Clayton, hardly ever talked. Drummer Larry Mullen Jr. was great looking. Even though they were lumped in with new wave, as soon as he could, Bono described his band as "punk"—even though, from the very beginning, Larry Mullen had asked Bono, with some trepidation, "We're not a punk band, are we?" Bono also told me, on many occasions over many years, "We're really the world's loudest folk band."

In May 1983, I was at a Mexican restaurant on New York's Upper West Side when U2, whose music I had heard about but had not yet heard, walked in. They were accompanied by their tour manager Dennis Sheehan, who I knew well from his days as the road manager for Led Zeppelin and the Scottish singer Maggie Bell. I don't remember exactly what happened or who said what, but I recall that when introductions were made, the then twenty-three-year-old Bono kissed my hand. This was no spontaneous, casual gesture. He was aware of columns I'd written in the *NME* about the Ramones, Patti Smith and the Clash. That hand-kissing would continue for the next three decades.

That week, I went to see U2's concert at the Palladium on 14th Street. During the show, Bono practically climbed up onto the lighting rig. U2 played loud, straight-ahead rock and roll. Their songs had melodies. Bono had a charismatic stage presence. They were a breath of electric guitar fresh air in a world that, at that time, was filled with synthesizers and dance pop. Two weeks later, at the US Festival in San Bernardino, California, the day after I'd been there with the Clash, I sat down backstage with Bono after U2's set. He was exhausted and hoarse; he was losing his voice. "I spent a lot of money to see a throat specialist," he said, "and he basically told me to shut up." I would quickly learn that for Bono, this was an impossibility.

In addition to the discussion about the Clash's onstage fight the day before with their road crew, we talked about Bono's onstage antics: climbing along the railing, leading the audience in singalongs and waving flags. He told me he was afraid of heights, but he climbed to the top of the stage because he wanted to engage the people all the way in the back who were in sleeping bags or buying hot dogs. "You saw the joy in the crowd," he said. "They lifted me up and carried me. The people I respect—like Bob Dylan and John Lennon—they gave us their feelings because it was the truth. Our songs are a reflection of what's going on in our lives. We take the music very seriously, but we don't take ourselves all that seriously. We don't have a poker up our backsides. Great music is possible. We don't want to just have people get up and dance."

We talked about the New York punk scene, and I told him I'd send him some tapes I'd made of Patti Smith and Television. That day at the US Festival, I asked Bono about U2's reputation as a "Christian" band. "People don't fully understand U2," he said. "They're always reaching for a label. I'm nervous about that—calling us a 'political' band, a 'spiritual' band. I'm frightened of all that. We're four people. We're not hiding under haircuts. We're not clothes hangers. We play music. We're U2."

While Bono claimed that their attitude was punk, their music decidedly was not. I was surprised that he chose to identify with punk rock, because, if anything, their music sounded slightly reminiscent of Echo and the Bunnymen. But, even with musical influences of Irish bands such as the Waterboys, the Boomtown Rats and the Alarm, U2 sounded like no one else. They always had those melodic choruses that were described as "soaring" and "anthemic." Occasionally, their rhythm was off and they didn't play exactly in time. But they were exciting. On that day at the US Festival, Bono actually said to me, "I'm not the best at selling the group"—which was hilarious, because the most striking thing about U2, aside from their actual talent, was their actual ambition, fueled by Bono's elaborate sales pitch. The reason some bands survive for years and others do not most often has to do with the drive, the lack of mistakes, the absence of drugs, the smart business decisions, and the hustle.

o o o

In October 1984, I was staying at the Lenox, a small hotel on the Left Bank in Paris. It was inexpensive and filled with people who were there for Fashion Week—which, at the time, happened only twice a year. Also there were some friends, like the photographer Steven Meisel, his entourage of stylists, makeup artists, hairdressers and favored models, and the photographer Albert Watson and his wife Liz. I got ten tickets for a group of us to see U2 at the Espace Ballard—a cavernous tent outside of Paris. It was a time of excess in the music industry. It was not at all unusual to obtain ten free tickets to go to a concert, or to get a table for twelve at a club like the Ritz in New York City to see a band. Thanks to MTV exposure and radio airplay, U2 was now a big band. I had interviews scheduled with Bono and the Edge at noon the day after the show, at their hotel—the Warwick, on the Right Bank. Because of a demonstration on the Champs-Elysées and a taxi driver unfamiliar with the Warwick Hotel, I arrived an hour late. I was embarrassed, but Bono was barely awake. He wore a peach-colored, terrycloth bathrobe and clearly, nothing underneath. I was slightly hungover and forgot to bring a cassette with me for the interview. (Today, I bring three backup cassette recorders and many extra cassettes. And, to the amusement of every musician I've interviewed in the last two decades, I still use cassettes.) Bono and I went down the hall to borrow a cassette from Edge, who was in his suite, also wearing a peach-colored terry robe. I told them they looked like they were members of a cult. Edge kindly (and foolishly) turned over a tape of the band's soundcheck from the night before, which I used for the interviews. (Years later, listening to those interviews, I thought, what was I thinking? Until I heard half the soundcheck still intact on the tape.)

That day, while I drank coffee and Bono had tea, I asked him why he wasn't hanging off of things or waving flags around onstage anymore. "I find the greater the crowd, the greater the charge," he said, "but adrenaline can get me into trouble. One night I threw Larry's drum kit into the audience, and it came to blows with the band. Edge actually socked me on the jaw, and you know him, he's a real gentleman. If things go bad, everyone will be silent on the way back to the hotel and then there'll be a phone call from Adam. He's the diplomat, and he'll say, 'Can we have a word with you?' I'll have to go down there and face the firing squad. They'll just say, 'Come on, you don't have to do this, you must keep control of this thing.' It's supportive; they know that if I fall off the stage I'll break some bones. They tell me the music should speak for itself. A whisper can speak as loudly as a scream." He said when he went into the audience, his original intention was to make the point that there were no barriers. That the band and the audience were on the same level. But he realized that it had been misconstrued as "the man meets the people," that he might be expected to do it all the time, and that he'd have to top it every time. I added that those forays could easily turn into caricature. I asked if he felt that U2 was still considered a "serious" band. "Well," he said, "we're Irish," as if that explained everything.

When U2 first came to the U.S., they shared rooms in motels. Here, in Paris, each band member had his own suite. I asked Bono if he was getting used to hotel suites and limousines. "The first ride we had in a limo was in 1980," Bono said. "We arrived in Hollywood, and the record company laid on this long white stretch limo. We were completely red-faced riding around in it, but at the same time, sort of curious. I remember we went to an import record shop in L.A. that had been supportive of the band and we made the limo driver park around the corner and we all sort of slinked into the shop. We were so uncool. I try to avoid the rock and roll circus, which is a kind of clichéd lifestyle. We try to avoid clichés in music and in lifestyle. I'm not into that rock and roll star trip of surrounding yourself with people who applaud your every dull action as you invade yet another nightclub. We'll always be rock and roll stars as long as we don't become celebrities. That's dangerous. Did you see the Scorsese movie *The King of Comedy*?"

Bono talked—and talked—about music and the band's new album, *The Unforgettable Fire*. How he was still "hungry" and "thirsty" for U2's music. He said he felt that U2 was a soul band, and that soul music wasn't a case of black or white. Bruce Springsteen and Van Morrison were soul singers, he said. Soul was a decision to "reveal rather than conceal." He said that U2 had made straightforward rock and roll, but now it was time to stretch. They always wanted to "innovate and aggravate." In the past, he said, U2 had done music that was "no bullshit." Did that mean, I asked, that it was now time for bullshit?

Bono has always been one of those interviews—Patti Smith is another—where you could just turn on the tape recorder and probably leave the room for a few hours, come back, and he'd still be talking. If one of his "minders" didn't come in to nudge him about another appointment or an interview or a meeting, or if I didn't wrap it up, there's no telling how long he could go on. Some said he had the gift of gab. Others said it was a lot of malarkey. But in 1984, in that Paris hotel suite, he was eloquent, inspired, enthusiastic. And yet, while it certainly never came to pass, he actually told me he was considering not doing any more interviews. "Because there are a lot of people who have nothing to say," he said, "and they say it all the time. I don't want to devalue what the group has to say. And if you tell the truth, you will end up repeating yourself all the time." Bono was not yet the global spokesman he would become. He was not yet the businessman that he would become. We talked only about our shared interest in music. And he was honing what would become his trademark flowery pronouncements: "We want our music to be all things to all men," he said. "We want our feet on the ground as well as our head in the clouds." He admitted that they thought in terms of the Beatles. "If you've got to drop a name," he said, "drop that one." He said the only big band able to show so many different musical sides was the Beatles. Which was, he said, "an arrogant, pompous goal for little Irishmen like ourselves." He said U2 was always accused of being arrogant and pompous. By whom, I asked. "Well, people less kind than yourself, Lisa."

"I want to be a certain kind of person, a good person," Bono continued, "and I don't think I am one in my life. But when I get onstage, I'm a much better person, I'm the person I want to be." I ventured that at least he had the chance to be the person he wanted to be somewhere. Which was more real, I asked, onstage or off? It was like that Kafka story about a man dreaming he's a cockroach or a cockroach dreaming he's a man. "Exactly," Bono said. "But you know my favorite Kafka story? He met a little girl once who was crying and crying because she lost her favorite doll. And Kafka said to the little girl, 'No, your doll is fine, I've seen her, she's just taking a trip around the world and she's having a wonderful time.' The little girl looked at him with widened eyes and said, 'really?' And Kafka told her yes, it was true. And for years afterwards, he wrote her postcards from various places all over the world, signing the cards with the name of her doll."

Later, down the hall, I sat with Edge in his suite. "Our goal is to write the perfect album," he said. "Every time we go into the studio we hope we'll get closer to that. But I very much doubt we'll ever attain that goal of perfection. It's like Mount Everest. That must be a terribly depressing place; you've spent all your time preparing to get up there. And when you get up there, all you can do is walk down again."

○ ○ ○

I spent a lot of time with U2 in the 1980s, and Bono said many things to me that even at the time, I thought could eventually come back to haunt him. "Rock and rollers generally do their best work in their first ten years," he told me once, "and then they break up like the Beatles. Or they repeat themselves ad infinitum and just bore everyone to death. I just always believed that there was some special spark between us when we played and that we would continue to make records that people would want to hear. Plus, we were always on the lookout for the bullshit: like here comes bullshit 'round the corner. We want to protect our music and ourselves from all of that." On April 12, 1985, I took the fashion models Christy Turlington and Naomi Campbell to see U2 at the Brendan Byrne Arena in East Rutherford, New Jersey. Christy and Naomi were both around eighteen years old. We went backstage. Bono approached. All of a sudden, this man I'd known as a passionate lover of punk rock and a serious, earnest talker, turned into a major flirt. "Such lovely women," he murmured, kissing hands all around. It would be the beginning of a long friendship that Bono and his wife Ali have with Christy. Naomi was another story.

Bono and I often joked about the band's image: he told me he'd heard that he lived in a castle, drove a hearse, and read the Bible on a daily basis. He was eminently quotable, telling me (and probably anyone else who would listen) such things as "Our music isn't urban music—it's about rivers and mountains and sky and earth." He referred to the United States as "the promised land." And, "U2's music is too big to have a roof over its head." In 1985 he told me, "People think that I must be some sort of guru because I write songs like 'Pride (In the Name of Love)' and am attracted to people like Martin Luther King and Gandhi. But the reason I'm attracted to men of peace is because I grew up in a violent way. I despise the violence I see in myself. I'm much more the guy with the broken bottle in my hand than the guy who would turn the other cheek." Of the hours and hours I have on tape with Bono, he kept returning, year after year, to similar declarations: every time they went to make an album, U2 wanted to stretch, to make something different, something special. The albums had to be pried out of their hands. They never quite got the sound they wanted. Each night onstage they wanted it to be the best concert they ever played in their lives, but they never quite did it. They hadn't made their best record yet. The best was always yet to come from U2.

Of all the bands and musicians I've talked to, every single one of them, in the beginning, wrote songs for themselves. They had no idea if they'd get an audience. The entire career was a dream, a fantasy. Then, there was always a series of steps. First, they'd get on a stage in a bar, or a small club. Maybe they'd perform other people's songs. If they were lucky, they earned around $50 a night. More often, they got free beer and each band member got $10 for dinner. They might have to pool the dinner money to buy gas for the van for the ten-hour ride to the next show. If there was a next show. When they got to the next club, often, there was no soundcheck. There might be eight people in the "audience" who stood around and watched them. This could be followed by a seventeen-hour ride through the desert—or the Everglades, or a snowstorm in the Midwest—to the next "show." Maybe some fans would let the band sleep at their house. Or, band members would take turns driving the van while others slept. If enough money was made from those small shows, the band could stay in a cheap motel where four or five people would share one room. If and when they made more money, two people would share a motel room. Song demos were made in makeshift studios. Band members— or their first manager, or a girlfriend, or a fan—would stuff envelopes and mail those demos to record companies. In the 1980s, the 1990s and even early on in the 21st century, a demo from a new, young, "baby band" could sit in a pile on some record executive's desk, unlistened to for months on end. Many of the piano players in cocktail lounges in strip malls, or cover bands in a local bar on a Saturday night, started out with the same dreams. One band in thousands makes it. Or, someone can come along, believe in the band, and help make something happen. In the case of U2, this was Paul McGuinness—their first, and longtime manager. Talking to me in 2004 about the early days of U2, Paul McGuinness said, "I didn't want to go and see them because I didn't like the idea of punk rock. I thought it was coarse." He said when he finally did see U2, they were doing exactly what they do now—"Only badly." Every record label initially turned them down, but he thought they would be huge. It probably helped, he said, that he was naive.

In 1987, I talked at length to Larry Mullen Jr., who rarely did interviews. Larry was amused that people thought he was the dumb, pretty one who just played drums. While Larry credited Bono with having the "vision" for the band, Larry actually started U2 in his parents' kitchen when he was seventeen. To my mind, Larry, who is stubborn and argues constantly with the other band members, is the conscience of U2. Talking about their early days, he said, "All the record companies in Ireland turned us down, and when we went to London, they turned us down as well. In a way, it was great that we were turned down, because right from the start, we were able to see the business for what it was. My parents were concerned, especially since I was seventeen and had never been out of the country before. London is like the big, bad world. Sex and drugs were very much a part of rock and roll. But coming from Ireland, and being brought up Catholic, I made a decision that I was young and impressionable, I'd read about what drugs did, so I just said no. Edge had a major conscience call about how the rock and roll lifestyle could work hand in hand with the Christian faith. I know he went through a very difficult time trying to figure that one out. We all questioned it. But in the end, it just seemed like the right thing to do." (In 2004, Edge told me that he never thought it weird that the band had religious beliefs or that they didn't have a lot of drugs or groupies around. "You have to understand," he told me, "we were from Dublin, not a city where rock and roll existed like New York or London or Hamburg. Dublin had its own cultural resonance. The biggest influences in our lives were the trouble up North and a lot of religious bigotry. We related more to Bob Marley than to the Grateful Dead. We saw that you had to take everything into your life; you couldn't exclude politics, you couldn't exclude religion. We didn't edit ourselves. It was all part of what made a complete band. We didn't even have to think about it. It was a natural thing. It was only when we left Ireland and were exposed to the media elsewhere that we realized we had to be careful. A lot of time it was blown up into a creepy thing.")

In 1987, Larry told me that he felt punk rock was hypocritical. "The punk movement was a great movement," he said, "and it was a great time to be in London. But it started as a revolution, and in the end, it became as bad as the old stars that were up there." In 1987, Bono said, "We came out of punk rock, but I hated the posturing of British punk rock. This faux leftist thing that was going around. People were talking about revolution, but not paying their road crew very much, or mistreating them. I don't know what was going on with the Clash that day [in 1983] at the US Festival. I'm sure I was being pretty pious, and they were the greatest rock and roll band, but I didn't want to hear people talk to me about revolution and then beat up on their road crew. I'd like to think that we took the love that came out of the hippie movement of the 1960s, and the anger that was part of 1970s punk. Our music is a combination of love and anger."

In 1987, I saw U2 several times. They released *The Joshua Tree* which included the hit singles "I Still Haven't Found What I'm Looking For" and "With or Without You." It was U2's first Number One album in the U.S. In my enthusiasm, I told them that they might be the first band who combined the commercial success of the Beatles with the innovation of Television. They liked the comparison. Bono and I talked about how the band looked like "the Brothers Grimm" in their dark, serious, Anton Corbijn photos. He promised me that they still had a sense of humor. As if to prove it, he registered in hotels under the name Tony Orlando. He told me, again, how punk rock had inspired him, how rock and roll had opened his eyes. He talked about how it took U2 years to live down the reputation of being a "born again," "Christian" band. He said that people could talk about sex or S&M and get into areas that they think are taboo, but that he, personally, never thought those were taboo. "But if I try to articulate a feeling inside myself, or sing about a belief that I have in God," he said, "people start getting nervous. They start sweating and leaving the room, and our manager starts scratching his head. But I'm a singer in a rock and roll band. I'm not a politician or a prophet. When we play, it's not Sunday school. I don't want to use the stage as a soapbox."

In 1987, when U2 was in Las Vegas to film the video for "I Still Haven't Found What I'm Looking For," they went to see Frank Sinatra at the Golden Nugget. He introduced them from the stage and announced that U2 was the biggest rock group in the world. But, he added, "They sure don't spend their money on their wardrobe." Later that year, Bono and Edge both told me they had met Sinatra in his dressing room and talked after the show. They talked about the Tommy Dorsey Orchestra. Buddy Rich had just died and Sinatra told them how he had once shared a room with Buddy Rich and they used to have arguments about whether or not to open or close the windows. Frank Sinatra was my favorite singer. The only time I had an opportunity to interview him was for Andy Warhol's *Interview* magazine and we were told that Sinatra wanted to approve all the questions beforehand. Andy and I refused. What idiots we were. I should have done anything to get into the room. I once wrote a *New York Post* column about how, even though Sinatra reportedly hated rock and roll, all the rock and roll musicians adored him. He wrote me a lovely letter and made sure I always had tickets to his New York shows. In 1993, Bono went to Sinatra's Palm Springs house around the time the two of them sang vocals (although not in the same studio) for "I've Got You Under My Skin" for one of Sinatra's duets albums. Bono promised me that one day he would describe Sinatra's house to me in detail and tell me all about Frank. He still hasn't.

By the 1980s and certainly the 1990s, the element of surprise in rock and roll had pretty much disappeared. It was rare to discover a new band either by word of mouth, or stumbling across a great album cover in a bin in a crummy little record store, yard sale or even at Tower Records. MTV had changed everything. It wasn't anywhere near what it would become two decades later with YouTube and Twitter, but nothing was a secret anymore. Things got big, and bigger. And in U2's world, nothing would be as overblown as their Hollywood movie, *Rattle and Hum*. On November 1, 1988, U2 held the premiere of *Rattle and Hum* at the Astor Plaza in Times Square. It was a ninety-eight-minute film that felt like three hours. The movie, directed by Phil Joanou, was an attempt to infuse a soulful, funky, bluesy American element to U2's body of work. In a way, it was their *Exile on Main Street*, but far more pretentious. When the Rolling Stones recorded *Exile*, that double album was an homage to American blues and country music. When it was released, it was a commercial flop and a critical disaster. Years later, it was declared a masterpiece. *Rattle and Hum*, a black and white movie about U2's 1987 tour of America, has still not been re-thought in flattering terms. It featured scenes with the band taking a walk in Harlem, singing with a black gospel choir, recording at Sun Studios in Memphis, and sitting by the Mississippi River. They were filmed at Graceland, staring at Elvis Presley's grave (the *Spinal Tap* reference may, or may not have been, intentional). The four band members wore oversized overcoats. Bono was lit as if he were Greta Garbo. There were images of Bono in a cowboy hat, references to Jerry Lee Lewis, a duet with B.B. King, and songs that sounded like the Velvet Underground. One song, "Angel of Harlem," sounded like a J.Geils song. The band looked uneasy throughout the film. Larry, especially, was not smiling. There was dizzying camera work and an abundance of dramatic Bono closeups. The whole thing was such a mess that some good songs got overlooked. "That whole time in Hollywood," Bono would tell me afterwards, "we were just trying to let everything out. It was fun and frolic and we had to go through it. But we were nothing like the megalomaniacs that some of the media said we were. All we did was make a record of new songs we liked. We were in love with American music; we were fans of Johnny Cash." Edge said, "I realized we were in trouble when Paramount showed me the twelve-foot-high poster of me with my stubble airbrushed out. I just went, 'Oh shit, we really got this one wrong.' But by then it was too late."

Possibly because of the negative press they got from *Rattle and Hum*, U2 decided to try something new. In 1990 they fled to Berlin to record with Daniel Lanois and Brian Eno—the producer who made such great albums in the 1970s in Berlin with David Bowie. I remember thinking at the time that it was a pity that U2—despite the fact that they didn't write or record it—couldn't perform Pink Floyd's *The Wall* by the site of the Berlin Wall. Roger Waters had already beaten them to it.

In 1992, in one of our talks, Bono said that "rock and roll has gone Broadway. Dance steps and Buck's Fizz and that whole cocktail mentality, where you don't take anything seriously. We grew up in a completely different time." And every time we ever sat down to talk, Bono would continue to say U2 hadn't done their best work yet, their best work was to come, they hadn't really begun as a band. In the 1980s, he said U2 was a four-legged table—each band member held the other up. In the 1990s the refrain was the same. Ditto the 2000s. They were all there to support each other. No one is a selfish member of the band. He may be the frontman, but there is no star. U2 is the star. Bono told me he once went two days without talking—which I found hard to believe. He said he could be inarticulate at times. He said he was motivated by "fear." When he finally admitted that the band was ready to play stadiums, he said, "The energy of rock and roll was always about sliding down the surface of fantasies. Elvis was important not only because he was Elvis, but because he was that big. There was a momentum that was part of rock and roll and it was about size. For us, rock and roll was always about playing with the big boys." He said Paul McGuinness was always telling them that they needed to supply the demand; that by playing smaller venues, the ticket scalpers were having a field day.

"Here comes success / Here comes my Chinese rug," Iggy sang in "Success," one of my all-time favorite songs. By the 1990s, U2 was huge. I'd seen so many bands go through the stages from struggle to success, and the pattern was usually the same. In Stage One, they were young. They were sexy. They had nothing to lose. They wore some version of their everyday clothes onstage. It took two weeks to make an album. Then came attention (if it came) and some success. In Stage Two, a band moved from a van to a tour bus, or to coach seats on flights from city to city. If they got really big, edging towards Stage Three, it was more "cost effective" for them to charter their own plane. The rationale was they could fit twelve people on a private jet for the same price as twelve first-class tickets. Sort of. Plus, they weren't hassled in airports. Each band member had a bodyguard. The band had large dressing rooms backstage. In arenas, there were private dressing rooms with even more private inner dressing rooms, with security guards standing outside the doors. There were extra rooms off the backstage hallways to house the trunks with the band's traveling stage wardrobe. Their production team had an office backstage. There was a "green room" with food and wine for their guests. Jack Nicholson attended the shows. It took around six months to make an album. And then, full-fledged Stage Three or maybe Stage Four of all this was the move to stadiums. More of their fans could be accommodated. It supposedly thwarted the ticket scalpers (except it didn't). The band had a stylist who oversaw the band's onstage costumes. And finally, the band made crazy money. Along with those multi-million-dollar-grossing stadium tours came the houses in Malibu. Or, in the case of U2, a compound in the South of France where the band and their wives and children decamp for the entire summer. (Coincidentally, U2's houses are in Eze, a few miles away from Villa Nellcote—where Keith Richards lived and the Stones recorded *Exile on Main Street* in 1971.) By now, it might take well over a year to record an album. And even though U2 has always espoused a more serious intention, and conducted their business in a more dignified and non-hedonistic vein, they had all the accoutrements that accompany bigtime rock success—including, but not limited to, the plane, the police escorts, and the complicated, political hierarchy of the backstage pass.

Backstage passes reflect status. The first time I was made aware of this was when I traveled with the Rolling Stones in 1975. The entire touring party had laminated photo passes that allowed us to go anywhere backstage. This became the norm for a major group. Clubs and smaller halls didn't always have this pass setup, but as soon as a band made it to arenas or stadiums, the elaborate pass situation was standard for what goes on behind the scenes. The first, and lowest backstage pass is the stick-on "After Show" pass for the "green room" mob scene. This literally is a square or circular or triangular piece of fabric with paper on the back that you peel off and stick onto (and ruin) your clothes. Next is the stick-on "VIP" pass for the "pre-show," "green room" mob scene. (I always thought it would be funny if some band had a pass that led to a door that opened right into the parking lot outside the venue.) The next level is the laminated "VIP Guest" pass for a "band room." It isn't really a band room, it's a "meet and greet" room where the band—or in the case of U2, Bono—might make an appearance before the show. (Early on, Bono told me that he was fine performing in front of thousands of people, but he got nervous if he had to meet five people in a dressing room. Obviously, he got over it.) After the VIP guest pass comes the "Staff" laminate, with no photo, that allows the bearer to move freely around the backstage area—except in the band's dressing rooms. Then, there is the "All Access" photo laminate, but you still might need an "escort" with a better pass to take you into the band's dressing rooms. And then, there is the top pass: the "All Access" laminate for friends and family that allows you to go anywhere, including the band's dressing rooms and the stage. But still, there might be a sticker or a star on this pass that alerts security just how far you can go: into the band's private, inner dressing rooms or just the band's private, outer dressing rooms. The whole structure is byzantine, and familiar only to people who've been through all these maneuvers. I recall many a time seeing someone proudly waltz backstage with a stick-on pass on their jacket or jeans, only to watch their face fall when they saw someone else with a laminate. Or those with non-photo VIP laminates glance enviously at those with the photo laminates. The entire pass arrangement is a visual indication of just exactly where you stand with a group. John McEnroe and I became friendly because of just such a situation. In 1978, the Rolling Stones were performing at Madison Square Garden. John was backstage. I was writing for the *New York Post*, and I was a huge McEnroe fan. I went up to introduce myself to him. He sneered when I mentioned the *Post*. I pointed to his stick-on pass and pointed to my all-access laminate. No words were needed. It literally broke the ice; we've been good friends ever since.

There is a different pecking order with each band, each arena, each stadium. One band's all-access laminate means nothing at another band's show. The musicians, of course, never wear their laminates. (When Pearl Jam's guitarist Stone Gossard once went onstage wearing his, I assumed it was meant to be ironic. And at the Grammys three years ago, security guards literally stopped Eminem from going backstage because he wasn't wearing his "credentials.") Then, there are the wristbands. The wristbands—paper or plastic—allow you onto the soundboard. The soundboard is a raised platform either behind or slightly above the actual concert sound equipment. Depending on how complicated or computerized the band's technology is, there can be multiple soundboards on the side of, or underneath, the stage. There is also a soundboard near the back of the arena or the stadium, a mile away from the stage. It has no seats (although comfy sofas and chairs were on the soundboard at Madison Square Garden for the Jay Z and Kanye West "Watch the Throne" concert). In the case of U2, the band's special guests watch the show from the sound-board, protected from the general public. Sometimes in stadiums, there are two soundboards. The color of your wristband determines which soundboard you get to stand on. At a U2 show, the "good" soundboard will have Christy Turlington, Jimmy Iovine, Jay Z, and old friends of the band like the Irish musician Gavin Friday or writer/publicist B.P. Fallon. The "bad" one might have lower-level record company executives or staff. This all sounds ridiculous. But it's akin to a front-row seat at a fashion show or a seat at a better table at a dinner party. The entire thing is often fraught with anxiety, drama and dread. But it is a very big deal for those who need the pass for their egos, or to move around freely to do their actual work.

And at the end of the show, the band may not hang around for any green room pleasantries after all. Instead, they may decide to do that "runner" and race to limousines lined up right behind the stage to get the hell out of the venue. This presents yet another hurdle. If you're included in the band's party, or had secured a ride with them to the show, you have a seat in one of their cars or vans going back to the hotel. Or to the airport, if you're going with them to the next city. For some, this is a convenience. For others, a coup. And by the end of the 1980s, U2 drove in a flotilla of limousines with a police escort that accompanied them to and from their stadium shows. At that time, Bono told me that while he used to find that sort of thing embarrass-ing, now he found it funny. "During the '80s, we knew we were taking rock and roll seriously and we knew it was against the tide. With suc-cess, I found everything funny. The limos and the police escorts and us four jerks. But people won't let us have a sense of humor."

U2 had the same manager for 35 years. All four band members share equally in the money. It may be one of the very few (if not only) major rock bands where not one member has been tossed out of a nightclub or arrested for drugs, gun possession, or punching a photographer. No band member has had to hide stories from a wife about visits to a strip club. None of the four original members of the band has ever (publicly) quit the band. No one has overdosed, committed suicide or died. They never backed themselves into a corner by saying they didn't want to sing a particular song when they reached a certain age. On paper, this makes them sound duller than they actually are. They've certainly had their share of blowups and meltdowns, personal tragedies, breakups and doubts. The difference with this group is that somehow they've managed, despite the increasing public persona of the lead singer, to keep most things private. Or, as they say in basketball, "in-house."

On March 12, 1992, I accompanied U2 on their plane from New York City to Hartford, Connecticut, for a show on their "Zoo TV" tour. We stayed at the J.P. Morgan Hotel, and Peter Wolf from the J.Geils Band was there. We all gathered in Bono's room. Peter played rare Hank Williams radio show tapes and talked about how, after a drunken bender, Hank Williams made repentant records under the name Luke the Drifter. I told Bono about the Alan Lomax "Sounds of the South" recordings. We stayed up all night, talking and listening to music. It was like being in Keith Richards' room on the 1975 Stones tour—without the drugs. By now, the band's touring party numbered seventy people. The "Zoo TV" tour was a technically ambitious trek designed to promote their *Achtung Baby* album. There were huge video screens, computerized effects, five onstage telephone hookups to the White House and to Sarajevo. Pizza was delivered onstage mid-concert. For some reason, Bono dressed up as characters: for the song "The Fly," he wore black leather and wraparound glasses. As "MacPhisto," he had a gold lamé suit, lipstick, eyeliner, and red horns on his head. It was not a good look. On August 12th, after the band's show at Giants Stadium, back in the city, Bono talked until four a.m. in the bar of the Rihga Royal Hotel. As always with me, he talked about punk rock and the band's beginnings: "We were in high school and we heard this guy was making a movie of James Joyce's *Portrait of the Artist As a Young Man*," Bono recalled, "and he was coming to our school to see if he could find young actors. We also heard he had an in with a TV station and we thought if we could impress him, we could get on this TV show that was like Britain's *Top of the Pops*. We were very young, we played cover versions, and while we found it easy to write our own songs, we couldn't agree on how to end them. So we just did two Ramones numbers, at the end of which he said, 'Very good, and you wrote those yourselves?' We mumbled we did. Years later I told that to Joey Ramone, who asked me, 'Who's James Joyce?'"

o o o

In 1991, defending the lavish spectacle of their "Zoo TV" tour, Bono talked to me at great length about how they had gone out with minimal shows in their early days because "that was the picture we were painting back then. It was stark. We were staring down the greed of the '80s—Oliver Stone and the Material Girl and all that. But we're not a one-line joke. Now the stage is like a huge playground, like Disneyland on acid. In the past, our influences were more classical—an author like Flannery O'Connor or the poetic spirit of the blues. Now they're more pop; Disneyland, the American elections, TV evangelism, pornography, remote control technology."

In June 1993, Paul McGuinness called to tell me the good news: Adam Clayton was in love. He and Naomi Campbell were engaged. It'll end in tears, I told him. "Oh Lisa," Paul said, "you're so cynical. Adam has never been so happy." I knew Naomi in the 1980s through my friendships with her first agent Bethann Hardison and the photographer Steven Meisel. I encouraged her singing aspirations. She accompanied me on numerous occasions to various concerts, and I accompanied her to a boxing match in Atlantic City when she was "dating" Mike Tyson. When Naomi realized at that fight that she was not sitting ringside—Robin Givens was—there was drama. There was often drama in Naomi's world. But I knew her when she was very young. Many of her hopes and dreams had not yet been dashed. She wanted to meet Michael Jackson. (Within six years, she would appear with him in a video and they became friends.) Naomi was, of course, a beauty, with a knockout body and a real little girl flirt personality. She also was erratic and given to fits of (well-publicized) anger. None of this boded well for Adam who was basically a sweet man and probably had no idea what he was getting himself into. During that phone call, Paul also asked if I'd like to come to Paris to see the band perform an outdoor gig with their opening act, the reunion of the Velvet Underground. Of course I would.

On June 23rd, I took an all-night flight to Paris. I didn't sleep and arrived jetlagged and completely wiped out. I was staying at the band's very fancy hotel, the Royal Monceau, around the corner from the Arc de Triomphe. Almost immediately upon my arrival, I got a phone call from Paul inviting me to lunch. Someone must have dropped out of his original plan, because we were going, he told me, to Joël Robuchon's restaurant Jamin. It was, apparently, the most famous restaurant in Paris, and it was, also, just days before it was due to close. I have never been, nor am I to this day, an adventurous eater. This is an understatement; I have a friend who claims that I eat like a twelve-year-old whose parents are away on vacation. Pizza is my favorite food. I don't eat fish. I have never tasted it and I don't want to. Well, I'll have caviar. Or the occasional shrimp cocktail or smoked salmon. But for me to dine in a serious restaurant is just a waste. Nonetheless, there was no way I was going to turn this down, even though I had no idea who this cook was.

In a semi-daze, I accompanied Paul and Ian Flooks, U2's European concert agent, to the small restaurant on Rue de Longchamp.

Later that week Bono would tell me, "We owe a lot of our good taste to Paul, who would rather starve than not eat in a Michelin-rated restaurant. From hanging around him, I knew more about good red wine than amplifiers when I was twenty." Rock and roll has never been a world filled with refined culinary experiences. At least not the people I'd been around—with the exception of a few good meals I had in the presence of Mick Jagger. At best, on the road, you remembered a good spot for ribs in San Antonio. Or a clean Taco Bell in a Nashville strip mall. Or a specific steak at the Pump Room in the Ambassador East in Chicago. Or those donuts at the Café du Monde in New Orleans. It wasn't really until the late 1990s or later that all this silly food stuff started to become a Thing. While big bands had previously traveled with their own drug dealers or "doctors," now they started traveling with their own chefs. And of course, as the bands aged, along came the cleanses and the detoxes and the grass-fed beef. But that day in Paris, I realized how far U2 had come. The food we ate in Joël Robuchon's restaurant was delicious and decadent, whatever it was. For all I know, in my state of semi-delirium, I might even have eaten some fish. By the end of the meal, my head was buzzing. It was the closest I'd come to a psychedelic experience since I took mescaline once in the late 1960s. Following the meal, I left Paul and Ian and decided to walk. I got lost and wandered around Paris for a few hours until I got in a taxi and went back to the hotel. My strongest memories of that Paris trip were that meal, the hotel spa, and telling Naomi that she'd better not break Adam's heart.

Before the band's concert, I went to Bono's suite to do an interview. Perhaps because of the presence of Naomi and Christy Turlington (who had posed with Bono on the cover of the December 1992 British *Vogue*) in the band's entourage, U2 now had paparazzi following them everywhere. Bono's suite was crammed with flowers, champagne, and major fruit displays. I asked him: what's with the supermodels and the cover of *Vogue* and the luxe hotel? "I'm very fond of Naomi and I've always had beautiful women as friends," said Bono, whose own beautiful wife Ali was out shopping with their young daughter Jordan. "I thought doing the cover of *Vogue* was a very funny thing to do; any U2 fan would find it funny. Every big group collects celebrity-hunter, rock and roll part-timers, but we have an audience to whom our music really means a lot. They know we're not a regular rock band. Besides, we've always stayed in good hotels in good cities. In order to stay in the Sunset Marquis in L.A. when we first came to America, we would stay in hovels—sharing rooms—for weeks." (When Adam and Naomi eventually broke up several years later, the rumors were that her high-handed behavior was at odds with a U2 world that did not include ordering people around. Later, Adam would tell me about that period and the paparazzi: "It's not really my cup of tea; I definitely prefer to live my life in a more private way. At the end of the day, tabloid stories are hurtful.")

Ostensibly, we weren't in Paris to shop, eat, or swim in the hotel pool. The show was the reason we were all there, and for me, the actual show was a disappointment. It was held far from Paris at a huge, unremarkable outdoor space called Hippodrome de Vincennes. The opening set by the reunited Velvet Underground was not the magic I had hoped for. Lou Reed and Nico rehearsing in my living room on West 83rd Street twenty-two years earlier had been more hypnotic and memorable. The (briefly) reunited Velvets were managed by Lou's then-wife Sylvia Morales, and John Cale and Lou were barely speaking. John complained to me that Lou was jumping into limousines with Bono, and that Lou treated John, Sterling Morrison and Maureen Tucker as his backup band. Bono, however, was enthusiastic about the Velvets, saying every night was like going on "after the Beatles." As for U2's set, I watched it from a soundboard almost a mile away from the stage. It was undoubtedly a thrill for the paying customers, but by then, I was at a point where perhaps I had seen too much and knew too much. I didn't feel the excitement. While the songs and the performance might have been good, maybe it was unrealistic to think that a band can matter—the way they once did—when it's out of context. U2 no longer were the young, passionate rock band that came along at a particularly dull, superficial time in popular music. Now they were mainstream. They no longer were the band that sounded like no one else. In fact, because of their success, dozens of bands sounded like them. Then too, there's that Chinese rug that Iggy sang about. Bono insisted that they were winking at success, they wanted to take the piss out of everything, they had their core values intact and so forth, were starting to ring hollow. It was a year after the Rodney King riots in Los Angeles and five years after NWA's "Fuck Tha Police." Fifteen years after its inception, hip hop was finally edging its way into popular music and it felt much more relevant than songs about the IRA. Nirvana had startled people with "Smells Like Teen Spirit." Trent Reznor's industrial, aggressive Nine Inch Nails caused a sensation. Even Bob Dylan had re-invented himself with an outstanding performance at a Woodstock anniversary concert and would, four years later, release an amazing album, *Time Out of Mind*. As a fan, I wanted U2 to still matter. As a band, so did they.

o o o

On March 1, 1994, at Radio City Music Hall, Bono presented Frank Sinatra with the Grammy Lifetime Achievement Award. It would be the first of many flowery, hyperbolic induction speeches from Bono, who was quickly becoming the toastmaster general of rock and roll. Introducing Sinatra, Bono said, "Frank walks like America . . . cocksure . . . a man heavier than the Empire State, more connected than the Twin Towers. As recognizable as the Statue of Liberty . . ."

Paul McGuinness, *New York Post* columnist Cindy Adams and I
watched the show on a TV monitor in a small backstage makeup
room. Bono did a grandiose, hyperbolic, four-minute introduction.
Sinatra came onstage and seemed unsure of where he was. He
rambled. He might have been drunk. Or medicated. It was awkward.
He told bad jokes. He talked so long that those of us backstage in the
dressing room muttered that someone should get him off. It was sad.
But when he walked backstage, holding the pointed, Lucite award in
his hands, he looked at his wife Barbara and said to her—with that
unmistakable Hoboken inflection—"You could give someone a real
ka-nock on the head with this."

o o o

On February 12, 1997, U2 held a press conference to announce their
"Popmart" tour. The press conference was held at the giant chain
store Kmart on Astor Place in New York City's Greenwich Village.
In the midst of noontime shoppers and surrounded by cash regis-
ters and polyester lingerie, the four members of U2 stood on a stage
under a sign that read "POP GROUP." In the "audience" were over
100 journalists from around the world, music industry types and
Allen Ginsberg. Bono announced that they were into "trash" and
"kitsch," and promised that everything would be "bigger, better,
taller and wider" than anything they had done before. He referred to
the concerts as "the Superbowl every night." Larry appeared uncomfortable. Among the props U2 planned to take with them on the road
were a 150-square-foot, 65,000-pound video screen, 1,000 lighting
fixtures including 5,000 feet of disco rope lighting, a plexiglass dance
floor, a 12-foot-high illuminated stuffed olive on a 100-foot-tall tooth-
pick, a 35-foot-high mirrorball lemon and a 100-foot-high Golden
Arch. In keeping with the band's tarted-up new image and upcoming

disco-supermarket theme, Edge wore a glitter shirt. "We still have the same ideals," Bono proclaimed. "Our music is still painfully insufferable and earnest, but we finally figured out how not to look like it. Kmart seemed like the right place to announce this, because we too, are a multi-outlet outfit." Afterwards, when I mentioned to Bono that it seemed strange to have held this press conference on Ash Wednesday, he said, "Ash Wednesday and Kmart—that just about sums us up."

The media missed the intended irony of the "Popmart" tour. Many people thought the tour was actually sponsored by Kmart. The shows got off to a dodgy start. On one early show, in a true *Spinal Tap* moment, the band got trapped inside that 35-foot-high lemon. Special planes were needed to transport all the equipment from city to city and the daily operating costs were $250,000. I asked Bono why they hadn't scaled everything back after their previous over-the-top "Zoo TV" tour. "That would have been too predictable," he said. "We've been through this at least five times—where small is big. The worship of the garage comes from people who never started out in one or can't get out of it. We did."

During that tour, I accompanied the band to Hartford, Connecticut, to see a show. Bono was defensive about the seeming dichotomy of serious ideals alongside this glitzy Las Vegas presentation. "What's wrong with wanting to be a big commercial band and also an art project?" he asked me. "The notion that you can't do that is retarded [you could still say that then]. If you are a writer and you write a book that captures the public's imagination and it becomes a best seller, does that take away from the book you wrote?" And he added, "I don't think we're old fashioned, but I think we're out-of-fashion. I start getting worried when U2 is in fashion." By that time, he constantly wore those tinted, wraparound sunglasses. I asked if he was trapped by them. "Are you kidding?" he said to me. "This is my way out. It's a mask." I said I thought stadium shows were dated. "I think they're really, really dated," he said, "which is why I think a band like us can take this tired old '70s format into the next century."

In February 2001, I saw U2 at a Grammy rehearsal at the Staples Center in Los Angeles. During the band's soundcheck, Bono spotted me and started singing what would become a constant refrain whenever he saw me: "Lisa is a punk rocker," to the tune of the Ramones' "Sheena Is a Punk Rocker." Afterwards, we talked, and I told him that Mick Jagger had once told me the most important thing for a lead singer was to have "a lot of front." He laughed and said, "I've certainly got a lot of front." He said he stopped dying his hair black because he remembered that I had told him he was beginning to look like Roy Orbison. After the Grammys, at Universal Music chief Doug Morris' party at the Cicada Restaurant, I hung out with Bono, Dr. Dre and Eminem. Both Bono and Dre had posed for *Vanity Fair*'s first music issue cover earlier that year. Eminem had shockingly lost the Best Album Grammy that night to Steely Dan. Dre introduced me to Eminem as "my girl," which was his seal of approval. I talked to Eminem about how his loss to Steely Dan kept his outsider status intact. That conversation was the highlight of the night.

o o o

By now, Bono was taking time off from the band to raise money for AIDS relief in Africa. Enlisting the assistance of Harvard professor Jeffrey Sachs and Kennedy family member Bobby Shriver, he lobbied to eliminate $354 billion in Third World debt. He met with world leaders—including President Clinton, Tony Blair and Republican Senator Orrin Hatch—who told Bono that he too, was a songwriter.

Bono gave a speech at the United Nations. He had a private audience with Pope John Paul II at the Vatican and gave the Pontiff his wrap-around sunglasses. (He once gave me a pair too; he must have had boxes of them.) Sometime in 2000, we met in the bar of the Mark Hotel on Manhattan's Upper East Side to talk about his escalating activism. Bono told me that the Pope gave him a rosary, "and we took pictures [with the Pope wearing the sunglasses], but they've disappeared. Apparently his courtiers do not have the same sense of fun that the funky Pontiff has." Funky Pontiff? I asked, in disbelief. "Oh, I disagree with the Pope's position on contraception and the like," he said quickly, "and I'm not a disciple. But I think he's a sincere man." He told me that U2 had finished a new album—*All That You Can't Leave Behind*—and, knowing that I would welcome this news, he said the band planned a more intimate, scaled-down world tour that year.

In May 2001, I went to see U2's "Elevation" tour at Chicago's United Center. By now, all the band members were in their forties. They had performed in 256 countries including, in 1997, Sarajevo—after the end of the war in Bosnia. There was a heart-shaped "mosh pit" at the front of the stage; I told the band it was like having CBGB's within the massive arena. The band walked onstage with the lights on. During the show, Bono took a large spotlight and shined it on the audience. This simple, inexpensive lighting effect was far more dramatic than anything in their last two big productions. I was, once again, excited. And then, on October 24, 2001, at Madison Square Garden, in a chilling, emotional moment, the names of all the victims of 9/11 rolled on a screen behind U2 when they performed "One" (one of the most beautiful ballads ever written and, ironically, about a breakup). The band dedicated a song to Joey Ramone, who had died of lymphoma six months earlier. Reportedly, Bono had called Joey on his deathbed. Given Bono's busy humanitarian schedule at the time, one could only imagine how many assistants it took to place that call.

Backstage, after the show, an over-protective U2 staffer made Joey's mother and brother wait far too long to see Bono in his dressing room.

At Paul McGuinness' fiftieth birthday party at the Park Restaurant in New York City in June 2001, I made a toast, commending the band's organization on their kindness. I noted how considerate and thoughtful they had always been to the press, which certainly was not the norm. And I added that I was certain this was because their management company was staffed mostly by women. Not run by women, mind you, but there were many women who worked closely with, or rather for, the band. This was unusual in rock and roll. As a member of the press, you often had to fight your way past a rude, unruly male staff—and the British were the worst—to get whatever it was you needed to do your job, which, incidentally, helped the band publicize their career. With U2, it was seamless. Their road manager, my old pal Dennis Sheehan, was a doll. There were a lot of fantastic women—Sheila Roche, Susan Hunter, Keryn Kaplan, Catriona Garde and Regine Moylett, to name a few—who worked for the band. But when I stopped to think about it, I realized that these women were all quite possibly rewarded less than men in similar positions. And of course, they worked harder.

In 2002, U2 got eight Grammy nominations for their album *All That You Can't Leave Behind*. They won four awards, but lost the Best Album Grammy to the T Bone Burnett–produced soundtrack album for the movie *O Brother, Where Art Thou?* That album was released on Lost Highway Records, a small label run by my friend Luke Lewis— who also put out records by Lucinda Williams, Ryan Adams, and Willie Nelson. Once again, I was at Doug Morris' Grammy viewing party at Cicada. Jimmy Iovine—whose artist Eminem lost the year before to Steely Dan—was apoplectic. Jimmy had been U2's producer and now was the head of their record label, Interscope. Bono once described Jimmy to me as a "nutcase, and I love him." At the party, Jimmy was screaming at Doug: "This is the second year we've had this party in this restaurant! This place is a jinx! We're never having a party in this place again!" Almost a year later, at the Golden Globe Awards, U2 won Best Song for "The Hands That Built America" from the Martin Scorsese movie *Gangs of New York*. In his acceptance speech, Bono used the word "fucking" as an adjective and afterwards, it caused a furor with the FCC. At the Academy Awards that same year, U2 lost the Best Song Oscar to Eminem, who was home asleep in Detroit. After the awards, the entire U2 entourage— wives, friends, management—arrived at the *Vanity Fair* Oscar party at Morton's. Gracious in defeat, Bono told me, "[Eminem's] 'Lose Yourself' is a great song." Everyone drank, and smoked, and the U2 entourage was the last to leave. The next day, Paul McGuinness called to say, "I think that was the best party we ever went to in our lives."

In July 2004, Bono was "nominated" a third time for the Nobel Peace Prize, which he did not win. U2 was about to release a new album, *How to Dismantle an Atomic Bomb*. I knew the band was in Boston on July 27th for some Kennedy event and I phoned Paul McGuinness to ask if I could pop up there and talk to Bono. Paul seemed surprised that I would just get on a plane or into a car and come up that night. He thought it was very "rock and roll." There had been a time, I told him, when he wouldn't have blinked at this concept. But to this day, Paul occasionally tells people, with something akin to wonderment, how I went up to Boston on a moment's notice and how rock and roll it was. The Democratic Presidential Convention was in Boston that week; Senator John Kerry got the nomination. When I arrived at

Boston's Symphony Hall, it was all decked out in red, white and blue balloons for a party honoring Senator Edward Kennedy's forty-two years of public service. (Senator Kennedy showed up after his speech across town at the Convention. He changed into a white dinner jacket, and led the Boston Pops in the "Stars and Stripes.") The room was filled with 2,600 political contributors, Kennedy friends and family members and Ben Affleck and Glenn Close. But as is often the case at such events, Bono, an actual rock star, was (after the Senator) the main attraction. Dressed in black and wearing his now ever-present sunglasses, Bono walked onstage to join conductor John Williams and the Boston Pops Orchestra. He appeared slightly insecure onstage without his band. He sang U2's "Pride (In the Name of Love)" with the Boston Pops and then, accompanied by Yo-Yo Ma and the orchestra, "The Hands That Built America." He got a standing ovation. And, as he walked offstage, he muttered to me, "It's a long way from CBGB's."

After the event, Bono, his wife Ali, Paul McGuinness, Bobby and Maria Shriver, and assorted friends and associates all hung out in a suite of rooms on the fourth floor of the Fairmont Copley Plaza. I had been wanting to talk to Bono for a while about his political work. I was disturbed by his swanning around the White House and at prayer breakfasts with George W. Bush. "It's classic rockstar syndrome," Bono said. "I want to have fun and I want to save the world. The band has been incredibly tolerant. Let's face it, this is pretty unhip work, some of these people are just so uncool. [The band] is occasionally frustrated and annoyed, but they're also very proud, and therefore, they financially support my work. Because if it takes two years to make a record that should take one, that's two years of their lives that they too, are investing in this other stuff." I asked why, at this stage of their career, did an album take two years? "Great hangs back until very good gets tired," he said. "Who wants a good, or even very good U2 record right now? What's the point? We need eleven great reasons [new songs] to leave home."

I asked Bono how he could possibly balance such great riches with his insistence that he was, at heart, a punk rocker. "The bubbles might go to my head occasionally. And the altitude sickness . . . it's called vertigo," he said, deftly tossing in the title of the first single from the band's new album. "For us, coming out of punk rock, we despised bands who thought it was just enough to turn up," he said. "That fat rock and roll thing . . . they got the house and the car but lost everything else. Imprinted in us was that the only justification for success is not being crap. There's a deal with your audience: we have this life and we don't have to worry about the things they worry about—medical bills, where the kids go to school—and in return, don't be dull, don't give us your second best."

And then he said, "I've noticed with men, as they get older, they rid the room of argument. They want to be lord of their own domain, and they eventually push out of their lives people who challenge their points of view. I noticed this with my father, cousins, uncles, brothers. They end up in a room where everybody agrees with them, which is like going solo. I think that's a mistake." Did this not apply to him too? I asked. No, he insisted, he was constantly surrounded by others' opinions, by friction. "Friction keeps you sharp," he said. "I would say I need the band more than they need me, especially as a musician—because I haven't got the sophistication to play the melodies I make up in my head. But I also need them emotionally. A lot."

As we ate pizza and drank wine, I told him I thought that he was now in the celebrity category that for years he said he wanted to avoid. "It comes in handy here and there," he said, "and it's an annoyance here and there. But I'm not sure I'm very good at it. We don't get the paparazzi, we don't get all that kerfuffle. When the guys go back to the *New York Post* and say, 'Here's a picture of Bono,' they don't go, 'Wow.'" I laughed and said that's because he's out all the time, hence, he's no big deal. "No," he said. "It's because it's not our world. There was a time when we were playing with celebrity, we tried it on like a party dress and I enjoyed it actually. But it is not the way people relate to us."

Then I segued into an area I had avoided for years. I told him that women were always asking me how Ali could put up with Bono's rumored (and unsubstantiated) philandering. I said that I personally thought Ali, who always appeared to me to be somewhat cynical, was probably happy to get him out of the house. "I'm glad you spotted the cynicism," he said, "because she is serene, but she also is a great skeptic. Ali doesn't need the favor of anyone. She's very complex." Also beautiful, I added. He said, "I know this sounds like a line, but she doesn't see herself that way. I met her when we were thirteen, and she was an academic. Her mother made her clothes; she wore Wellington boots, and I found that absence of vanity very attractive. She understands mysterious distance. A lot of the relationships I see are like 'Where were you? Who was there?' type of thing." I venture that most marriages in rock and roll don't last and it's often because of that choking thing. "She's the least choking person," Bono said. "It's sometimes unnerving, because I'll be about to go away on a tour and she's standing there in the doorway with the kids with a big smile on her face, waving. Whatever it is, it's immensely attractive. And sometimes hurtful. You know, performers are not the most secure people in the world. Why would you go on a stage if you were of sound mind? In a very, very, very deep place, I'm secure. And on the surface, secure. But somewhere in there, I need 20,000 screaming people a night to feel normal." I asked him what he was like when he returned home from a tour. "You find yourself on the dinner table," he says, "maniacally swinging a lightbulb, telling jokes that aren't funny."

I asked him—again—how he could possibly justify his association with George W. Bush. Artists should not go into that White House, I said. To which he replied, "I'd do *anything* if it meant he'd give more money to help people in Africa." I continued to challenge him about Bush until I said I could no longer argue with him. "It's not an argument," he said. "It's a debate. Irish people debate." But, I said, Orrin Hatch??? "I have huge respect for Senator Hatch," he said. "Huge respect. I know it's strange from someone coming from a Labor family, from the Left such as myself, but I've discovered you can disagree with someone's position and still respect them for holding it if it comes from real conviction. I've met a lot of people who are conservative who are really true to their code—and others who are just greedy. Look, does an AIDS sufferer in Africa care that the ARVs that are keeping him or her alive were paid for by a dollar from the pocket of a person who might be preening sometime in the future? I don't think that person taking a twenty-cent pill gives a damn about that, and I don't think they should. So I don't either."

Soon after that conversation, I talked to Paul McGuinness, Larry and the Edge about how Bono's political work affected the band. Paul said that Bono was very careful to lobby every political leader around the world. That his efforts were always bipartisan. And that yes, it could put him in some pretty strange photographs and some very uncomfortable juxtapositions, but that he was certain Bono would say the embarrassment was compensated by the things he achieved. Edge told me, "It doesn't necessarily help our band that Bono is so well known now as a political activist. It's great on one level, but being photographed with George W. Bush and the Pope—I don't like it particularly and he knows it. I asked him, whatever you do, please don't be photographed with George Bush Jr. [*sic*], and he said, 'You know Edge, I hear what you're saying, but this is really important.' And at the end of the day I had to agree that if you can help hundreds of thousands, maybe millions of people's lives . . . I just worry that with political work, it's a murky business. You never really know if the deal you're getting is the deal you think you're getting. He's had to make certain compromises I'm not sure I would be comfortable making." And Larry said, "We've all asked him if this is something he can defend, and he's said, 'I've been to Africa, I've seen people dying from starvation, I've been to AIDS hospitals and seen people dying from AIDS. If I have to have lunch with the devil himself to get people to help and to do something, I'll do it.' You can't really counter that."

In 2005, in their first year of eligibility, U2 were inducted into the Rock and Roll Hall of Fame. The running joke was who was going to induct them, since Bono couldn't really introduce his own band. In 2008, they jumped on the Obama bandwagon and performed at an inauguration special aired on HBO. They released an album (*No Line on the Horizon*) that was, Bono emailed me, a "knockout punch." He reminded me that I had asked him, after *How to Dismantle an Atomic Bomb*, when the band was going to musically "take things up to the next level." He said this was the "next level," and would send me an advance copy. In 2009, after the album hadn't done well, he told me at great length one night how it was one of their most misunderstood albums ever. And that it had been their most critically acclaimed, which was not entirely accurate. Since then, the party line from the band's camp has been that the album was meant to be "experimental" and "underground," but was promoted out of proportion. The band themselves went on a huge "360" tour in 2009 to promote that album. In March 2009, I saw them in New York when they performed for an entire week on the David Letterman show. During a rehearsal, Bono saw me sitting in the orchestra and once again, started singing "Lisa is a punk rocker." On September 24th of that year, I went with

Rick Rubin to see the "360" concert at Giants Stadium. Bono gave onstage shout outs to such New Jersey notables as Bruce Springsteen, Jon Bon Jovi and *The Sopranos*. Rick and I moved to the soundboard just in time to see Mick Jagger, Nicole Kidman and Keith Urban leave. U2 then threw two Stones songs into their set—including the 1978 disco hit "Miss You"—a song no one other than Mick Jagger should ever attempt to sing. Rick and I stood with Kanye West. It was a few weeks after his debacle on MTV with country pop darling Taylor Swift. We commiserated with Kanye for awhile. When the face of Aung San Suu Kyi, the jailed pro-democracy leader of Burma appeared on the giant video screens, and extras wearing masks of her face marched around onstage while the band sang "Walk On," Kanye said to me, "Who's that girl? I don't keep up."

o o o

By now, U2 were firmly in what I consider Stage Four of a band's evolution. They were a huge, huge, global superstar group. They made a ridiculous amount of money. They had, in fact, been criticized for moving some of their official businesses out of Ireland to the Netherlands to save on taxes. With age and financial success beyond anything anyone could imagine, people change. With adulation, people change. Priorities change. Three out of the four band members had children in private schools. They had multiple houses. They carried a large staff who also had mortgages and children with school tuitions. Edge was involved in some sort of lawsuit in Malibu for trying to build houses in a spot that some Malibu property owners protested would ruin the environmental lay of the land. Bono had joined forces with the venture capitalist group Elevation Partners. Along with Mario Batali, Jay Z and others, he invested in New York restaurants. The band owned a hotel in Dublin. With this sort of operation, it becomes difficult to know who to trust. The band trusts fewer people.

And for the most part, those they do trust are financially dependent on them. Musically, the band became more insecure. The signs were there. Bono always thought he could talk his way out of everything; he even had meals with critics who had unfavorably reviewed the band, trying to change their minds. They (meaning Bono) started to take the pop music temperature. Jimmy Iovine urged them to make dance records. The band meetings undoubtedly lasted longer. Their recording sessions dragged on for years. They weren't sure if they were still relevant. I had seen this before with others: Led Zeppelin in 1979 at Knebworth, the Rolling Stones (well, Jagger) even as far back as 1975.

On June 14, 2011, *Spider-Man*, the Broadway show with a score written by Bono and the Edge finally opened. When Paul McGuinness had called me several years earlier to tell me the good news— Julie Taymor was going to collaborate and direct—I told him it would end in tears. He told me I was crazy. For several years the show had been described as "troubled." It was savaged by the theater press in previews. Cast members flew around the theater, fell from cables, were injured, and sent to the hospital. On opening night, in a downstairs VIP green room were, among others, former President Bill Clinton, Mayor Bloomberg, Jay Z, Lou Reed, John McEnroe and Jimmy Fallon. I stood chatting with Jay, John and Lou. Bono wore a black suit and a glittery shirt that reminded me of the shirt Edge wore at the Kmart "Popmart" press conference. Bono saw us, came over, and seemed nervous. "My rock and roll friends," he said, and proceeded to do a short monologue on why this should not be considered a rock and roll show. I felt kind of sorry for the guy. He was putting on a brave face. Perhaps he actually thought the show was great. Or perhaps he was aware that tourists from Kansas would bring their children to see it in droves. This was not the Clash telling me they wanted to do a Broadway show someday in the future. Joe

Strummer didn't live long enough to do it. And if he had, who knows what he would have come up with either.

U2 is a great rock and roll band. They have a real body of work. They've influenced hundreds of bands—although Radiohead would never admit it, and Coldplay is U2 "lite." The chorus in Cee Lo's song "Bright Lights Bigger City" is note for note U2's "[She Moves in] Mysterious Ways." There is a Kia car commercial on TV that sounds decidedly like Edge's guitar runs in "Surrender." U2's "Elevation" is played at nationally televised NBA games. They're much more fun to spend time with than anyone might think—especially when drinking is involved. And especially Larry—who I'm always happy to see, much to the surprise of the band's own staff. Bono can be great company—when he isn't going on about Africa or that great guy Senator Bill Frist (who destroyed health care in his home state of Tennessee). And it's hard to consistently argue with someone who might have helped save some lives. His bandmates always told him the music should speak for itself. It's been four years since the last U2 album. I always said if I won the lottery I'd be off in a flash to the South of France. U2 won the lottery. They were in the South of France where, I'm certain, they continued to debate their future musical direction. And where, I'm certain, they listened—and listened, and mixed and re-mixed—the songs they recorded with the trendy producer Brian (Danger Mouse) Burton. And I wonder if Bono tried to convince the rest of the band—Larry especially—that it's time to also make some music that gets people up to dance. After all, wouldn't that be the punk rock thing to do?

Eight

Starting around 1999, whenever I was in Los Angeles, I visited Jimmy Iovine at his house in Bel Air. I'd known him for years—first, in the 1970s, as the guy who brought coffee to John Lennon at the Record Plant, then as an engineer and producer for Patti Smith, Tom Petty and U2. By the end of the 1990s, Jimmy was the head of Interscope Records, and had signed Tupac Shakur, Snoop Dogg, Dr. Dre, No Doubt, U2 and Eminem. In February of 2000, he started talking to me about the importance of Eminem. He compared him to Lenny Bruce. It turns out that many people think that there are many people like Lenny Bruce. Of course, there are not. Just being dirty, or cynical, isn't enough to qualify. Even the original Lenny Bruce wasn't what he's been made out to be. He was brilliant, funny, outrageous—but he needs to be viewed in context: it was the 1960s. The only comparison I could see between Eminem and Lenny Bruce was that Eminem said things in his songs that people may have felt—or thought they felt—but would never say out loud.

I hadn't really followed Eminem's career. I was aware of the jokey Slim Shady videos on MTV—when MTV still aired videos. They struck me as humor for kids. But in March 2000, when Jimmy played some songs for me from Eminem's *Marshall Mathers LP* prior to its release, I was immediately drawn to the combination of lyrical skills and rage. It felt like punk rock. And at the time, I thought of what hardcore singer Jello Biafra had said: "Punk will never die until something more dangerous comes along to replace it."

Eminem's lyrics, about incest, murder, rape and sodomy were described as a cross between *South Park* and *Raging Bull*. Apparently he was either the single most notorious character in popular music, or a genius. Or both. I started to investigate. I went to Interscope's offices and looked through an entire storage room with boxes of magazine and newspaper articles about Eminem. He was called a sociopath, a master storyteller, white trash, brilliant, homophobic, misogynistic, antisocial, dysfunctional, touching, inventive, heroic, twisted. He was compared to T. S. Eliot, Robert Browning, Howard Stern, Mark Twain, Andrew Dice Clay, Rimbaud and yes, Lenny Bruce. I was intrigued.

I began to pay more attention to rap. Rick Rubin told me that when he started Def Jam Records in his NYU dorm room in 1982, "If you loved rap, you couldn't understand how people could not love it." Run DMC's Darryl McDaniels has said, "I never in my wildest dreams ever thought that hip hop would be as big and as powerful and magnificent as it is. To me, it was just something that was big in my basement." By the start of the 21st century, rappers had sold millions of records and infiltrated white suburban households. But big, white rock bands still filled stadiums on a regular basis, and the Grammys didn't air the Rap category on their prime time, network telecast. When I saw Eminem perform "The Real Slim Shady" at the MTV Awards at Radio City Music Hall in September 2000, with dozens of Eminem look-alikes, I thought, here is a rock star. Once again, things had become boring and predictable. And I was, once again, attracted to the outsider, the misfit, the "rebel." It would take four years before I sat down for a real talk with Eminem. In the meantime, I was hooked.

In February 2001, Lyor Cohen, who was then the head of Island Def Jam Records, told me I should meet Jay Z. We were at Petrossian restaurant on West 58th Street in New York, eating caviar. I asked Lyor, didn't Jay stab someone? Lyor took out his phone, called Jay, and said, "I'm here with Lisa Robinson and I think you two should meet. But she's afraid you're going to stab her." We arranged to go to a Knicks game on February 7th. On the way to Madison Square Garden, in his massive Escalade, Jay blasted Stevie Wonder songs and talked about the Motown and R&B music he had grown up hearing in his mother's house. Backstage at the Garden, Jay waited a while until courtside seats were available; he wouldn't sit anywhere else. We watched Dallas beat the Knicks and we talked basketball— about how it was a rhythm game and its similarities to hip hop. We talked about which basketball players listened to his music. And we talked about the Grammys. Jay said he and his fellow rappers continued to boycott the Grammys because the Rap category wasn't shown on the telecast. After the game, we went to Nobu in Tribeca for dinner. For years afterwards, whenever I saw Jay, we talked about basketball more than we talked about music. It took about six years before he realized that I knew what I was talking about. "I thought you were just trying to humor the colored guy," he told me. By the middle of the decade, Jay was a regular at the Grammys; the show had no choice but to air the rap awards. They needed stars like Jay and Kanye West and Eminem for ratings.

A few years later, Jay Z announced his "retirement" from recording and performing. He replaced Lyor Cohen (who went to run the Warner Music Group) as president of Island Def Jam. Both Rick Rubin and I asked Jay, why on earth would he want a job? We told him— you're Jay Z—the guy Rick always referred to as "the coolest guy in the room." Any room. One day, when I posed the job question again, Jay said that at the end of the deal, he would own his master recordings. Beyoncé had told me that Jay could just walk into a recording studio and rap on the spot; he never wrote anything down. I asked Jay how this worked. He said he didn't like to write things down because he felt "the lines on the paper put the words in jail. It traps you in there. The first couple of times it's difficult. I wrote one verse on my first album, but haven't since. It's just my process. Later on isn't the problem—by then I've done them over and over. It's the first couple of times doing it that's the difficult part."

o o o

With the exception of one year (2003) at Madison Square Garden, the Grammy Awards have been held at the Staples Center in Los Angeles for the last thirteen years. Backstage at the Grammy Awards is a high pressure, live TV situation. Dozens of major stars perform, present, win, or gracefully applaud on camera when they lose. Some have their own dressing rooms. Others are crammed together in shared spaces. First, before the actual show, there's the red carpet—which has become a show in itself. The red carpet at these award shows is hysteria incarnate. The setup is much smaller than it appears on television. All the various entertainment shows and media outlets are crammed into individual two-by-four spaces that resemble tiny horse stalls. Fans and paparazzi are screaming their heads off. Stars often exit the dressing rooms inside the Grammy venue where they've been all day, and pretend to make a new entrance onto the red carpet. A publicist whisks them along a row of press and photo ops. Then, they're escorted back inside to the relative peace of a dressing room.

Many of them change outfits to either sit in the audience, or get ready to perform.

In the 1990s, when the Grammys were held at Radio City Music Hall in New York, with an all-access pass, you could wander around at will. The dressing rooms were on four floors at either side of the stage. Perennial Grammy nominees like Michael Jackson, Whitney Houston, and Mariah Carey each had their own suites on the top floor. Lesser stars shared dressing rooms on lower floors. Backup singers and musicians were shmushed together in rooms in the basement. There were "green rooms" for stars to gather together—although few of them ever did. At some point in the late '90s, I noticed an "alcohol free" room. I never saw anyone in there. The laminated pass hierarchy started with "Talent"—which allowed you to go anywhere—and went all the way down to "Working Press," who were restricted to media rooms in the basement. A small makeup touch-up room for those going onstage was behind one side of the stage; another makeup room was on the other side for the host of the show. At Radio City, to get from one side of the stage to the other, you took an elevator down to the basement, walked around a huge maze, and then took the elevator back up to the other side. Or, you could walk behind a scrim on the stage in the dark—and risk possible injury as you stepped over a labyrinth of wires and cables. There were many times I stood in the wings to watch the show. After years of covering this event for the *New York Post*, I could have found my way around Radio City's backstage wearing a blindfold.

When the Grammys were in Los Angeles, I got to know the lay of the land first at the Shrine Auditorium, and then, at what now appears to be the Grammys' permanent home, the Staples Center. The dressing rooms at Staples are all on the same level. They wind along a hallway that houses the locker rooms for the sports teams. Award shows from Los Angeles start in the middle of the afternoon. This way, the broadcast to the real world—New York—is in prime time.

Dress rehearsals are in the morning, the parties go on well into the night, and the whole thing becomes an all-day endurance test. By 2008, after years of working the Grammy backstage, the thrill was gone. I put on high heels and went to watch the show at Doug Morris' private viewing parties.

o o o

In 2001, Eminem had been slammed for homophobic lyrics by gay rights groups, Lynne Cheney (wife of the then Vice President Dick Cheney) and members of Congress. Eminem anticipated a boycott by gay rights groups at the Grammys, so he suggested—almost as a joke—that the only way he'd perform was with Elton John. Eminem's manager, Paul Rosenberg, and Jimmy Iovine were on the phone with him when he suggested it. Paul and Jimmy paused. Then Jimmy said, "You know what? I know him. Let me call him and ask." Elton, who came out in the late 1970s, has a long history of supporting gay rights and runs a big AIDS charity. He thought the protest was ridiculous and immediately agreed to do the performance. So, in 2001, while I still was involved in what I referred to as Grammy "combat duty," I stood in the wings at the side of the stage at Staples Center with my friend, the Interscope executive Dennis Dennehy. And we watched Eminem and Elton perform "Stan." Eminem opened the show, sitting on a bed, singing the verse to "Stan." Then the curtain rose, with Elton—who sang the chorus—at the piano. It was an amazing moment. (Bono would have called it very punk rock.) I found it very moving. And it instantly shut everybody up.

o o o

In the 1970s, I spent a lot of time with Elton John. We traveled on his plane—the same one I'd been on with Led Zeppelin and the Stones.

I often went backstage before his shows to visit him and check out his elaborate wardrobe. His ensembles were completely over the top: a Donald Duck costume, sparkly suits and glittery platform boots from the famous London shop Mr. Freedom. In July 1976, backstage in Washington, D.C., I commented on how much stuff he carted around. "Oh who doesn't?" Elton said. "You can't tell me that Frank Zappa doesn't take a lot with him. He probably wears all this all the time"— his arm swept around at the racks of multi-colored outfits—"and then changes into a t-shirt and jeans when he goes onstage." Several days later, we were in Philadelphia, where because of his hit song "Phildelphia Freedom," he was getting the keys to the city. As the mayor introduced him, Elton whispered to me, "Could you see Keith Richards doing this?" In his dressing room, he proudly showed off his handbag collection to his friend Elizabeth Taylor. She shrieked with pleasure. He dragged me into a bathroom to talk about Iggy and Bette Midler and how great they both were. (To this day, Elton is among the first to know about a promising new band or singer.) I had never written about Elton's homosexuality because he hadn't publicly said anything about it. When he finally did come out, he talked to me at length about being "bisexual." He told me how moved he was by the letters he'd received from people who told him how frightening their lives were and how much he helped them by coming out. I was always surprised that no one wrote about how dishy and funny he was. He referred to the summer of the Bicentennial as the "Bisexual." Celebrities who came to his shows included Shirley MacLaine, Peter Frampton and Patti Smith. Patti told Elton she was sorry that she had said bad things about him in interviews, but that she loved, and masturbated to, his records.

In 1977, Elton told me he stopped taking drugs. He hadn't, as he admitted years later. He said that at first, becoming a star was like winning the lottery. Everything was excessive, over the top. He went to unbelievable extremes. He knew he was flamboyant, yet he never thought he was glamorous. He thought he was ridiculous. But he said he had to get it all out of his system, that he was having a ball. For someone who became so rich, so grand, so ultimately troubled with drink and drugs, his heart was always in the right place. So, while people who didn't know him might have thought his Grammy performance with Eminem was bizarre, or a publicity stunt, I knew it was just Elton stepping up to support someone whose talent he considered important. Watching the two of them from the side of the stage, I was mesmerized. And, as always when I see something I think is great, everything else seemed old fashioned.

After the 2001 Grammy show, when I sat with Dr. Dre, Bono and Eminem at Doug Morris' party, I had told Eminem that it was just as well he lost the Album of the Year Grammy to Steely Dan, because there was something to be said about not getting that mainstream stamp of approval. (Years later, Paul Rosenberg told me Eminem hadn't even known what Steely Dan meant. When he found out, his response was, "I lost to a dildo?") I asked Eminem that night if he read books. He said no. Where does this all come from? I asked. Dre said, "To this day, whenever he sits in front of me in the studio, he surprises me. Every time. I'm waiting for the lights to dim in the room." (Eight years later, Eminem would tell me, "I did well in English at school, and I've always had a large vocabulary. Plus, by the time I was eighteen, I'd probably read the dictionary front to back ten times.")

In 2002, Annie Leibovitz wanted to do a photo of Eminem. We were going to run it in our *Vanity Fair* music issue. I thought it would be historic if we added Dr. Dre and Rakim (of Eric B. and Rakim) to the picture: three generations of hip hop. At that time, Dre was working on a Rakim solo album, and I knew that Rakim was one of Eminem's heroes. I thought that if we did the three of them together, it might actually get done. Still, as I would learn, anything having to do with Eminem and Dre would take at least a year to accomplish. Eminem didn't like leaving Detroit unless it was to go on tour or to record in L.A. with Dre. It took months to get in touch with Rakim—who wouldn't fly, so it was an additional problem getting him to L.A. Eventually Jimmy Iovine, who ran the record label for all three, suggested doing the photo at his house. This way, he said, they wouldn't turn it down.

On May 31, 2002, Annie, her crew, Dennis Dennehy, Paul Rosenberg, Dr. Dre, Rakim, and various others assembled at Jimmy's house. We waited a long time for Eminem to show up. When he did, he was accompanied by Shady Records executive Marc Labelle, and his best friend, the Detroit MC Proof. Eminem introduced himself to the stylist and Annie's crew as "Marshall" and then went to take a shower. Proof played pool in Jimmy's den. Some of us sat on the patio outside. Dre looked around and said to Jimmy, "This is a nice house." Jimmy replied, "You paid for it." Annie set up a studio downstairs to take a tight portrait of the three hip hop stars. A bootleg tape from a live Bob Dylan concert was on the boombox that Annie's crew carried with them. I realized that at any moment, this music might put these guys to sleep—so I asked Marc Labelle to go out to his car to get more appropriate CDs. After the shoot, Dre and Eminem discussed what Eminem's next single should be (I voted for "Cleanin' Out My Closet"). Eminem came over to say goodbye. "Thanks. That was fun," he said, deadpan. I appeared startled. "I'm kidding," he said, and then smiled. Barely.

On November 6, 2002, *8 Mile* opened at the Mann Village Theater in Westwood, Los Angeles. The movie was based on Eminem's life. He was in every scene, and you could not take your eyes off him. At the party following the premiere, Eminem stood in a roped-off VIP section. Dr. Dre and I walked up to him. "Ahhh," Dre said, "the movie star." Eminem gave me that hip hop, leaning into my shoulder, clasping my hand, half-hug that caught me off guard; I had no idea how it was supposed to go. I asked him if he had any idea how good he was in the movie. "No," he said, staring at me.

After the enormous success of *8 Mile*, Paul Rosenberg and Jimmy Iovine agreed that I should interview Eminem. Paul Rosenberg is a cigar-smoking, sneaker-wearing, six-foot-five, bearded man. When I first met him, I thought he was intimidating, even slightly scary. He reminded me of Zeppelin's manager Peter Grant, without the groupies and the drugs. Intensely devoted to Eminem, Paul had a permanent poker face. He took everything in and said very little. He was often accompanied by a bodyguard. When I got to know him and we became friends, we shared a love of the Clash and of (his alma mater) Michigan State basketball, and its coach, Tom Izzo. Still, even with Paul and Jimmy and Eminem all on board, it took over six months to get the story underway. I wanted to talk to Eminem and to the three men I felt were the most important in his life: Paul, Dr. Dre and Proof.

In June 2004, Paul and I began a series of talks that eventually filled 150 pages of transcript. On June 30th, I went to the office of Shady Records (Paul and Eminem's label) and Goliath Artists (Paul's management company). The office, which took up an entire floor, was in a nondescript building in Soho. There was no sign on the door. I was let in by a large security guard. (When I got to know the guard better, we would argue about football and his beloved Dallas Cowboys—a team I loathed.) The first thing I noticed in the office was a Mountain Dew soda machine. The walls were lined with platinum records for *The Marshall Mathers LP* and *The Eminem Show*. There were plaques for other Shady and Goliath artists: Obie Trice, 50 Cent, D12, Cypress Hill. Framed photos of Dr. Dre hung on the wall, along with hip hop magazine covers and Paul's law degree. The bathroom had a Sex Pistols poster and one for the *Sid and Nancy* movie. An industrial-sized bottle of Listerine was on the sink. On the desk in Paul's corner office was a sculpture of two fists and some brass knuckles. Lined up against the wall were fifty-six unopened boxes of sneakers.

In the first of several long talks, Paul told me he was raised in a middle-class Jewish household in a Detroit suburb. His mother was a music teacher at his synagogue, and his father played the clarinet. As a teenager, Paul fell in love with break dancing and rap, and eventually became a rapper. He formed a group called the Rhythm Cartel. "My name was Kid Swift," he said, "and my friend Jake was Skinny Supreme. We were okay, not great. I was adequate." Paul said that he was almost an outcast for liking rap among his Van Halen–loving peers. But, he said, "I was totally obsessed. I always watched what was going on behind the scenes. I knew who Russell Simmons was, and I'd always pay attention to what Rick Rubin was doing. A white Jewish guy, producing rap records in the 1980s? It was bizarre." Coming from a family of doctors and lawyers, Paul was expected to be one or the other. He went to law school with the dream of becoming an entertainment lawyer; and he wanted to take the Detroit hip hop artists he loved and make them his clients.

Paul said that Proof—who was the hottest MC in Detroit—was the first person to tell him about Eminem. "Proof introduced me to everyone as his lawyer," Paul said, "even though I was still in law school at the time. One day at Detroit's Hip Hop Shop, Proof told me, 'Paul, you haven't heard this guy; white boy's better than you and Jake used to be.' So Em rapped there, and I thought he was cool. A few months later Em was there, selling his *Infinite* tape hand to hand for six bucks. I bought it, took it home, listened to it, and thought it was really good. Then I saw Em battle at the Hip Hop Shop and the Rhythm Kitchen and he just wiped everybody out." Eventually, when Paul got tapes from Eminem, "The thing that I really loved and I knew people were going to love about him, was that he would write a song and you would think, I can't wait to see what he's going to say next. Like, 'oh my god, did he just say that?' I would hang on every word. That, and combined with the amount of syllables he would rhyme in conjunction with each other—it was just crazy. That's when you really fall in love with him." Paul told Eminem he wanted to be his lawyer and get him a record deal. He brought Eminem's tape to every label. They all turned him down. In 1997, Paul and Eminem flew to L.A., where Eminem had been invited to participate in the Rap Olympics. Eminem came in second. He lost to someone named Otherwize ("Who has Otherwize never been heard from again," Paul told me). "He was totally crushed," Paul said. However, Paul gave a tape of what would become the "Slim Shady" album to "some kids from Interscope." The rest has been well documented: the kids from Interscope got it to Jimmy Iovine. Jimmy played it for Dr. Dre, who was one of Eminem's heroes. And Dre said, "Find him. Yesterday."

In 2004, Dre told me, "When Jimmy first played me Eminem's tape, I didn't think he was a white cat. It never crossed my mind. I guess at that time I must have thought he was a black guy, because I wasn't thinking that a white guy could rap that well. And I still haven't heard anyone come close." Dre was talking to me in his Los Angeles recording studio. He's almost always in his studio. That year, he told me that his record for hours logged in there was seventy-nine hours straight. In addition to his various production work for others, he had been working on his own album, tentatively titled *Detox*, for over ten years. Every time during the past decade, whenever I've seen Dre,

I ask when it's going to be finished. He always says, "I'm almost ready." The last time he told me he was almost ready was at the 2011 Grammy Awards, after he performed "I Need a Doctor" with Eminem. That song was basically Eminem's plea for Dre to get back into the rap game. Dre's idea of "getting ready" involved a physical regimen that included a great deal of weight lifting. When he came offstage with Eminem after that Grammy performance, I said, "I think you're ready."

Both Gwen Stefani and Mary J. Blige told me that Dr. Dre is the most perfectionist producer they ever worked with. He demands multiple—multiple—takes. But Dre told me, "Em is more of a perfectionist than I am. I don't know how we ever get records done." There's no question that Dre gave Eminem hip hop credibility. "But he would have been a really big success without me," Dre said. "I just made it happen sooner. He's got a real talent for melody. And he's two people: the comedian in the room one day and then this person who's pissed off at everybody the next day. He's a weird individual. But the controversy? I love it. This is the entertainment business. Without it, it would be boring as shit."

o o o

On July 23, 2004, I sat with Proof in a dressing room at 30 Rockefeller Plaza before his group, D12, was about to go on the Conan O'Brien show. Proof, born Deshaun Dupree Holton, was Eminem's best friend and the model for the Mekhi Phifer character in *8 Mile*. Eminem referred to him as his "rock," and his "ghetto pass." They met as teenagers when Eminem was passing out flyers for a show. Proof told me that he was impressed when, on the spot, "Em spit out 'first place' and 'birthday' in the same rhyme." Proof talked about how he encouraged Eminem to battle in the lunchroom of Osborne

High. He said that he, Proof, was still the best MC in Detroit, but that Eminem was the better songwriter. "I never thought about him being white," Proof said. "It was just incredible to hear that shit happening right in my face, you know what I'm saying?"

Proof and I talked for several hours that day. He talked about his obsession with the Grateful Dead's Jerry Garcia. I told him I'd send him some books about the Grateful Dead and an interview I'd done with Jerry Garcia backstage at the Fillmore East in 1970. I told him about Lenny Bruce—whom he'd never heard of—and said I'd send him some CDs. He talked about the similarities between punk rock and hip hop—the struggles involved with both, and how both started as underground movements. We segued into a major discussion about whether Blink-182 and Green Day were the cartoon versions of punk. And whether Slim Shady was the cartoon version of rap (this was years after MC Hammer and Puffy's *Playboy After Dark* persona, and years before Nicki Minaj). I asked how much of freestyle battling was really—even secretly—written down in advance. "You can freestyle not knowing what you're about to say at all," Proof told me. "That can be done. In battles, people can take from previously written material and throw them about and then go back to freestyle. But there are rules. The adrenaline is intense. You've got to stay flow-focused. I mean anyone can rhyme 'dad/bad/mad' but you've got to get crazy with it. Like if you said 'backflip/graphic' and I came back with 'flipping through gymnastics.' That's the skill, you know what I'm saying?" We talked about how Eminem didn't read. Proof said, "He's got a big-ass library and I asked him where he got all those books. Em said they came with the house."

Proof talked about their friendship. "Being Em's best friend is like being Tupac's best friend, Michael Jordan's best friend or Elvis Presley's best friend," he said. "Those are the only people who would understand. I don't even know how to look at it sometimes. I wish we could just go walk to the store or go play basketball in the park. We can't do any of that anymore. It's just crazy. I love the fact that I can go out of my driveway, go to a store at three in the morning, grab shit, put it in my basket, and no one is going to bother me. But he gets swamped. Everywhere. I remember one time he told me he was in the park with his daughter Hailie and she fell and cut her ankle. So he takes her to a fountain and tries to wash it, to keep it clean, make sure there's no dirt and stuff. And while he's doing that, people are asking him for autographs. This happens with him all the time. Any fucking where. I mean, most rich people, they can fly to islands, or go to their yachts. They have fun, right? Em can go to places like that because he's got the money, but everybody still wants to talk to him there, because he's so famous. He put himself in jail."

We talked about how they met and how Proof encouraged him. Together, they decided to quit school, become rappers, and get married to their girlfriends. "And then he goes and gets divorced," Proof laughed. "I was like man, what shit are you doing to me right now?" Proof talked about his own kids and how he cried when he took his son to school, because he was breaking the dysfunctional cycle of his own family. "For a black man to be there for his kid, it's just a beautiful thing," Proof said. "And not even a black man, just a man, to do the right thing. I feel like I beat it. It's great. And for Em, without Hailie, there is no Eminem. I know that sounds bananas, but the definition of focus is direct attention, and he gives direction attention to Hailie. That's the thing that matters to him most, you know what I'm saying?" Proof talked about how he and Eminem came together mostly because of their love of, as he put it, compound syllables. "We knew how to structure sentences with compound syllables," he said. "I couldn't stop thinking about how he rhymed 'first place' with 'birthday.' When I first saw him perform, it was like instant recognition. Our color just went right out the window." (The next time I saw Proof, at the MTV Awards in June 2005, he'd received my Jerry

Garcia and Lenny Bruce package and he thanked me, saying, "It changed my life." We always meant to get together again and talk some more. We never got the chance.)

o o o

Before I went to Detroit to talk to Eminem, I saw Jimmy Iovine again. He compared Eminem to John Lennon, Bruce Springsteen, Kurt Cobain and Bono. I said that, to me, he was like John Lennon, Keith Richards and Joe Strummer. Jimmy told me how, the night that Eminem won the Best Song Oscar for "Lose Yourself," he and Dre called Eminem in Detroit to congratulate him. His then-wife Kim woke Eminem up. "What's up?" he said. They told him. "That's great," he said, then immediately proceeded to tell Dre about a rap he'd just written about someone who, after it came out, would never be able to leave his house again. Jimmy told me, "To every kid who grew up in the '80s, rap was their rock and roll. And I've always looked for things that would move the culture. Death Row did that, Tupac did that. The Elvis Presley myth was that Colonel Tom Parker said if you could find a white guy who could sing like he was black, you'd make a fortune. But in rap, everyone said a white kid couldn't make it. Em may have been the only artist I ever worked with who wasn't motivated by money. He's still obsessed. He's still hungry. At first, people in the industry thought I shouldn't put his record out. I was like, what are you talking about? He's so gifted and talented. People realize it now. *8 Mile* changed everything. He keeps the lights on in our building."

On October 1, 2004, I hired a car and driver to take me from New York City to Detroit. It took eleven hours, but I'd rather sit eleven hours in a car than eleven minutes on a plane. Prior to my trip, I went to Paul Rosenberg's office to hear one of Eminem's new songs—a "protest" song called "Mosh." I went berserk. At a time when Bono was posing for photo ops with George W. Bush, Eminem had written an incendiary, compelling, passionate and intense anti-war, anti-racist song. I couldn't wait to get to Detroit to talk to him.

I hadn't been to Detroit in years. I went a few days before I was scheduled to talk to Eminem. I stayed at a hotel in Birmingham, Michigan, but I had a car take me all over Detroit. The driver's name was Matthew Calhoun, and he told me there was a store that sold $1,000 alligator cowboy boots. "People come from all over the country to buy those boots," he said. "The two-tone ones are $1,200, and the mink-lined ones cost up to $1,800. I've seen preachers and drug dealers side by side buying those boots," he said.

Eminem's Detroit was not the Polish area of Hamtramck with its groovy, alternative rock scene that spawned the White Stripes. A vintage clothing store on Joseph Campau Street in Hamtramck called Detroit Threads had framed photos of the Stooges and the MC5 in the window. The proprietor told me that his landlord's husband was in the bus scene in *8 Mile*. Eminem's Detroit wasn't over at West Grand Boulevard either— where Motown Records had brought "The Sound of Young America" to the world in the 1960s. Nor is it the college town of Ann Arbor where the Stooges, the MC5 and the White Panther Party all lived in the late 1960s. It's not the blue-collar environment of Mitch Ryder and the Detroit Wheels or Bob Seger or Grand Funk Railroad. And it has absolutely nothing whatsoever to do with Madonna, wherever she came from, before she fled for Times Square. Eminem's roots are firmly in the black neighborhood east of 8 Mile Road.

Marshall Mathers, born in 1972 in St. Louis, moved many times before his mother settled in Detroit. His father abandoned them when

Marshall was six months old, then re-surfaced thirty years later on the TV tabloid show *Inside Edition*—displaying baby pictures of the son he hadn't seen in three decades. Detroit is a gritty, suffering city. In 2004, downtown appeared evacuated. You could feel the poverty, the frustration, the fury, the desire to just get the hell out by any means necessary. Like other kids of his generation, Marshall fell in love with hip hop. He always had jobs, but rapping was the only thing he thought he could do well. He used to rap the food orders at Gilbert's Lodge, where he worked as a short-order cook. I went to Gilbert's, a large diner-type restaurant in St. Clair Shores. It's on Harper, between 8 and 9 Mile Roads, right in the middle of strip clubs, pregnancy crisis centers and beauty supply stores. Inside the recently renovated restaurant were large TV screens, an open kitchen, and a hunting lodge motif. Specialties were patty melts, french fries and deep-dish pizza. The people who worked there spoke highly of Marshall, even though they weren't thrilled with the ton of mail still sent to him there. Cindy Giraud, a bartender who'd been working there for seventeen years, said most of the mail was from Germany, and a lot of it was from young girls in "seductive" poses. "He was an average cook who made it big," Cindy said. "But nobody ever expects anybody to make it that big. He called the other night to say hi."

At 19946 Dresden, between Fairmount and State Fair, the brown-shingled house where Marshall used to live was empty. Several houses on the block had "For Sale" signs. I got out of the car and stood across the street. The house was the one that had been on the cover of *The Marshall Mathers LP*. It felt like I was visiting a historical spot—like the Motown Museum two miles away on West Grand Boulevard. Except that this house was, at the time, not preserved. It was empty, and boarded up. It's since been sold.

On October 3, 2004, Eminem and I sat down to talk in his studio. In 2004, in addition to the small studio where we talked, he had one in his house so that he could make beats, or record tracks any time of the day or night. The studio has always been his sanctuary, his safety zone. For Eminem, to even go out to a Taco Bell in Detroit is a production. First, he has to tell his security guards he wants to go. Then, they have to get the car. Then, they have to get in the car, and drive to wherever. Then, a security guard has to scope the place out, to make sure that it appears "cool"—which means there aren't any obvious nuts loitering about. Or it's not too crowded, so Eminem can walk in and order something with a minimum of fuss. Once people started having cellphones with cameras, it was impossible to not be photographed. If his daughter was with him, she and his niece and their friends had to go in first, so she wouldn't be seen with him and wind up with her face in the newspapers. In the end, the whole thing was such a performance that it was always easier to send someone to get whatever it was he wanted.

When I walked into the studio, I didn't recognize Eminem. The man standing in front of me was not the vitriolic threat, or the jokester who made all those million-selling records. Nor was he the guy I'd talked to before—backstage at the Grammys, at Doug Morris' party, or at the *8 Mile* premiere. Seeing someone out of context is often a surprise. It's like seeing Mick Jagger at a dinner party as opposed to backstage getting ready for a Rolling Stones show. He's a different guy. Without the showbiz aura. And, in "real life," they always seem shorter. This guy standing in front of me was Marshall Mathers: polite, soft spoken, lucid, direct. Everyone around him called him Marshall. Or Em. He wore a red warm-up suit, gray t-shirt and red, white and black Nike sneakers. A patterned scarf was on his head, covered by a red baseball cap worn backwards. His hair was bleached blonde, and he wore wire-rimmed eyeglasses. (Years later, after he had revealed his addictions to Vicodin, Valium and Ambien, I listened back to the tapes of our talk that day, trying to ascertain if he'd been stoned. I doubt it, but it's possible that he was on pills, or that he was a really good actor. It certainly wouldn't have been the first time I was fooled by a musician.)

I told him that I couldn't believe how great his song "Mosh" was, as well as its accompanying animated video. I said I considered it one of the most important, intense anti-war (and anti-Bush) songs I'd heard. In fact, it made all these "non-partisan" musicians look like wimps. This was not a time to not take a stand. I said I thought "Mosh" was a hardcore version of Bob Dylan's "Masters of War"—a song that Eminem had never heard. "I've never been one to be all that political," Eminem said. "Most of it is in the song and I would prefer to leave it at that. But my personal opinion—and I'm just one person who happens to speak to a lot of people—is that we live in the best country there is, and this guy is fucking it up. There's people over there [in Iraq] dying and we can't get a straight answer why. Obviously, I wasn't around for Vietnam, but it's almost becoming like Vietnam 2. This is the first year I've registered to vote. I want to vote, and I want to get him out of office. But he's created such a fucking mess over there, I don't know if it can be fixed." He added that his personal take was when 9/11 happened, it was an attack on America from Bin Laden, and "we went after someone [Saddam Hussein] who we hadn't heard about in fucking ten . . . twelve years. It's like two people are standing here and one punches you in the face. You don't do anything back to him—you punch the other guy in the face." We discussed the Republican convention in New York City with its penned-in "free-speech zones." We discussed how that concept applied to music and lyrics; that the whole country was supposed to be a free-speech zone.

Eminem talked about Proof and what it was like being a white kid doing black music. How Proof told people the white kid was cool. We talked about freestyle and he admitted that sometimes people wrote things down in advance. But, he said, "If a guy came back with something off the top of his head he'd always win the battle. You can tell if the lines are too perfect. Proof had such a big name and was so respected, not only in my neighborhood, but he was the best in the city—just for going off the top of his head." He talked about rap battles as a sport—like boxing or football—how it was psyching out your opponent. He got butterflies when he used to do it, he said, and yes, he was crushed when he lost the Rap Olympics. "Losing a battle was absolutely crushing. But I took the feedback and put it back in my music. Yeah, I am white trash. I'm whatever you're gonna say about me, I am that. I started taking the disadvantages and using them to my advantage."

The previous year, Eminem had been arrested for a felony weapons charge following an altercation outside of a bar. His ex-wife Kim was in jail for drug possession. "It was the worst year of my life," he told me. "I was never as scared as I was when I was standing in front of a judge with my life in his hands." He talked about his daughter Hailie. She was born on Christmas and, he said, it was the best Christmas present he ever got. When he went on tour, she would line up items from the house as an obstacle path in front of the door. It was kind of a joke, he said, but not really. Once, when he was leaving to go on tour, she gave him a special coin. He had it silver-plated and put on a bracelet ("Like those Tiffany bracelets you see people wear"). He said that he had always been responsible, always had some sort of drive. "I had a job as soon as I was able to work," he said. "I was thirteen years old when my little brother was born and I've always been a father figure to him. My little brother went through protective services and the court system—I wanted to pull him out of that. When Hailie was born it was another kick in the ass. I thought

I had to do something because otherwise I'd be caught in that cycle of dysfunction that the rest of my family was in. I just wanted to be the one to make it."

He told me he recently bought a big house from the man who owned Kmart, but he hadn't moved into it yet, because he wanted his kids to stay in the school they currently attended. (In addition to Hailie, who was almost nine at the time, he had adopted a niece and his younger brother.) He said that as a child, he had to move, change schools and make new friends so many times, he didn't want that for his daughter and his niece. "It's a cliché," he told me, "but I want them to have everything I didn't have." At one point during our talk, an assistant came in to ask if we wanted any food from Wendy's. Eminem ordered a cheeseburger and another Mountain Dew—which he'd been drinking nonstop. I ordered french fries and a Diet Coke. When the food arrived, Eminem noticed immediately that there was no cheese on his cheeseburger. We discussed how we were both picky eaters. I then went off on a tangent about how it makes perfect sense that I don't like to fly. If you can't even get a cheeseburger the way you order it, I asked, how are we supposed to expect that airplane pilots know what the hell they're doing?

I asked him why he still lived in Detroit. "Just to stay grounded. This is all I've ever known. All I ever wanted to do. I've seen the world, I've played all over. It's great to visit, but this is where I want to live. I don't want to go to L.A. and get caught up in the party scene. All I ever wanted to do was to make a living from music and be able to support myself and have a future for my daughter. Getting this big—I never planned it." I asked him, now that he had gotten this big, what kept him going? "I just have fun with it," he said. "And I like the feeling of being able to sign other artists and help people who had the same struggle as me. It's not like I want to be some big-business monger and run a label. It's more like putting a smile on someone's face, when you see somebody with talent who deserves to get the same shot that Dre gave me. Just being able to do that adds to my drive." Talking about Dre, he said, "He saved my life. Literally saved my life. Just by giving me a chance. I could never repay what he gave me. Dre was going to be OK regardless of whether he found me or not. If it wasn't me, he would have found somebody else. I call him 'bossman'—not in the sense that he's my boss, but if he ever needs me for anything, I'm there."

We talked about lyrics. I told him how Rosanne Cash told me her father, Johnny Cash, didn't mean it literally when he sang, "Shot a man in Reno, just to watch him die." She said she thought everyone knew that he was playing a part. "Nobody ever thought Dad wanted to go out and shoot someone," Rosanne said. Eminem said, "Everybody's got a dark side to them, and there's a sense of humor about me. When I get really comfortable and open and relaxed is when you see that come out. When people first meet me, they're a little taken aback because I'm so laid back. But that's a wall I've put up; like how much do I want to reveal to this person I may never see again? How much do I want them to know about me or what I'm like? I'm not very talkative until that door opens." And, he added, "Sometimes it's like how can I tap into someone else's dark side, or sense of humor? Let's see what kind of button I can push here. If you laugh at it, you're just as guilty as I am. It's just that I had the balls to say it."

Given that his love of rap was so connected to language and to words, I asked if he ever regretted his lack of formal education. "I felt like I was too smart for school," he said. "I hated everything about it. I hated crossing 8 Mile and going into Warren—which was hillbilly territory—and getting called a 'wigger.' And the fact that I lived in a black neighborhood but went to a white school. The names people called me; the way I was looked at—like I was trying to be something I was not. But hip hop gave me a voice. And now, being able to make music whenever I want to—it's a dream come true." I asked him if, given the slew of problems that came along with his success, would he take any of it back? "I would take a lot of it back," he said. "I would take it back to where I would make a comfortable living. Where I would just make music that people would appreciate and still just to be able to walk to a mall, to a store." We talked about love, and how hard it was for him to meet a woman he could trust. He told me that his ex-wife Kim had been there in the beginning; that no one ever could have gone through what they went through together. Now, he never knew if a girl liked him for him, or because he had money, or because he was Eminem. I suggested that perhaps he should date famous women. He said he tried that, they were crazier than he was. We talked about groupies on the road and he said he wouldn't say he had never taken advantage of the situation, but that he thought it was all a bit . . . sleazy. He talked about his musical influences— Tupac Shakur, Rakim, Public Enemy, Big Daddy Kane, Kool G Rap, Beastie Boys, LL Cool J, Masta Ace, Dr. Dre and NWA, Treach, Nas, Run DMC, Biggie Smalls, and Jay Z. I noted that he didn't seem to be into the "bling" aspect of hip hop. He didn't display an elaborate watch collection or show off his cars, personal gym or houses on *MTV Cribs*. He didn't attend Puffy's White Party. "To each his own," he said. "But I can't say that's my lifestyle, it's not the one I chose. I have a nice house, and Dre bought me a car for my thirtieth birthday. But I don't like all the glitter and the glamour."

We talked about his performance with Elton at the 2001 Grammys. "The idea just flew out of my mouth one day on the phone with Paul and Jimmy. I knew the notoriety of when Elton came out, and how people respected him for it. His attitude about it was almost punk rock. I mean there's got to come a time when you stop worrying about what people think or it'll drive you fucking crazy. The second I stopped caring what people thought about me, people cared about me. I figured out how to flip it. People said I was selling so many records because I was white. But I remembered there was a time I couldn't get a record deal *because* I was white. If you got twenty people in this room, imagine how many people would have different opinions about me. At the end of the day you're your own individual and if I were to say 'rape your mother,' and you're crazy enough to do it because I said it, then you've got a problem to begin with."

o o o

By 2005, after spending a year immersed in hip hop, there was only one rock musician who really interested me. Trent Reznor, who had been in Nine Inch Nails—actually he *was* Nine Inch Nails—was a big star in the 1990s. His music combined melodic metal, industrial, and hard rock. He had a bad reputation. He'd had a well-known alcohol addiction and was now sober. In early 2005, Dennis Dennehy played me NIN's great new album *With Teeth*. On February 13, 2005, Dennis introduced me to Trent at a Grammy after-party at the then unopened Soho House in Los Angeles. I was surprised to discover that Trent was funny, charming, articulate. Totally unlike his public image as some sort of dark, scary drug addict visionary. A few nights later, Trent, his manager Jim Guerinot, Dennis and I went to dinner in L.A. at Madeo's. I decided to do a story on him for *Vanity Fair*—I was going to call it "The Last Rock Star." And then, months later, because of various in-house issues, the story never ran. But Trent was another one of those musicians who revived my interest. And, even though it was not the height of his youthful fame, he still mattered.

On May 15 and 16, 2005, I saw NIN at the Hammerstein Ballroom in New York City. Also in the audience were David Bowie—who had been Trent's idol, mentor and friend—and Chris Rock—who agreed with me that it was the best live show of the year. Trent had the theatrical frenzy of Iggy and the rage of the hardcore/punk group

Bad Brains. On June 5th of that year, Trent and I did the first of several very lengthy interviews at the Beverly Hills Hotel. We sat, both of us dressed in all black, in a beige room looking out at the hotel's pink bungalows. A wedding was taking place on the lawn and I recall murmuring, "hope springs eternal." Trent talked about his early classical music training. He talked about how, when he initially rented a house on Cielo Drive in Benedict Canyon in the early 1990s, he hadn't known it was where the Manson murders took place. He talked about math and machines and how the record companies didn't have a clue about how to exploit the Internet. It was the day after the MTV Movie Awards. Trent/Nine Inch Nails had been scheduled to perform "The Hand That Feeds"—a song critical of the Iraq War—on the show. But he pulled out when MTV wouldn't allow the band to perform in front of a backdrop of President George W. Bush. His public statement at the time was, "Apparently the image of our President is as offensive to MTV as it is to me." And I remember thinking that here were these two musicians—Eminem and Trent—who had come out with strong anti-Bush statements. Where the hell was everyone else?

On September 3, 2005, on NBC-TV's live telethon to raise money for Hurricane Katrina victims, Kanye West stared into the camera and, with a stunned Mike Myers standing by his side, said, "George Bush doesn't care about black people." Before that, Kanye had said, "I hate the way they portray us in the media. If you see a black family, they're looting. See a white family—they're looking for food." What happened to New Orleans was a disgrace. The images on television were heartbreaking and enraging. And now Kanye was added to my very short list of those angry enough to take a stand. It wasn't the 1960s, and probably none of this would really change anything. But when George W. Bush said a few years later that the worst moment of his Presidency was when Kanye said that on TV (really? the *worst* moment?), I was delighted that Kanye had caused this man even one bad minute.

○ ○ ○

On April 11, 2006, Proof was shot and killed in a fight at the CCC Club in Detroit on East 8 Mile Road. It was a place known for violence, but Proof always liked to hang out in local clubs. Eminem, already addicted to massive amounts of Ambien, Valium and Vicodin, was understandably distraught after Proof's murder. Seizures, ambulances, hospital stays and stints in rehabs followed. This is a scenario I have witnessed too many times. It starts out innocently enough with an insomniac, or a light sleeper, who needs pills to fall asleep. It winds up with death. Or, in Eminem's case, two hours away from death. When I saw him again, on October 15, 2008, it was at a launch party for his book at a sneaker store in downtown New York. In attendance were LL Cool J, the actor Michael K. Williams (who played Omar on *The Wire*), and 50 Cent. Eminem made a brief appearance and gave me that leaning into my shoulder, half-hug. I expressed my sadness about Proof. I told him how great I thought he looked. "Don't believe everything you read about me," he said, and disappeared into a back room with 50 Cent.

A few years later, in an email interview we did after the release of his *Relapse* and *Recovery* albums, he admitted he had to learn how to rap again after getting sober. "On *Relapse*," he wrote, "I was more concerned with maintaining my 'bugged-out' subject matter. Whereas on *Recovery*, it was more about the songs. Right now, I've resolved a lot of my issues. I'll always have conflict, but I'm more comfortable with that. See? More resolution right there. In the past, it's been like okay, heard the song, joke's over. This time I wanted people to hear the songs over and over and discover new shit every time." I asked him what got him through his addiction, his overdose, Proof's murder, and the past few years. "I've always had a close circle of friends who have stuck with me and looked out for me," he wrote. "And of course I have my kids. If it wasn't for them, things would be very different. I hate to sound corny, but they really were a big part of pulling through. I grew up without a father, and I couldn't let that happen to them. No way."

∘ ∘ ∘

In 2009, when Kanye West left the country for a year following that infamous Taylor Swift MTV brouhaha, he emailed me that he was living in Rome where, he wrote, "there aren't any paparazzi." I emailed back that he ought to see *La Dolce Vita*, the Fellini movie that invented the word. When he was back in New York, I visited him on August 18, 2010, at Electric Lady studios in Greenwich Village. He told me that there was a time when he felt he'd replaced George Bush as the most hated man in America. I told him I still thought he had spoken the truth: George Bush didn't care about black people, and Beyoncé's video was better than Taylor's. "Well, it was very punk rock and revolutionary," he said. "And idealistic, and very angry in a way. But the timing was in poor taste, I realize that." We talked about rap, and his musical goals. "I want to take it back to the essence," he said. "Like the people who brought soulful knowledge—like RZA and Q-Tip. At a certain point, you've got to find a better way to do it. It's like people in basketball who dunk and hurt their wrist and come down on their knees too hard. At a certain point, your knees are going to give out. Some of my social and public persona knees are starting to give up. I still want to run the game; I've just got to not get kicked up so hard." And we discussed his penchant for award show onstage outbursts. I suggested that perhaps he took such shows too seriously. "But these things mean something," he said. "You'd like them to have some accurate representation."

And so, on February 11, 2011, at a Grammy rehearsal at the Staples Center in Los Angeles, I saw Eminem again. He and I were at the backstage Artist's Entrance at the same time. The security guards wouldn't let him in because he didn't have his laminated pass. "I can't get in because I don't have my credential?" he asked. I offered to vouch for him. It took about two minutes before this was cleared up and he was allowed inside. I told him that I thought the Chrysler ad that had run on the Superbowl—the one with him at the renovated Fox Theatre in downtown Detroit, with the gospel choir, and the scenes of the city—was incredibly moving. It had made me cry. "I'm sorry," he said. No, I said, it was a good thing. "I know," he said, deadpan. Then he smiled. He looked extremely fit; he had been running eighteen miles a day on a treadmill. I also knew that Elton had helped him—quietly—with his sobriety.

This time, Eminem was nominated for the Album of the Year Grammy for *Recovery*. It was, clearly, the album of the year. When Arcade Fire was announced as the winner, Dennis Dennehy and I, standing backstage in the wings, looked at each other, stunned. I couldn't believe that once again, the best man did not win. First Steely Dan in 2001, now this—although you could hold a gun to my head and I wouldn't be able to name that 2001 Steely Dan album. I told Dennis that Eminem just shouldn't show up at the Grammy Awards anymore. The last time a rap artist won for Album of the Year was Outkast in 2004. They wanted Eminem on the show for the same reason they wanted Jay Z or Kanye West (both of whom had performed a standout version of "Swagga Like Us" in 2010 with M.I.A., Lil Wayne and T.I.). They needed them for ratings. They still wouldn't give them the big award.

Seven months later, on September 13, 2010, I stood on the soundboard in Yankee Stadium at the first of two sold-out concerts Eminem did with Jay Z. It was not far from 1520 Sedgwick Avenue in the Bronx, where thirty-three years earlier, Kool Herc had started block parties with a turntable and a microphone—and hip hop was born. Eminem made note of this from the stage. He seemed grateful to be performing again. He had not lost one bit of his intensity or his power. It reminded me of all those other times something or someone had taken my breath away—the Clash in particular. It had been a long time since I'd seen anyone perform in a stadium who still mattered like this. Eminem's set was stripped down, bare, intense, manic. I hadn't seen anything quite that furious since the Bad Brains' raging set at the Ritz in 1986. And considering that Eminem once told me he couldn't sing when I told him he could sing, he sang the choruses on "Not Afraid" without sounding sappy. Despite the stadium show, the huge success of *Recovery*, and the fact that he was named the best-selling artist of the decade, I thought that Eminem probably felt the same way he did in 2004. I had asked him then if he still felt that he was an underdog. "Always," he said. And I remembered something Jimmy Iovine said to me in 2000: "It'll be ten years before another artist this talented comes along again."

Nine

On September 11, 2011, Lady Gaga and I were in a suite at the Mandarin Oriental Hotel, sixty-five stories above New York's Columbus Circle. Earlier that afternoon she had cooked me a pasta meal at her parents' apartment, about ten blocks from the hotel. The previous day, we had spent the afternoon at a dive bar on the Lower East Side with some of her old friends. Now we were in the midst of a three-hour interview and we were talking about hanging out with celebrities. She said that Hollywood felt like a Kegel exercise. "It's like my vagina inhales," she said. "I get so nervous." Nervous? "Not nervous," she said, "just uncomfortable. You know when you're speaking with someone and you just know they're not listening to anything that you're saying? They're just waiting their turn to talk. I get very confused. It's just not my style. I don't like fake people. I don't surround myself with people who just tell me what I want to hear all day. I work hard and I make records, and I'm passionate about music. It doesn't get me off to have champagne with celebrities. It's like a tribe; why would I gather with people that I don't know? I have made some wonderful friends among the previous generations of music and I've been very lucky that they really love what I create. It's always nice when you meet someone that you revered your whole life, and they are so wonderfully nice." What happens, I asked, when you meet somebody you revered your whole life and they turn out to be horrible? "It's devastating," she said. "It's absolutely devastating."

I knew she was referring to the M word—my nickname for Madonna—who, along with David Bowie, Freddie Mercury, John Lennon and Britney Spears, Gaga had loved as a child. Madonna had seemed especially petty about Gaga's song "Born This Way," claiming—and not quietly—that it sounded suspiciously like her own "Express Yourself." I asked Gaga about this "controversy." She was diplomatic. "What I have arrived at as a performer," she said, "is that you must create what you know is your vision, and execute it exactly as you see it. If someone thinks it's like another artist, or it reminds [them] of something they've seen before, then that's what shall be. It's not my responsibility to teach people how to excavate art and music. It's my purpose to entertain." You expected the comparison? I asked. "I anticipated that something might occur," she said. "And I don't give a shit. People will see what they choose to see. I have never questioned the integrity of my creations. I love what I have made. And to create a stir with a pop song is pretty fuckin' exciting, if you ask me."

o o o

Aside from the Italian heritage and the dyed blonde hair, Gaga was nothing like Madonna. Lady Gaga has a great voice. She can really play the piano. She writes hit songs with undeniably catchy choruses. She is connected to her audience. She is warm.

One afternoon, way back in 1983, Madonna was at the East Side Manhattan apartment of fashion photographer Steven Meisel. Steven and I were friends at the time. He was going to take the photo for Madonna's *Like a Virgin* album cover. He wanted me to talk to her. He put her on the phone. "I want to rule the world!" she squealed.

Those literally were the first—and may have been the only—words out of her mouth that day. Later, we did one interview, on July 25, 1984, at the Warner Brothers Records offices at Rockefeller Plaza. We talked for almost two hours. I recently listened back to that tape, and my impression remains the same now as it was then: to me, she seemed humorless, a determined woman who decided music was the way to go. It would help her rule the world.

Madonna was the only one in thousands of interviews that I did over four decades who gave me absolutely nothing. She talked for a long time. She told me her story. But it all sounded like boilerplate. She wanted to come to New York City ever since she was five years old. She had never been on a plane before. She came here with just $35 in her pocket. She felt too guilty to ask her father for money. She said she struggled for years. She came here wanting to conquer the city, and, now, she told me, "I feel like I own the joint." Her personal life was topsy-turvy. Boyfriends always picked fights just before an audition or a big show, she said, and it fucked her up. "I've gone on-stage with tears in my eyes." Despite that sole heartfelt admission, it was a businesslike business conversation. No passion. She talked about album sales. She talked about her "image." She said she knew she could sing (not the majority opinion) and ultimately, she wanted to be a great actress. She had a problem, she said, when radio programmers found out she was white. She said they thought she sounded black. (This was news to me.) Maybe she was in a bad mood. Maybe she just didn't like me. At any rate, we just didn't hit it off.

Twenty-five years later, in 2008, Madonna was inducted into the Rock and Roll Hall of Fame. It was the same year that Leonard Cohen finally got in. Lou Reed inducted Leonard. Following Lou's introduction and Leonard's acceptance speech, Leonard, Lou and I walked backstage to the kitchen in the Waldorf Astoria Hotel ballroom. Madonna was standing inside the swinging door, getting a makeup touch-up before she was inducted by Justin Timberlake. We wanted to see Damien Rice's performance of Leonard's gorgeous song "Hallelujah" on the TV monitor. The three of us were immediately stopped by Madonna's bodyguards. Just as I was about to flip out, Madonna's manager Guy Oseary—to his credit—told them to leave us alone. We stood and watched the TV. Madonna stood behind us, talking loudly and chewing gum.

After Madonna's 2012 Super Bowl appearance, one prominent music journalist who shall remain nameless (Jim Farber) told me, "Well of course she lip-synched. And thank god. Can you imagine if she actually sang??" And he likes her. Adores. Madonna did little to conceal her ire over the success of Lady Gaga's "Born This Way." As she reportedly lip-synched her way around the world on tour, she performed a version of "Express Yourself," then segued right into Lady Gaga's "Born This Way." Lady Gaga's "Born This Way" was, Madonna told Cynthia McFadden on *20/20*, "reductive." Then she smirked and added, "Look it up." And despite her gay fans, one gay superstar (Elton John) told me, "Madonna has never done anything for the gay community except take their money." Elton had been particularly catty, but on point, about Madonna when he compared her to a "fairground stripper." When she started out, in the 1980s, Madonna took a little bit from the Paradise Garage gay disco scene, a little bit from the Beastie Boys, and a lot from Steven Meisel—and mixed it all up into a watered-down, commercial stew.

o o o

Every success story has an influential mentor, or a scene. Often, it's someone, or something, that happened years before. "New" things happen by osmosis, insidious influence, obvious imitation, or all of the above. In the early 1980s, at the same time that AIDS started to appear in New York City, there was a small scene that was a pale imitation of the 1960s Andy Warhol Factory scene. It grew out of the wittier, smarter, Max's Kansas City crowd and the New York Dolls and David Bowie. It wasn't about money. It was to some degree, about fame—but an extremely limited and underground fame. As is often the case with anything original, it was too outrageous for the general public. This was Steven Meisel and his crowd. The circle of people around Meisel at that time was tiny. It consisted of a few fashion professionals, models, music insiders and drag queens. It included the platinum blonde transsexual "model" Teri Toye, her platinum blonde sister Tami, pianist Richard Sohl, designers Stephen Sprouse and Anna Sui (years before they were famous), makeup artists Way Bandy, Francois Nars (when he was just starting out), Kevyn Aucoin (when he was just starting out), hairdresser Oribe (when he was just starting out), and various others. It took place between Meisel's photography studio on Park Avenue South, Ricky Sohl and Teri Toye's fifth-floor walk-up on West 85th Street, and Sprouse's West 57th Street workroom. "Events" were held just for fun, and captured by a home video recorder. These situations were created simply as excuses to dress up and to do hair and makeup. But it was all taken very seriously, yet not seriously enough. There were Christmas "specials" and, most importantly, Halloween specials. Everyone would scream and pose and perform. For hours. I recently watched some of the tapes we recorded during that time. Half the people in them are currently dead. But I still remember the energy. And I remember the smell of the inks Sprouse used for the graffiti he sprayed on his early clothes. Everyone wore black. This was years before the salespeople in Barneys, or hairdressers in high-priced salons wore mandatory black. Some of the men wore wigs and headbands. Sprouse had been an assistant to Halston, but also made clothes for his Bowery neighbor Debbie Harry during the CBGB's days. By the 1980s, he was making black clothes, but also did minidresses and matching graffiti tights in the brightest neons—hot pink, chartreuse and orange.

At that time, the straight New York art scene included the painters David Salle, Francesco Clemente, Robert Longo, Jean-Michel Basquiat and Julian Schnabel. Andy Warhol was still alive. So was Keith Haring. The Odeon restaurant, owned by brothers Brian and Keith McNally and in the middle of nowhere—currently Tribeca—was considered the height of something "new." It was one of the first restaurants, as opposed to a bar or club, to be considered a happening spot. But the next twenty-five years of fashion and music were changed by the more underground, and ultimately more insidiously influential scene going on with Meisel and his acolytes. Steven anointed hairdressers Oribe and Odile, makeup artists Francois Nars and Kevyn Aucoin, and young models Christy Turlington, Linda Evangelista and Naomi Campbell. (Do not think that the very young Beyoncé wasn't practicing Naomi Campbell poses in front of her mirror in Houston.) If you weren't involved in this, you probably weren't aware of it. Or aware of how it seeped in and created change.

To be in a scene in New York then—or at any time for that matter—was completely different than if you came to New York, wrote about a scene, and thought you were in that scene. It was not unlike CBGB's when writers from *New York* magazine came down (and it was definitely considered down) to do a story. Those writers were tourists. And it was a different world at that time. Those 1980s nights were not planned. There were no red carpets. No events were manned by a team of clipboard-bearing publicists. No one was hawking a fragrance. Those nights were born out of fun, passion, sex and ambition.

One night in 1984, I left Area around three a.m. with the makeup artist Way Bandy. Area was a club all the way downtown in the middle of nowhere on Hudson Street—currently Tribeca. The club featured "performance art" spaces behind big glass windows in the hallway. Way was a famous makeup artist who could actually paint a completely new face on someone's face. He was Southern, very tall, very grand, very good looking. Of an indeterminate age, he had dark hair and perfectly smooth skin. He wore makeup. He always wore black. Occasionally, Way would dress in drag and assume his alter ego "Margo George"—"the owner of the first, and most prestigious, modeling agency." On camera as Margo for those little home videos, Way wore a black shift dress, a short black wig, and earrings. He held a live chihuahua in his lap. And, in a tone of voice akin to Gloria Swanson's in *Sunset Boulevard*, he would tell tales about Mae West's funeral. This all was happening almost a generation after Andy Warhol and Candy Darling and Jackie Curtis and their "real" movies. There were maybe thirty people in this scene. Still. One night, Way and I—accompanied by the often-shirtless model Attila, who had waist-length hair and was the boy of that minute (and I mean literally that minute)—went to an all-night coffeeshop (now it would be called a diner) on Sixth Avenue. It was in the West 50s, around the corner from Way's apartment. We walked into the place and the waiter took us to Way's regular booth. The waiter said to Way, "Mr. Bandy, is everything all right?" Way raised his arm, twisted a lightbulb that was shining too brightly above the booth, took the bulb out of the socket, and said, "*Now* it is."

With the onslaught of MTV, the visuals became as important as the music. The fashion world merged with the music world. Paula Greif, an art director who worked a lot with Steven Meisel—particularly on

Madonna's *Like a Virgin* album cover—directed one of the first videos for MTV. It was the Smiths' "How Soon Is Now?"—done with eight millimeter film, utilizing very fast cuts. I always told Paula that all of the videos that followed over the next two decades were her fault. Of course, she didn't get any of the credit. Or the blame.

Richard Sohl, who played piano for Patti Smith, had his own drag alter ego: a Swedish model named Astrid. "She" was famous for her poses: "The Prayer," "The Search." I interviewed "Astrid" for *Interview* magazine. Many readers thought she was a real Swedish model. The fledgling photographer David LaChapelle dressed up like Steven Meisel on Halloween and knelt at Steven's feet at Area. There would be no Steven Klein today had there not been Steven Meisel then. (Of course, Richard Avedon had famously remarked that looking at Meisel's photographs was like drowning, and watching his entire life pass before his eyes.) In the 1980s, Steven and Francois Nars collaborated on what is referred to as a "story" in fashion magazines: a series of pictures for Italian *Vogue* of women who appeared to be in the post-operative stages of plastic surgery. They had bandages all over their faces. Fast forward to Lady Gaga's "Paparazzi" video. Most Gaga fans don't know much—if anything—about any of this. They may not know about the British performance artist Leigh Bowery, or the theatrical German musician Klaus Nomi. Or *Paris Is Burning*— the movie about drag queens "vogueing." They might not be familiar with Peter Hujar's photo of Candy Darling in full makeup, dying, in the hospital (although Antony of Antony and the Johnsons used the picture for an album cover). But it all comes from the same seed. On May 1, 1984, "street" fashion and underground music merged at Stephen Sprouse's fashion show at the Ritz, on East 11th Street. Teri Toye sashayed down the runway in day-glo sequin minidresses to hysterical cheers from a packed house—and screams of "Necrophilia!" from the poet Rene Ricard. All of this was accompanied by hardcore punk music that I compiled for the show's soundtrack. It was one of those moments when it felt like a real change was in the air and fashion would never be the same. Of course, that didn't happen.

o o o

Much like I did with Eminem, I started to pay attention to Lady Gaga after she was already a huge star. After she had supposedly shocked the world. And after, because of some costume changes and so-called "re-invention," she was compared to Madonna. I did not find her shocking. I thought she was hilarious. Costume changes were ho-hum. Thirty-five years earlier, David Bowie changed costumes. To say nothing of his own supposed "re-invention." It's certainly what Teri Toye and Richard Sohl would have done if they'd had the money. Granted, Gaga went to sartorial extremes. There were, at various times, the red lace gown, veil and crown combo, the rubber dress worn to meet the Queen of England, the underwear worn in public, the hat made of spinning metal rings, the dress with matching Damien Hirst–designed piano, and later on, that dress made out of raw meat. But Lady Gaga—born Stefani Joanne Angelina Germanotta, in 1986, on Manhattan's Upper West Side—was always more interesting than her wardrobe.

When Gaga left home at eighteen, after she dropped out of NYU's Tisch School of the Arts, she moved to a one-room, walk-up apartment on Stanton Street. The area around Stanton and Rivington Streets wasn't built up the way it is now. Gaga hung out in bars like St. Jerome's—where she befriended the DJ/go-go dancer Lady Starlight. St. Jerome's was also where her boyfriend, the bartender and heavy metal drummer Luc Carl held court. In earlier decades, before nearly every bartender was "really" a musician or an actor or model, bartenders were stars. Along with the wet, crumpled-up dollar bills in tips they took home every night, they got the girls. At St. Jerome's, the bartender with the heavy metal hairdo was the king of the joint. And just like Eminem, who kept returning to his ex-wife Kim because she knew him before he was famous, it's significant that well into her stardom, Gaga kept going back to Luc.

It took almost a year to set up an interview with Lady Gaga for *Vanity Fair*. Finally, we set a date for April 25, 2010, in Los Angeles. And since this was Los Angeles, it only made sense for us to talk at my favorite L.A. spot, the Beverly Hills Hotel. I like to plan things way in advance. The people in the Gaga camp never plan anything— except a tour—until it's right in front of their faces. Interscope's Dennis Dennehy, as he had with Eminem, had the thankless task of organizing this with me. So, after close to 1,000 emails, we decided that Bungalow 9 at the Beverly Hills Hotel would be a good setting. It was in between Bungalow 10, where Marilyn Monroe had an affair with Yves Montand in the 1950s, and Bungalow 8, where Elizabeth Taylor fought, got drunk and had sex with Richard Burton.

Dennis and I planned the ambience of the bungalow's living room: jasmine-scented candles for her, dimmed lights for me. Some food for her and a bottle of Pinot Noir for us both. Interviews are best done without food. The last thing I ever want is to transcribe someone talking with the sound of cutlery or clinking glasses in the background. Or worse, people talking with their mouths full of food. When I do interviews, water, which has become such a staple item of late, is usually the main course. Flat or sparkling, with or without flavors, or vitamins or electrolytes—whatever those are. Or Diet Coke— another current popular drug of choice. I've learned to never do an interview in a restaurant. I want as little distraction as possible. In a hotel, I don't want the TV on in the room even if the sound is muted; people's eyes wander. Especially rappers, who have ESPN on all the time. I won't let anyone else in the room when I do an interview. (The sole exception was the first time I talked to the then sixteen-year-old Justin Bieber, who was required by law to have another adult present when he talked to a journalist.) Before the interview starts, I turn the air conditioning way up to make the room as cold as possible. Then I turn it off, lest the hum is heard on my tape. I try to organize a room with a conference table or a sofa, table, and chair that faces the sofa. I place three cassette recorders and external microphones in a strategic arrangement on a table. If one of these machines screws up, I still get a tape that works. Since so many people laughed at me when confronted by my old-school, analog equipment (Beyoncé and Kanye West in particular), I decided, for the Gaga interview, to add a small digital tape recorder to my arsenal. My husband Richard showed me how to use it. And, of course, after the hours that Gaga and I sat and talked, the cassettes from my Sony tape recorders were all fine. The digital one hadn't worked at all.

Lady Gaga had been in rehearsals all day with director/photographer Steven Klein for her "Alejandro" video. She wanted to come to the bungalow, take a shower, eat something—in private—and then change. I assumed that meant into something more comfortable. Silly me. When she walked in, holding on to Dennis, who introduced us, she was tottering on ten-inch heel-less boots. She was covered from head to toe in black lace netting, and a transparent catsuit adorned with rhinestones. Her fame, by this time, was so much larger than life that it was bizarre to see that even with those boots, she was teensy. She seemed nothing like the woman who had been described in thousands of press clippings as outlandish, a drag queen, hermaph-rodite, trashy, grotesque. She seemed like a cute girl in her twenties who had really good manners. "Hi, I'm Gaga," she said, and we shook hands. She sat down. She stared at my tape recorders. I muttered my usual shtick about how once I interviewed John Lennon and the tape recorder didn't work and he had me come back the next day to do the interview again. (I'm not even sure anymore if this ever happened or not. But it makes for a good story and an ice breaker.)

We talked about New York. I said that I too, had grown up on the Upper West Side. I too, had been born at Lenox Hill Hospital—albeit many years prior to her birth. I sailed right into David Bowie and Freddie Mercury references and told her all the things I heard in her music. Within minutes, we had a connection. Gaga started to sip wine with the veil still over her face. I murmured that she should just take it off. She did. And we talked for close to three hours. Unveiled.

She talked about her family and being a bad kid and sneaking out of the house to go down to clubs on the Lower East Side. She talked about relationships. She said at that time, she was semi-celibate, "Because," she said, "if I sleep with someone, I feel like they're going to take my creativity from me through my vagina. Like it would deplete the energy I could put into my next song." I asked if it was possible for her to meet someone new and fall in love. "It's not like when you're younger and nobody knows who you are," she said. "You're in a bar and you meet a nice guy. Maybe a week goes by and you sleep with him, and it's not a big deal. Now if you let somebody into your world . . ." she trailed off. I asked if she trusted anyone. "I don't trust anybody," she said. "I don't trust that wine glass. And I don't know if I ever will. But it's okay. It's the tradeoff."

She said she was always determined, but she'd had some horrible times, including "the worst day of her life." On the worst day of her life, she said, her mother screamed into the phone and came to get her out of her Stanton Street apartment. They went to West Virginia to visit her grandmother—who let her cry for two days, then told her to go back to New York and "kick some ass." She said that when she hadn't had any money, she used to make clothes with sequins and a glue gun. She said she went to a school where the girls were all rich. But her parents had to work really hard to send her and her younger sister Natali to private school. She talked about how she had been "a theater girl," and was made fun of for getting dressed up to go to school. "It was not an environment that fostered any kind of creative energy," she said. Her mother would put curlers in her own hair every morning, she said, put lipstick on, and then pass the lipstick to Gaga. "She really taught me about my womanhood and femininity. I used to put my makeup on every night before I went to bed. It made me feel like a star. And I'd be ready for school the next morning. And I used to pray every night that God would make me crazy. I prayed that God would teach me something, that he would instill a lunacy in me—something that all the people I loved and respected had. I was very afraid, I had no courage, and it took me a long time to get to this. I had some very special moments when I lived alone. It was just me and a bed and my keyboard. I had a turntable next to the toaster. Somehow, this was where I started to know I would be okay. And I was fearless."

"My talent is twofold," Gaga continued. "I'm very disciplined, and I'm gifted in music." I asked her when she realized how famous she had become. She said it had been recently, on tour in Australia. "I got out of the car and the screams were so loud, it was a roar. Somehow, that night, there were more fans waiting for me after the show. It was insane. And I thought to myself, how can I be better for you? I want to say and sing the right things for you and I want to make that one melody that really saves your spirit one day. I know people say I'm pretentious, but this all really matters to me. I'm sitting here with you today as if I've sold no music and no one knows who I am. I'm hungry, starving, for more inspiration. For more music."

By now she'd had a few glasses of wine. She reached for her white Hermès Birkin purse. Japanese fans had written all over it (shades of Stephen Sprouse and those Marc Jacobs/Louis Vuitton graffiti bags). She wanted to show me its contents: a plastic bottle of water, a wig, Chanel "Gardénia" perfume, a Chanel sleep mask, seven pairs of sunglasses, a tiny Michelangelo "David," and some talisman that was blessed in a Buddhist temple to keep her healthy. (I was reminded of Patti Smith in her bedroom, over thirty years ago, showing me various items blessed by assorted saints and shamans and whatnot.) Gaga produced some acid reflux medication and Xanax—which she took, she said, for anxiety. "I was placing some in my hand this morning and I said to Steven Klein, 'I just knew this day would come.'" We discussed some of the crazy rumors about her—for example, that she was actually a man. "Well," she said, "there was this video from the Glastonbury Festival and it did actually look like I had a penis. What's funny about it is that people have come to my show and they still don't know . . . the beauty of it is that nobody gives a shit. They say, 'I don't care what she is. I like her.'" Eventually, we wrapped up the interview. It was dark outside, and we had been talking for close to three hours. After she left, I did what musicians call an "idiot check": I looked around all the rooms in the bungalow to see if anything was left behind. In one of the bathrooms, some metal-studded underwear and a G-string contraption lay on the floor. I took it and put it in the Beverly Hills Hotel pink plastic laundry bag. The next morning, I brought it to the photo shoot and handed it to Gaga, who shrieked with pleasure. "My favorite!! I wondered where I left that."

○ ○ ○

Photo shoots, along with recording sessions, were fun at first. Now, after having been at hundreds of them, the thrill is gone. With women, the hair and the makeup takes hours. There are racks and racks of clothes. In the 1960s, musicians like Janis Joplin and Jimi Hendrix had style, not stylists. In the 1970s, Mick Jagger and David Bowie wore designer clothes and had makeup artists on tour. But other than those two, and maybe Elton John in the 1970s and Duran Duran in the 1980s, musicians simply looked the way they looked. Well, the New York Dolls wore makeup. But they did it themselves and it was funky—but chic. The photo shoots I oversaw in the 1970s for *Rock Scene* were casual, often spontaneous. I'd tell the New York Dolls to pose in front of Frederick's of Hollywood's lingerie emporium on Hollywood Boulevard. Bob Gruen took pictures. I lined Led Zeppelin up alongside the wing of their private jet at Teterboro Airport in New Jersey. Bob Gruen took pictures. I find it hilarious that these photos—done on the fly in ten minutes—are now considered "iconic." At the end of the 20th century, when I became involved with *Vanity Fair* photo shoots, I likened my job to that of a fluffer on a porn set. I chatted up the musician. We talked about music. We gossiped. It was a warmup. It created a more comfy atmosphere. It is a role that continues to this day.

The photographer for the Gaga *Vanity Fair* cover shoot that morning was Nick Knight, who had worked on the videos for her live show. "Gaga was on my radar," Nick said. "She just seemed to have a lot of energy and a huge love of life—you don't often see that." Nick and I talked about how antiquated fashion shows had become—especially those tents in New York and Paris. Nick's website SHOWstudio featured a live stream of Alexander McQueen's 2010 fashion show. The finale of that show was the "premiere" of Gaga's song "Bad Romance," and, Nick said, "When we did the McQueen show online, it really caught how things are changing. The show—conceived by McQueen—was brilliant. His clothes were brilliant. And then the Lady Gaga moment happened. I didn't even know there was going to be a Lady Gaga moment. I thought we were having some other music at the end of the show. It wound up being like inviting 10,000 people to something, 100,000 people showed up, and all of them tried to get in the door. The site crashed. I knew that Gaga had a massive following, but basically, because of her, Alexander McQueen's clothes were put in front of two and a half million people. It was that kind of fashion moment turning point," he said. "Fashion will never be the same again." But of course, fashion will be the same again. It always is.

Several months after I'd seen Gaga at the Beverly Hills Hotel, we had a chat on the phone. She had recently caused tabloid sensations: attending a New York Mets baseball game wearing only underwear and giving the finger to the paparazzi, wearing a beekeeper's hat at her sister's high school graduation, and supposedly fondling her breasts at Yankee Stadium when she met the team after a game. She called me from the Brooklyn apartment of her on-again, off-again boyfriend, Luc Carl. She told me he'd gone out to get her some food. She reported this in a breathless, little girl voice. It reminded me of Patti Smith on the phone with her then-boyfriend Fred "Sonic" Smith, over thirty years ago.

Luc returned and she put him on the phone to say hello. He said hello. I said hello. She got back on the phone. We discussed her latest press coverage. She said she'd been ambushed by photographers at the Mets game. All she'd wanted to do, she said, was go to a game with some friends for one of their birthdays. "Of course I was drunk when I went to Yankee Stadium, I was with my girlfriends. But everyone was so nice and sweet. I have no idea where that thing about fondling my tits came from. People want to make me out to look like I'm a slutty Italian girl—which I am—but I wasn't doing that after the game. Why would I rub my tits in front of Yankees? I'm not interested in dating any ballplayers." She continued, "Look, I'm not an idiot. I know I'm a public figure and I'm going to be recognized if I wear a bikini or a potato sack. They're going to write the story they want to write. But the tradeoff is I get to go and see the Yankees.

And what the Yankees mean to me in my soul as a young person from New York is more important to me than my reputation in the tabloids. My real fans know who I really am. My music and my performance is what really speaks." We talked about how her idea of a great day off was to get trashed in some dive bar. I have to see this, I said. She said she would take me. She talked about her parents' apartment and mentioned that they had several floors. I said that sounded like they were rich. "They got a deal," she said. "You should come see it." Most people say this stuff to journalists and they never follow through. She did.

o o o

On August 28, 2011, Gaga performed on the MTV Video Music Awards dressed as a guy—her alter ego, Jo Calderone. Depending on your age and point of view, she resembled either the *Karate Kid* actor Ralph Macchio or Marlon Brando. She did a remarkable acting "performance" with her hair slicked back, a Brooks Brothers suit and a plain white shirt. She wore prosthetic male genitalia under her trousers. She smoked a cigarette—the thing that seems to cause the most shock these days—and swigged from a bottle of beer. Jo was, undoubtedly, the type of guy Gaga knew well. "He" was a combination of many of the men in her life. I was amused by the totally befuddled looks on the faces in the audience, most notably on Justin Bieber, Katy Perry and Britney Spears. With this performance, Gaga instantly made Katy—who wore a yellow block on her head—and the pink-haired Nicki Minaj, look dated.

Two weeks after the MTV Awards, I asked Gaga why she created Jo Calderone. "When I first invented Jo," she said, "it was an exploration in gender identity. I thought that whatever the reason, there is something about my aesthetic as an artist that is unrelatable. I am continuously poked about who the hell I really am—when I am truly being myself. So I thought, wouldn't it be an interesting cultural exercise to create someone that's not me, that's infinitely more relatable than me. A blue-collar Italian guy in a Brooks Brothers suit who just wants this girl to stay the hell home. Jo is so easy to have a beer with. So easy to talk to. I remember when I was writing the script, working with my acting teacher Larry [Arancio], I said to him that one of the things I do a lot is cover my face when I have an orgasm. Like I'm ashamed or something. It took a performance art piece for me to understand all the things about who I am. I learned about how I am in bed. I learned about how I'm less able to be private in private, and more able to be private in public. When I'm onstage, I'm so open and giving and so myself. And when the spotlight goes off, I don't know what to do with myself."

Earlier that year, Gaga and I had talked about what we could do to make yet another magazine story about her interesting. I was tired of reading the same stuff about how devoted she was to her fans. I wanted to see her parents' apartment and her Lower East Side hangouts. I knew that to some degree it would be staged. But I still wanted to meet some of those so-called old friends she claimed she still saw when she was in New York. She suggested that she cook a meal for me. We agreed to both the bar hangout and a home-cooked meal at her parents' apartment. Then of course, it took almost four months to get this together.

On September 10, 2011, we were in New York City, in an SUV on our way downtown. Gaga was in the front passenger seat with her legs akimbo, up on the dashboard. She always sat like this in cars, she said, so she didn't feel "cramped" or "trapped." We stopped on East Houston and Avenue B. She said she wanted to get out and walk. She teased her two security guards for wearing suits and being "too conspicuous." Meanwhile, she was decked out in a black lace, see-through dress with black bra and bikini underpants. Long blonde wig, sunglasses, full makeup, and a black latex cape. Mile-high, black Louboutin pumps, a boxy pocketbook and long glass earrings. We walked down Clinton Street to 176 Stanton Street. This was the building where she had lived in the one-room apartment with the bed, the toaster and the turntable. She pointed out the liquor store across the street where, she said, when she was really fucked up she would order in a bottle of wine. She told me she never did laundry when she lived down here, she wore the same t-shirt every day, and she stank. We walked past a park where Dominican families hung out. She told me the rats that scurried across the street had been huge. She pointed out various landmarks: a beauty supply store that had closed, a Mexican restaurant that had closed, a biker bar where she used to stand in the doorway and take drugs. She conducted this "tour" with a certain degree of affection, possessiveness and pride. "This is where I really got my education," she said.

When people recognized her and asked if they could take a picture or get an autograph, she said yes every time. But we were not mobbed. "People are too cool," she said. We peered into St. Jerome's at 155 Rivington Street, but it wasn't open yet. At four in the afternoon we wound up at The Johnsons, a dive bar on Rivington Street. It was fairly packed. We took seats at the bar. I said perhaps it was a bit early to start drinking. "Are you kidding me?" she said. "Back in the day, this would be late." Waiting for Gaga at the bar was her friend Breedlove, a musician who also did the makeup for the Broadway show *Wicked*. The two of them reminisced about the days when they hung out in this bar "waiting for Judy," their code name for cocaine. Also with us was Bo O'Conner, Gaga's best friend since she was four years old (and the only person who called Gaga "Stefani" in all the time I spent with her). I ordered a beer. Gaga ordered the first of what would be several shots of Jameson's. Breedlove left to go do the makeup for that evening's performance of *Wicked*. And then Gaga's friend Lady Starlight—a tall brunette whose real name is Colleen Martin—showed up. For the next few hours, Gaga, Starlight and I talked about performance art and rock and roll. No one bothered us. Occasionally someone would come over and ask if they could take a photo with their phone. A few paparazzi gathered outside. If this was central casting, Gaga had done a good job. It really did seem like just another Saturday afternoon in a local bar. At no point did Gaga complain that she couldn't go out in public or have any semblance of a "normal" life. The other patrons were busy with their own conversations. It appeared as if they couldn't have cared less that sitting at the bar was one of the most famous women in the world.

Gaga went outside to smoke a few times. I muttered how I couldn't believe these girls had to grow up in a city where you couldn't smoke in a bar. Frank Sinatra, I said, is rolling over in his grave. Gaga and Starlight did some head banging to the AC/DC, Iron Maiden and Slayer songs played on the jukebox. They told me about an Australian band they loved called Airbourne who had a fake Aerosmith logo and sounded like AC/DC. We talked about Freddie Mercury, David Bowie, Patti Smith, Led Zeppelin, Florence and the Machine, Blondie, Kanye, Beyoncé, and Michael Jackson. And, as Michael Jackson had decades earlier, the two of them asked me more questions than I asked them. Once again, my "history" gave me a particular passport. I knew David Bowie. Gaga, who idolized Bowie, had never met him. She asked me what he was really like. I said he was really like what he seemed. Just like you, I said. She told me she couldn't believe I had traveled with Led Zeppelin and Van Halen and I had never wanted to sleep with any of those boys. I told her she wouldn't have wanted to either. That David Lee Roth used to have roadies pull girls out of the audience to give him blow jobs. "He could have pulled me out of the audience," she said, joking. I think. Obviously, we were sitting in that bar because I was doing a story about her. I was getting what is known in journalism as "color." But after a few beers and no tape recorder, it turned into more like just an afternoon with three women of different generations talking about their love of rock and roll. This tends to be a universal language.

Gaga and Starlight talked about how they first met. Gaga recalled seeing Starlight go-go dance at St. Jerome's. "There was just something . . . off about it," Gaga said. "She had these awkward-on-purpose moves. It was uncomfortable. It was just so shocking in a completely natural way. She was so unapologetic and interesting. I wanted to be like that." Starlight explained: "I guess what people liked about my performance was that it was kind of confrontational. It was meant to confuse people. Like I was in a bikini and supposed to be sexy, but I would actively do things that were not sexy. I'd be go-go dancing, then I'd just sort of freak. I'd fall on the ground, then go back to go-go dancing. It was a very aggressive, fuck you attitude."

The following day, on September 11th, I went to Gaga's parents' apartment in a beautiful art deco building on the Upper West Side. Her mother, Cynthia Germanotta, an elegant blonde in her mid-fifties, opened the door to their triplex apartment. Cynthia was wearing all black, with black-rimmed eyeglasses and perfect makeup. It was obvious to me that she had been Gaga's first style inspiration. Gaga was at the kitchen sink. She was wearing a black Chanel dress, a platinum Daphne Guinness–styled wig, sky-high Louboutin shoes, full makeup and glass earrings. She was chopping cherry tomatoes for a homemade pasta sauce. *Kill Bill* was on a computer monitor screen with the sound down. I brought the family a box of Ladurée macarons, which Cynthia put on top of a box of Dunkin' Donuts. Gaga took the pink Ladurée ribbon off the box and wrapped it around her hair.

There was a garden patio off the living room. Cynthia pointed out small fig and lemon trees, and the herbs she grew herself. Gaga gave me a tour of the apartment. She took me upstairs to show me her childhood bedroom, where she currently was sleeping on an air mattress. Why on earth, I asked, would she sleep here on the floor instead of a hotel suite? "I'm in hotels all the time," she said. "When I can, I'd rather spend more time with my parents." Her father Joe came upstairs from the basement. He wore a red polo shirt and blue jeans. "That's a nice dress," he said to Gaga. Joe Germanotta, from New Jersey, was a Bruce Springsteen fan (it's the law). He was the owner of the *Darkness on the Edge of Town* boxed set on the windowsill next to the piano. Gaga told me that for her father's fortieth birthday, he requested that she learn to play Springsteen's "Thunder Road" on the piano. Gaga, Cynthia and I talked about how someone had tried to talk Gaga out of having saxophonist Clarence Clemons in her "Edge of Glory" video. Gaga said they wanted her to use a model, a "Clarence type" in the video. The director thought Clarence wasn't sexy. We all agreed that Clarence was sexy.

The living room had a beige sofa, some comfortable chairs, and was monopolized by a black grand piano covered with framed family photos. This piano was the same one Gaga had played as a child. At this time, I was the only journalist who had ever been in this house, or spent time with her parents. I watched Gaga make the sauce. She put leeks and spices and tomatoes in a big pot and stirred. She asked if I liked whole wheat pasta. She made a salad. In all of my years doing this job, and all of the people I've interviewed, I cannot remember one other musician who cooked me a meal. I'd been in other families' houses—the Jacksons' comes to mind—and I've had countless meals with bands backstage, and in restaurants and hotels all over the world. But this was a first.

The basement was Joe Germanotta's domain. It had wine-making equipment Gaga had bought for him, big leather chairs, a huge TV and boxed sets of *The Sopranos*. The walls were covered with Gaga's gold and platinum albums, tour posters, and laminated backstage passes. Cynthia apologized for the "mess." She said they had all of Gaga's "stuff" because their daughter still had not purchased a place of her own. We discussed the reports of Gaga apartment-hunting in Manhattan and looking for a house in the Hamptons. "Gypsy queen couldn't take the leap," Gaga said. "I need an underground garage. I'm not going to pay ten million dollars for something. I'm not ready. I can't commit to being an adult."

At the kitchen table, Cynthia read me a letter she got from the White House praising Gaga's efforts fighting the "Don't ask, Don't tell" policy. She showed me boxes of Gaga's fan mail that came to their house. I read them an email I'd received from a sister of a friend, a twelve-year-old girl named Maddie Polkinghorn. She wanted me to tell Gaga that there was a boy in school who had been bullied because the kids thought he was gay. Gaga had inspired her to act. She told the school director, the school devoted a day to anti-bullying, the bullying subsided, and Maddie's mother told her: "Gaga would be very proud." Gaga sat and held her mother's hand while I read this email aloud. She cried. She's either a truly wonderful actress or this really matters to her. Or both. I would like to think that this matters to her. I'd occasionally like to believe that not everyone is a phony. Cynthia told me about the Born This Way Foundation she and Gaga had formed to try to combat bullying. I saw such a sense of parental pride and love here that it was hard to imagine the "bad kid" who infuriated her parents when she dated much older guys. Or the girl whose father talked her out of taking cocaine by telling her of the dangers of the drug. Of course, I wasn't born yesterday. For all I know, the entire family might have had a huge screaming fight before I arrived. But I saw not one hint of discord.

Eventually, we sat down at the table, held hands, and Gaga said grace. (Later, knowing my atheist tendencies, she told me, "I'm sorry I made you pray today.") We all had second helpings of the pasta.

"You've got a hit," her father said to her about the sauce. Joe and I talked about how it was a lonely life on the road and how either he or Cynthia try to go with Gaga when they can. He told me about the restaurant he planned to open, named after his late sister Joanne. We talked about (college basketball) March Madness and the Yankees. Joe told me he was purchasing four seats from the old Yankee Stadium to put in the garden of his restaurant. Following lunch, Gaga went to the piano to play us a half-finished new song called "Princess Die" about celebrity deaths. Her parents stood and watched her. I asked if it had always been this way—the two of them standing at the piano, watching her play. Always, they said. "We didn't push it," Cynthia said. "She was determined. But we wouldn't have encouraged her to pursue this if we didn't think she had the talent."

o o o

"We haven't had one of these since Eminem," Interscope Records' chief Jimmy Iovine told me about Gaga. "Someone who moves the culture." Over the course of that September 2011, I talked to a lot of people in Gaga's life. Both Vincent Herbert—who signed her to his record label at Interscope—and her manager Troy Carter have backgrounds in R&B, rap, and what the business calls "urban" music. Troy is a thin man who looks about eighteen (I was shocked to discover he had a son about to go to college). He said at first, "People would walk by me and talk to the security guard. Maybe they thought I was a production assistant on the set. But the bottom line is that Gaga was just looking for someone who cared. She didn't care that I had worked with [only] rappers before. It was me showing up with a plan. I think we've been able to break boundaries. There are no limits to music. Whether you're doing pop or rap or electronic music, it's all about the soul behind it."

Troy told me that Vincent had called him up and said he had a girl he wanted him to see. "She walked into my office wearing fishnet stockings, no pants, and sunglasses," Troy said. "She had dark hair. She walked in a superstar. She had too much confidence. She just needed somebody to protect that vision for her. She was very, very specific about what she wanted everything to look like, to sound like, and it felt very original. But at the same time, it was scary, because it wasn't what pop music was supposed to sound like. Top 40 radio told us we should just try to get played on the dance stations. I knew she was going to be big, but I had no idea it would get this big, or that it would happen so quickly. When she started, she didn't sound like anything on the radio. The key to her is that her music never fit the fashion."

Vincent Herbert said that the minute he met her, he knew Gaga was a star. "She told me she wanted to be the biggest pop star in the world," he said. "She wanted to sell ten million albums and she would be the most loyal artist I would ever work with. And that was 'hello.' I knew she'd be the Michael Jackson of this generation." When I asked Troy if Gaga got antsy after three days on vacation, he laughed. "Three days? Or three hours?"

I went back to St. Jerome's to look at the room, and then had a long talk with Lady Starlight. The "stage" where she had danced was a tiny bench in the back of the bar. "How hilarious is that stage?" she said. "Gaga and I never did an actual show there together, but occasionally, she would get up and go-go dance with me. I think a big part of why my go-go dancing was unique was my knowledge of and love for the music. It's like hearing a vinyl album instead of an MP3. The audience doesn't always consciously pick up on it, but they feel the difference. I made myself look ugly sometimes. I guess when you think about it, it's very similar to Gaga, except that she knew how to conform in a certain way to make people accept the message. I was in the sexy bikini, but when I got onstage, I wasn't just a girl up there grinding and trying to get tips."

When she and Gaga started to perform together, Starlight said, "I influenced her not to be afraid of anything. Go to whatever lengths we need to go to make people shocked and upset. I would have worked with her no matter what her music sounded like, because I just liked her. She has this positive energy and a can-do attitude about everything that is so inspirational to me. And she has not changed. A lot of pop stars just want to be pop stars because they want to be famous. She wanted that, but her main goal was to be able to sing and write music and just be an artist. I always knew Gaga would be famous and successful because of her voice and her drive. But I thought her talent could be a disadvantage. I didn't think it was possible—not just for her, but for our culture—to ever get excited again the way they have for her. I thought people were so jaded that no one would ever care about anything enough. Isn't it funny that we have to be surprised that someone with actual talent becomes a celebrity? It should be a given."

The words "performance art" have, for years, caused me to roll my eyes. Yoko Ono, the naked cellist Charlotte Moorman and all that 1960s avant-garde self-seriousness was never my cup of tea. However, once, I went to a show at the experimental Living Theater, where founders Julian Beck and Judith Malina encouraged the audience to come up and roll around on the stage. Many in the audience did, including me. Many in the audience got naked. I did not. But I remember Abbie Hoffman being there, and there was something liberating and fun about it. Of course, what that all got watered down to was the Broadway musical *Hair*.

I recently saw a documentary on HBO about the performance artist Marina Abramović. She said, "When you perform and you have a knife, it's your blood. When you're acting, you don't cut yourself. It's ketchup." At the 2009 MTV Awards, Gaga sang "Paparazzi," and, at the end of the number, she was "killed." (She told me that she thought it would be interesting to see what she looked like dead.) She was dragged up to the top of the stage by a rope. She was "bleeding." Ketchup. Of course there is no way that Gaga would—or should— actually cut herself with a knife and bleed onstage. But even with that ketchup, she made enough of a point that it actually shocked some people in that crowd. As she did two years later with the Jo Calderone performance. Most performance artists are considered freaks. Until they get older. Especially the women. Now that Yoko Ono, Patti Smith and Marina Abramović are too old to be thought of as sexual in this culture, they get respect. The Marina Abramović film documented her history and her 2010, three-month-long show at the Museum of Modern Art. One at a time, 750,000 people lined up to sit across from her and stare into her eyes for a few minutes. In the film, someone said, "The audience is her lover." Marina Abramović said she hears their pain, their loneliness, their fears. Without saying a word, just looking at the person in front of her, she made very moving connections. After seeing this, I emailed Starlight, who was on tour with Gaga in Eastern Europe. I knew that Gaga had been inspired by Marina Abramović, and I assumed that Starlight had been too—I told her I saw a direct line here. Granted, Gaga throws in the commercial songs and the big pop production numbers. Still, some of this gets out to the world.

o o o

After we left her parents' apartment on September 11th, Gaga and I went to the suite at the Mandarin Oriental Hotel. When we got there, I reiterated that I myself, would have been perfectly happy not only to spend the night there, but to permanently move in. "Not if you

314

had to spend most of your life in hotels," she said. She added that she planned to return to her parents' apartment that night to sleep. We ordered wine, the usual waters, and a plate of crudités and assorted fruits and nuts. We picked at the fruit and the crudités. We took our shoes off and drank the wine. We finished all the food. She showed me photos on her phone of her new boyfriend, the actor Taylor Kinney. And then, we talked for close to three hours.

I asked her about every single tabloid rumor I'd heard about her. No, she said, she wasn't using Rogaine. Yes, she said, she had been to a sex club in Berlin where there were paper towels and toilet paper hanging on the walls and beds everywhere. She and her friends had had a great time. I asked if she took advantage of the sexual opportunities. "No," she said, "that would have been very difficult for me." I brought up her past references to abusive relationships. Had a boyfriend actually ever beaten her up? "No," she said, "but mentally and emotionally . . ." she trailed off. I asked if her relationships were always monogamous. "Yes," she said. "I don't really believe in having sex without monogamy. I don't enjoy it. That's just my personal belief. The trouble with men is that some of them are really bad. I mean I could put some people in jail, is all I want to say. The damage that was done to me at such a young age was irrevocable. Psychological, mental, emotional. And the inability to even know what happiness feels like with a man. I only know the happiness of putting a smile on someone's face from the stage." She started to cry. I don't know if it was the wine, or we were two women talking about emotional stuff, or what. (I remember Stevie Nicks burst into tears sometime in the 1970s during an interview, when I asked her if Fleetwood Mac was breaking up. But I attributed that at the time to cocaine.)

I asked Gaga if she would give back all the fame, all the love from the fans, if she could find happiness with a man. No, she said. I asked what if she had no fans, no money, no fame. Would she still want to make music? Yes, she said. She did not, like Eminem, say she wanted less of all this. "Of course I want this," she said. "It's not about what my fans give to me. It's what I think I can be for them. The difference between being with a fan and a lover is that with my fans, I know what I mean to them. But I have never felt cherished by a lover. It starts out good. And then the guys, they get really crazy." Maybe you're picking the wrong guys, I said. "That's what my mother says," she said. "Look, I'm very loyal. I've seen my parents married now for almost thirty years. And my grandparents on one side for sixty years, and fifty on the other side. I just believe it's a woman's duty to stick it out no matter what." Duty? Stick it out? She said she saw her parents fight a lot when she was a kid, especially when she was dating older men. She said she doesn't know how she got through some of the things she got through; there were times when her parents looked at each other and said, what did we do wrong with her? "My mother might tell you no," she said, "but my mother is just so lovely, so optimistic. She's sunshine, my mother."

I asked her if she got all girly and submissive in relationships. She said, girly yes, submissive no. She liked to do certain things for men— like cook. "But let's not overgild the lily," she said. "I'm not a pushover. And even though I'm from New York and I can see you coming from a mile away, I try to find the most beautiful thing about you. It's just the way I am. If I let someone into my life, I will cherish them and take care of them. I'm a very loving person." She said she was attracted to "creative types" who were jealous of her effortless ability to create. "What intimidates them is not my purse, it's my mind. I once had a man say to me that I would die alone, in a house bigger than I know, with all my money and hit records, and I will die alone. He said, 'I will be the last person who will love you for who you really are.'" She continued: "But even when something bad was happening, even in that very stressful, worthless moment, when I felt I had nothing to offer anyone, I always thought, I'll show you. And now, when I fight with someone in a relationship, I think, how would my fans feel if they saw me, as a female, allowing this to go on? And then I get out. Then," she laughed, "after I leave, they want to marry me." I thought about all of the female musicians I'd talked to over the years—Sheryl Crow and Bonnie Raitt, Linda Ronstadt and Chrissie Hynde, Patti Smith and Debbie Harry, Joni Mitchell and Tina Turner, Jennifer Lopez and Gaga and Katy Perry and so many others. None of them had an easy time with love. All of them were victims of bad romance.

I asked Gaga if she was, as had been reported in some tabloids, bulimic. If she threw up to stay thin. "Sometimes," she said. But she was very clear that that, along with her smoking cigarettes, was not something she was in a big rush to encourage her fans to do. I asked about the fake English accent I'd heard her put on in some televised interviews. She told me that she sometimes got nervous. She got panic attacks. I told her that once, when she was on *Saturday Night Live*, at the end of the show when they all lined up to say goodnight, I noticed that she was standing by herself. She looked alone and vulnerable. All the guys were hugging each other, but no one was hugging her. For just a few seconds I could see a glimmer of the girl who felt unpopular. She thought about this, then said, "Well, I think maybe people are afraid of me." I asked if she'd ever been in therapy. "Anytime I ever tried anything like that," she said, "they always wanted to talk to 'the real me.' And I thought, fuck off. What do you know about me? Just because I have a wig on my head doesn't mean that I'm not a real fuckin' person."

It was starting to get dark. We hadn't put on any lights, and our talk was winding down. She said, "I'm in a state of genuine gratitude and I have a sense of humility about my work and about the love being channeled back into me. What I often see occur in the world of music is that people smell the money. They don't smell the love. It's that thing that's invisible."

o o o

A few weeks after I'd spent time with Gaga in New York, she was on Staten Island, directing and starring in an "autobiographical" video for her song "Marry the Night." It was an elaborate shoot with many different scenes: a dance class, a re-creation of the stairs in her Stanton Street apartment where she lugged a keyboard up and down, "neighbors" coming out to look at her. Then, I found out what had happened on "the worst day of her life." In one scene, she was wheeled on a table into a women's clinic. She was seen in a hospital bed. That was followed by a scene where an actress who played her best friend Bo took Gaga back to her (re-created) one-room apartment. Gaga got into bed and then, got a phone call with the news that she was dropped from her record label. In her trailer before she was about to shoot this scene, there was some discussion about how far she should go with all of this. "I want it to be humiliating," she said. "It can't be safe." She sent someone to a local mini-mart to purchase a sanitary napkin or a diaper. And while she never actually came out and said specifically what had happened, it seemed to me that this could have been a miscarriage, or an abortion. Followed, on the same delightful day, by being dropped from her first record label. As we discussed the various possible undergarments she could wear, she joked: "People will probably think I had my dick cut off." (In the finished video, what actually happened is still left to the imagination. Some people think it was a suicide attempt. For all I know, it might have been.) As she prepared to film that scene, she took a swig out of a bottle of Jameson's, turned to her choreographer Richie Jackson and me, and started to cry. "I'm re-living the worst day of my life," she said. "We're already walking on thin ice with this video. It's chaotic and sad. We could fake it and be safe, but I don't want it to be safe. I can't do anything halfway."

When we talked at the Mandarin Oriental on September 11th, Gaga told me she was already planning her "Born This Way" world tour. She said she wanted to perform in China. Are you nuts? I asked. They'll put you in jail. "I would go to prison for my music," she said. I said that it was all well and good to say this in such a cavalier fashion while sitting in a luxury hotel. The reality of a Chinese prison would not be the fantasy prison in her "Telephone" video, with her wearing stiletto heels and sunglasses made of cigarettes. Of course, I said, she probably wouldn't even be allowed into China. But, she said, "I say this cavalierly and with tons of commitment and focus: I would consider it an artistic moment of love and commitment if I was to be jailed for my work. You can't write a song called 'Born This Way' and then just promote and perform it in places with more hospitable environments. The point of the song is to make a statement and enforce change." I told her that it was impossible, at age twenty-six, for her to know how she would feel about what lay ahead. I reminded her how, when we first talked, I asked her what would happen if she wound up another burnout, a crazy casualty. At that time, she said, "If I wind up a crazy casualty, then that's my destiny." This time, she said, "I'll say it again. Everyone takes me way too seriously. And not seriously enough."

Ten

In 1988 I took a trip down South. The purpose—ostensibly—was to find musicians for a little record label that Richard and I had at Sony Records. Walter Yetnikoff was the head of Sony Records at that time and a friend. He thought that since I went out every night to clubs, and Richard had produced albums, we could find bands and bring them to Sony. The venture was pretty much a non-starter from the beginning. No one at the label listened to our warnings that "alternative rock" was about to happen—especially with some little bands out of the Pacific Northwest, namely Mudhoney, Green River (an early incarnation of Pearl Jam) and Nirvana. But Robinson Records really began to unravel, and eventually folded, when Walter was fired in 1990. We had no "godfather" to protect us and had signed only a few commercially unsuccessful baby bands. Ahmet Ertegun had offered me a label a year or so earlier, but stupidly, I turned him down. Clearly, I bet on the wrong horse. And no, there was no "conflict of interest" concern—I never wrote about any of the bands we were involved with, and the music business was a business where the most powerful lawyers routinely represented all sides in most deals.

But in 1988, I still thought this was a going concern, and I decided to travel as a combination tourist and talent scout, to see what was going on outside of New York City. I started out in Nashville, where I met up with the British engineer and producer Glyn Johns—who was there to check out some local group. Glyn was a friend who had worked on Led Zeppelin's first album, the Stones' *Exile on Main Street* and various albums for the Who and the Eagles. He also engineered *The London Howlin' Wolf Sessions* album in 1970. That featured the blues giant Howlin' Wolf with British musicians Eric Clapton, Steve Winwood, Ian Stewart, Charlie Watts and Bill Wyman. I wanted Glyn to produce a re-make of that album with some old blues musicians and the young guitarists Stevie Ray Vaughan, Jimmie Vaughan, Joe Perry, Eddie Van Halen and Slash. Walter Yetnikoff said he'd put up the money for the project.

At that time, I wasn't familiar with Nashville. I didn't know about the famed Ryman Auditorium, which was the original home of the Grand Ole Opry shows. I didn't know about the Hatch Show Print poster shop on Broadway with the old printing presses in the back of the store. Or the historic dive bar, Tootsie's Orchid Lounge—and its walls covered with photos of the great country singers who had performed in the place. All of this would come much, much later. As I've said, I grew up thinking the South was full of hillbillies and bigots. Images of the Klu Klux Klan and civil rights marches were imprinted on my brain. I thought most Southerners were Jesus freaks who didn't have a full set of teeth. The few times I'd been to New Orleans or Atlanta in the 1970s and '80s were with Led Zeppelin or the Rolling Stones. When traveling with those bigtime bands, my experiences were mostly high-end. Or, we flew in, they did the show, we flew out. Before this 1988 trip, my travels had been specific: I "covered" a concert, or a tour. I did interviews. There was a story, a deadline. This trip was different.

I had a few vague plans. In Nashville, in addition to seeing Glyn, I arranged to meet up with Duck Dunn, the bass player for Booker T. and the MG's. Duck played on many of the great records that came out of Stax Records in Memphis—among them "Hold On, I'm Comin'" and "I Can't Turn You Loose." He also played bass for Isaac Hayes, Muddy Waters, Eric Clapton, and Bob Dylan. Most notably, he had created the bass line for Otis Redding's "Dock of the Bay." And Duck made no secret, especially after a few alcoholic beverages, that he considered that bass line the melody of the song—for which he never got the credit; but Duck had finally achieved some well-deserved worldwide acclaim with *The Blues Brothers* movie. Duck and his wife June visited me at the Vanderbilt Plaza Hotel. We stayed up until three a.m., drinking and watching TV. I made some Video 8 tapes of that night: Duck wore white shoes and noodled around on his bass guitar. We watched Chrissie Hynde on TV sing the great Lorna Bennett tune "Breakfast in Bed." I talked about Chrissie and Ray Davies and how badly that had worked out. Duck talked about Otis Redding and the Staple Singers.

Following my brief two-day stay in Nashville, I went to Memphis to see Jim Dickinson. Jim was the musician who brought the great bluesman Furry Lewis to meet the Rolling Stones' plane when we landed in Memphis on July 3, 1975. Jim had played piano on the Stones' "Wild Horses" track, and on a Flamin' Groovies album Richard produced in 1969. Jim played on Stax sessions, had been a member of the band the Dixie Flyers, and was a walking blues encyclopedia. When I got to Memphis, I made the obligatory trips to Sun Studios and Graceland, then I met Jim at Ardent Studios. He talked to me about the local blues legends R. L. Burnside and Junior Kimbrough. He talked about Merle Haggard, Willie Nelson, Kris Kristofferson and Keith Richards. He described all of them as soul musicians. Then, he told me I should drive down Highway 61 from

Memphis to New Orleans. Jim said it would be a heavy, haunting, transformative trip.

Other than part of a title of a 1965 Bob Dylan album, I truly had no idea what Highway 61 was, where it was, or why it mattered. I didn't know that it was called the Blues Highway. Or that it had been the road taken by Delta blues musicians from the cotton plantations up to Memphis. And so I drove, or rather, since I was from New York City and had never learned to drive a car, I was driven, down Highway 61 from Memphis—through Clarksdale, Leland, Robinsonville, Greenwood, Vicksburg and Baton Rouge—to New Orleans. In the car, I listened to tapes of Southern field recordings made in the 1950s by Alan Lomax. Lomax had recorded Negro spirituals, white church music, and chain gang chants. One gospel song in particular— "Why I Like Roosevelt," by the Soul Stirrers—moved me to tears. I played it over and over again. That music had an eerie, emotional pull. I think even if I hadn't been playing the tapes in the car, I would have heard that music. It was in the air. As foreign as that church music and those Southern field chants were to someone from the Upper West Side of Manhattan, it all hit me in the heart. Then, in the ears. It was primal, familiar. It was like hearing a train whistle in the middle of the night. Something from your childhood that you didn't really remember where it came from but somehow, it connected.

The highway was flat. The soil alongside it was dark. There were signs for crossroads—like the one where Robert Johnson supposedly sold his soul to the devil. (This was the same absurd myth that had been attributed to Jimmy Page—only Jimmy supposedly made his deal with Aleister Crowley). There were shacks. I saw one with a hand-painted sign that said "School." In 1988. I was stunned. This was not the same as driving in the Northeast. It felt like another planet. I couldn't help but think that only thirty years earlier there were chain gangs and signs at gas station rest rooms that said "White Only." I did not drink on this drive. I was not on drugs. I did not go to juke joints. I don't remember a lot of it. I videotaped much of the trip but many of those Video 8 tapes are unmarked or lost. But I do, however, remember thinking that Jim Dickinson had been right: it was an almost hallucinatory experience. It was hypnotic, mesmerizing. I felt the intense, almost physical presence of the blues.

I had heard there was a blues museum in Clarksdale. At that time, it was on the second floor of the local library. This was years before Clarksdale had a proper Blues Museum—thanks to help from actor Morgan Freeman, who also opened his Ground Zero blues club in Clarksdale. A woman who worked at the library got a key to let me in to the large, dusty, second-floor room. Various historical blues artifacts were on display. I thought about the extravagant I. M. Pei building in Cleveland that housed the Rock and Roll Hall of Fame. This blues museum was shameful. I was angry. Then, sad.

o o o

Road trips in a car, or in a van with a band, are romantic only in memory. I am always amused when I hear bands affectionately reminisce about the early days before their careers took off. When they played small clubs and could see the faces in the audience. When they shared a close camaraderie during years of struggle. It is absolutely true that massive success brings out the worst in some people. But there is nothing charming about arriving at a budget motel on a highway in the middle of the night. Lugging a suitcase up a flight of stairs into a room that has roaches crawling up the walls. There is little pleasure in driving through the Florida Everglades with signs that warn "Beware of Alligators." For me, such travel was eye-opening. It was, as Keith Richards has always said about a variety of things, "The price of an education."

Driving with bands in vans across America, I often wound up in motels that provided you with one small "bath" towel. The phone and TV barely worked. The vending machines by the stairs were empty. There were lines of scary-looking trucks parked right outside the room. But to me, coming from New York City, from a family that had never owned a car or never took a cross-country road trip (our biggest foray was from the Upper West Side every summer to Fire Island), I found the whole thing exotic. Especially the open-all-night truck stops. These massive complexes actually had showers, although I can't imagine ever using one. The huge diners served breakfast all night long. It took me awhile to realize what was going on with those truckers parked at the side of the road—the hookers and whatnot. But the best feature of these establishments were the gift shops. All those Harley-Davidson t-shirts, trucker's hats, chrome-plated medallions of silhouetted naked girls, and little license plates on key chains. There was an abundance of novelty items. For me, this was an exciting retail experience.

In New Orleans I checked into the Royal Orleans Hotel in the French Quarter where I had stayed with Zeppelin in 1973 and the Stones in 1975. The second time I heard Led Zeppelin sing "It's been a long time since I rock and rolled" was onstage in New Orleans. And it was rock and roll. Not rock 'n' roll, the way newspapers and copy editors have butchered the phrase over the years. You need the "and" in there as much as you need the "roll." Because there's been way too much rock, and not enough roll. "Rock" is up and down. "Roll" is side to side. It has to be slinky. In New Orleans, I walked around the French Quarter and ate at tourist traps like Antoine's and Galatoire's. I didn't go to any dives. I remembered the first time I was there, in 1973, with Zeppelin. Then, I wandered around the Quarter and heard songs like "Iko Iko" blaring from jukeboxes in bars. I visited clubs like the Gateway and the Nite Cap—where Frankie ("Sea Cruise") Ford and Ernie ("Mother In Law") K. Doe performed. In 1988, it wasn't the same. Ahmet Ertegun wasn't there to take me to Cosimo's studios to see Professor Longhair play piano. I only saw Professor Longhair once. Still, I never forgot it. I thought about Ian Stewart, who had died in 1985. I remembered one night in the summer of 1975, when Stu sat in the lobby of the 1776 Inn in Hampton Roads, Virginia. He was alone, at the piano, playing Fats Domino's "Blueberry Hill." I had talked to Led Zeppelin a lot about Stu, who had played piano on "Boogie with Stu," on Zeppelin's 1975 *Physical Graffiti* album. I am in no way a musicologist. I was a fan who felt connected to the music. And somehow, through a series of what Keith Richards would call lucky accidents, I got connected to all the music that was connected. In the South, and in New Orleans especially, there were ghosts everywhere.

After New Orleans, I went to Austin, Texas, to visit the songwriter and guitarist Stephen Bruton. For me, Stephen Bruton was the only reason to ever go to Texas. I had met Bruton through Earl McGrath in the 1970s. Bruton had played guitar with Bonnie Raitt, Bob Dylan, Willie Nelson, and was Kris Kristofferson's best friend. He was close with Bobby Neuwirth and T Bone Burnett. He was the inspiration for the character Jeff Bridges played in the 2010 movie

Crazy Heart. Bruton was handsome, elegant. He wrote songs about drowning beneath bridges burned and learning to live with what you need to live without. He had lived through heartbreak and hard times. Originally from Fort Worth, he had a distinctive Texas twang. I spent an afternoon at his house and taped him singing his songs and playing with his beloved dog Greta. That Video 8 tape has survived.

Bruton took me to Antone's—a small blues club which was, at that time, on 5th Street. At Antone's I met Hubert Sumlin—who had played guitar in Howlin' Wolf's band. Hubert was fifty-seven years old. He wore a suit and tie, a fedora hat, and had a twinkle in his eye. He was missing some teeth. He always had a drink in his hand. He was adorable. The seventy-five-year-old piano player Pinetop Perkins was there too. Pinetop had been born on a cotton plantation. In 1942, when he was stabbed in the arm in a bar fight and couldn't play guitar anymore, he started playing barrelhouse piano, and replaced Otis Spann in Muddy Waters' band. Pinetop was another one of those old bluesmen who wore a suit and tie, hat, and always had a drink at the ready. I met the guitarist Matt Murphy and saw the very young Charlie Sexton play guitar—years before he joined Bob Dylan's band. I thought about what Keith Richards said to me in 1975 and repeated constantly over the years: no guitar player ever picked up a guitar thinking they'd get rich. It was a calling.

It was relatively easy to meet these guys at Antone's who were, essentially, blues legends. The dressing rooms were like those at CBGB's, albeit slightly cleaner. Dressing room protocol has changed so much over the years, but at that time, in this blues club, it was loose. There was an easy access. Usually, unless you're family, a close friend, management or a major celebrity, you don't go into the dressing room to see musicians before the show. (Except that way too often, a loved one picks a fight right before the show and throws the whole show off.) The only sensible reason some people drop by (or barge into) the dressing room before a show is to let the band know you were there. Record company executives are expert at this move. A pre-show appearance insures that you can flee during, or even before, the show. A quickly muttered explanation, or excuse—"I know it's going to be mobbed afterwards, so I wanted to say hi now"—doesn't fool anyone.

At Antone's, it was fun to hang out in the dressing rooms late into the night with a beer, or a glass of whiskey, and listen to these guys talk. They all loved women. They all had stories, many of which involved a jealous husband and a gun. The entire area around 6th Street in Austin was full of bars and live music. One night I was walking around 6th Street when I heard a band playing Johnny Thunders' "You Can't Put Your Arms Around a Memory." I couldn't believe that anyone in Texas would know one of my favorite songs, written by the former guitarist of the New York Dolls. It was played by Javier Escovedo who, along with his brother Alejandro, had been in the band True Believers. It was a hot night. I was in Texas. But just hearing that song, I felt like I was home.

o o o

In the mid-1960s, I met Ramblin' Jack Elliott in Greenwich Village. I have absolutely no memory of how I met him. I was young and had not been hanging out in folk clubs on Bleecker Street. I had been sneaking into jazz clubs to see Thelonious Monk and Stan Getz. Nevertheless, I met Jack Elliott. I remember his cowboy hat and his rasping voice. I remember sitting with him at a party, or in a deserted bar on MacDougal Street—or both—while he played acoustic guitar. Hence, I was somewhat shocked when I first heard Bob Dylan doing Ramblin' Jack's act. Of course in the end, it didn't matter if Dylan ripped Jack Elliott off or if they both stole from Woody Guthrie. It was osmosis. Everyone was feeling the same thing at the exact same time. Dylan was just so good. Unlike those purists who were enraged, I welcomed it in 1965 when he "went electric" at Newport. It was the late-1960s Dylan that I liked; the one with the black and white clothes and the sunglasses and the cigarette and the attitude on television talk shows. I practically memorized his 1965 *Highway 61 Revisited* album.

Somewhere along the way I stopped following Dylan's recorded work. But in 1994, when he got onstage at the Woodstock 25th anniversary festival, he was on fire. He seemed to have something to prove. He had been fat. His son Jakob had had a big hit with his band, the Wallflowers. Now, Dylan the elder was slim. He wore a western-style suit and a cowboy hat. He played great. He totally reconstructed his early songs—to the point where they were virtually unrecognizable. It was like watching a great artist re-paint his paintings right in front of you. I met Dylan a few times—once with Walter Yetnikoff and another time backstage in his dressing room at Madison Square Garden. You never knew which Bob Dylan you were going to get. He could give you a limp handshake or a flirtatious grin. He could look right through you or have a spark of recognition in his eyes. For years, he was one of the few I never really wanted to interview. He jerks journalists around. Whether it's for his own amusement, or he's bored with the questions, or it perpetuates the "enigma," it doesn't matter. For me, it was preferable to remain a fan from afar.

In 1998, Bob Dylan won the Grammy for Album of the Year for *Time Out of Mind*. That night, I stood backstage with photographer Kevin Mazur and Dylan's publicist Larry Jenkins. Dylan and Daniel Lanois (who co-produced the album with Dylan and quickly jumped onstage with Bob to get the award) waited for Sheryl Crow (who had presented him the award). Dylan knew that a girl in the photograph would make for a better photograph. He was, and still is, one of the few of his generation who had grown old but had not grown old and irrelevant. He was then, as he is now, a combination of Muddy Waters and Hank Williams, Little Richard and Johnny Cash. Highway 61 revisited.

As a passionate sports fan, I am mindful of what Yogi Berra once said: nothing slows a game down like speed. It is the same with music. Count Basie and Keith Richards both have said that the most important notes are the ones you don't play. There needs to be space. And nowhere was this more evident than in the recording studio, watching what used to be called records being made. In the 1990s, I spent a lot of time in recording studios. Because of Richard's experiences with the Flamin' Groovies, Lou Reed and David Johansen, I was familiar with the recording process. But until you've spent hours, days—or rather nights—in studios, you can't possibly know how tedious it can be. How it can destroy the soul. Now musicians make music anywhere with a laptop and Pro Tools (although, of course, with vinyl making such a comeback, it wouldn't be a surprise if musicians— other than Jack White and Neil Young—bring analog back). But then, it was a coup to secure a big budget from a record company to book studio time at one of the "elite" studios like New York City's Record Plant or Hit Factory, Woodstock's Bearsville, or Los Angeles' Ocean Way. The whole recording thing was ego driven. Some of the most amazing music ever recorded was done quickly. Or with inferior sound equipment. Alan Lomax in the field. Led Zeppelin in two days. But in the 1990s, at a time of fiduciary excess in the recording industry, bands took months futzing around in the studio. Some still do. Some take years.

With some of the bands I've witnessed, a typical recording session might start at six p.m. For nocturnal types, nighttime was more desirable. It also was cheaper. Musicians could work all night, sleep all day, and not have to show up at the studio again until eight p.m. And yet, there still was always someone in the band who wouldn't show up on time. Jimmy Iovine once told me that the reason he quit producing records and became a record executive was because he got tired of waiting around in the studio for the guitar player to show up. Rhythm tracks—drums and bass—were usually the first to be recorded. Sometimes the band would play live in the studio, all together. Then the guitar parts would be re-recorded later. Presumably—although not always—those guitar parts would be "better." Rick Rubin has said that guitars can be recorded anywhere, but drums change from room to room. Producers often hate drummers. Funnily enough, they prefer a drummer who can keep time, as opposed to someone who has the right "feel," or had been in the band since the band formed in college. Or was the "live" drummer. (This was something that had never been a problem in Muddy Waters' band. Or at Motown or Stax. Or with the Rolling Stones or Led Zeppelin.) If the band's own drummer wasn't good enough to keep time in the studio, or refused to play with a click track (a sort of metronome), the drummer was replaced by a session guy—like perennial studio favorite Jim Keltner. Or a drum machine. A well-known heavy metal guitarist once told me that he, personally, had to re-do all of his drummer's parts in the studio. Microphones were placed in front of each piece of the drum kit with a precision that would not have been unfamiliar at NASA. I remember *many* nights of arguments in various studios about whether the hi-hat was too loud. Or the bass drum had the right "roundness." I remember one band that "needed" a special drum "tuner" who they flew across the country at great (and recoupable back to the record company) expense. All this stuff could, and often did, drive people insane.

For the uninitiated, should there be such a thing anymore, "tracks" are like little lanes on a highway, all next to each other. Even with 48-

track consoles that resemble something out of science fiction, the drum tracks alone—the hi-hat, snare drum, bass drum, cymbals—could use a dozen tracks. The lead guitar part had its own "lane." The rhythm guitars had their own lanes for overdubs. There could be ten more tracks for guitar overdubs. And it still wouldn't be enough. Tracks were left open for keyboards, percussion (tambourine, maracas, cowbells) and such. And then, of course, there were the vocals. This usually came last. In the case of singers like Aerosmith's Steven Tyler or U2's Bono, it *really* was last. Often, the lyrics weren't even written. I remember being in the studio with Audioslave when Chris Cornell hadn't finished lyrics and he just sang gibberish. Sometimes, gibberish remained. I don't care what anyone says, I personally think that "Stairway to Heaven" is just such an example. Certainly the lyric "I'm just trying to find the bridge" in Zeppelin's "The Crunge" must have been Robert Plant imploring the band to get him out of the verse.

After lead vocals, the band listened back. With rock bands, and certainly in the days before Auto-Tune could electronically "correct" out-of-tune notes (and give some people a career), the singer "punched in" words or lines that had melodically misfired. Then, there were vocal overdubs and harmonies. The final step is mixing. This is a process so byzantine, so fraught with drama, that it is a miracle any of these records ever got made. Mixing means putting all the recorded tracks together and getting the balance right. I've been in studios when bands have stormed out, had fistfights, or broken up over mixes. This, of course, was before computers and digital, but the process is still the same. I've been there when some bands have listened to fifty or sixty mixes of the same song until you just want to scream that no one could possibly hear the difference. Except that someone always does. If a single part is one decibel too loud or soft, it can throw the whole thing off. Or so the musicians think. The bass player wants his part louder so there's enough "bottom." The drummer thinks the cymbals can't be heard. The guitarist thinks the vocals are too loud in the mix. Depending on the band's budget, this undertaking could, often did, and still can take months. And none of this makes the actual songs any better.

Being in the studio, at night, secluded, cossetted, with food, drinks, or drugs, was at first, and for many still is a sexy, romantic experience. Not for me. Not anymore. I've seen hours wasted because friends drop by. Or parents want to visit. People outside the band think it's a party. I've seen producers lock bands in the studio and won't let them out until mixes are done. I've been there when a musician sneaks in to remix what someone else did the night before. I've seen people sit at a mixing board for so long they won't even get up to go to the bathroom; they literally pee in a jar.

And yet, in 1990, when I asked Glyn Johns to re-record *The London Howlin' Wolf Sessions* with young guitarists, I was excited. When Glyn wanted more money to do this than Sony was prepared to pay for a small blues project, I called Tom Dowd. Tom was an engineer and producer who had worked with Ray Charles, Aretha Franklin, Thelonious Monk, Charles Mingus, Booker T. and the MG's, Rod Stewart and many others. In 1974, I had visited him in Miami while he recorded *461 Ocean Boulevard* with Eric Clapton. Tom Dowd was happy to go to Chicago to produce an album that we decided would be a tribute to Muddy Waters. I tracked down musicians who had played with Muddy Waters: Pinetop Perkins, drummer Willie Smith and bassist Calvin Jones. We also asked Hubert Sumlin—who had been in Howlin' Wolf's band—to play guitar.

On June 17, 1991, we assembled at the old Chess Studios in Chicago. It took only two days with these guys to record the backing tracks for most of the songs in the Muddy Waters catalogue. Chess Studios, which had originally been at 2120 South Michigan Avenue in Chicago, was Muddy Waters' first recording label. Howlin' Wolf,

Chuck Berry, Bo Diddley, Ernie K. Doe and others had all made records for Chess too. The Rolling Stones recorded an instrumental track, "2120 South Michigan Avenue," on their 1964 *12×5* album. Sometime in the mid-1960s Chess moved to 320 East 21st Street. I don't remember where we recorded the tracks with Tom, Pinetop, Hubert, Calvin and Willie. But it was a recording session unlike any I'd seen with rock bands. The very early blues recordings were often done in a few hours. So were the Sun Studios records made by Johnny Cash, Elvis Presley and Jerry Lee Lewis. Our plan was to take the approximately twenty songs these guys did in just two days and have guitarists Slash, Eddie Van Halen and others overdub solos and vocals. Somehow, nothing ever came of this and the project was shelved. And for once in my life I, a collector to the point where my storage spaces and my apartment look like something from the TV show *Hoarders*, walked out of that studio without the tapes. They still cannot be found.

o o o

When I first went to Austin in the summer of 1988, I met James Cotton at Antone's. James Cotton is considered the best living blues harmonica player. According to Keith Richards, Mick Jagger is also a great harmonica player. Keith has often said that Mick's soul shines through when he plays blues harmonica. And the Stones are at heart, a blues band. In 1981, when the Stones played with Muddy Waters at the Checkerboard Lounge in Chicago, Ian Stewart sat in on piano. I remember how Stu took a drink out of a bottle of whiskey, passed it around, then carefully put the top back on the bottle so nothing would spill when he placed it back on the piano. Such was his respect for the piano. And for the music. And for Muddy Waters, who shared vocals with Mick that night. They were on a tiny stage. Mick held back a bit. He took the lead vocal only when Muddy told him to do so. Mick was thirty-eight years old. Muddy was sixty-eight. The Stones took their name from a Muddy Waters song. You certainly could have enjoyed the Rolling Stones without ever having heard Muddy Waters. Or Robert Johnson or Chuck Berry. Most of the Stones fans weren't familiar with the music that had inspired the band. But knowing what comes before enriches the experience.

Ian Stewart talked to me once about how bizarre he thought it was that, in the 1960s, the English white guys came to America and played American black music to American white people. After Stu died in 1985, Keith Richards talked to me for hours about Stu. For many years after the 1975 Stones tour, and many times, I talked to both Mick and Keith. I worked as a consultant with the band on their 1981 Hal Ashby–directed live concert movie *Let's Spend the Night Together*. I worked with Mick on his first solo album, *She's the Boss*. We spent a lot of time together. I did a lot of interviews with him. He picked my brain. I made a lot of suggestions. He ignored most of them.

During the 1980s, and well into the 1990s, the Stones were still active. They recorded new albums, went on tour, and talked to the press to promote those endeavors. Yet, after having spent hours and hours interviewing Mick, when people ask me what he's really like, it's still hard to explain. Keith always says that Mick is a "great bunch of guys." And it's true; one never knows which Mick is going to show up. He doesn't really let people in. And while I know he's been as candid with me throughout the years as he's been with any journalist, he doesn't really consider journalists "people." He often used words like "the gutter press." Of course, coming from England, and having been a victim of Fleet Street, this is understandable. Mick can be wildly entertaining and funny and smart. He can still light up a room. But also, he's insecure. Wary. He can't ever really get away from being MICK JAGGER. Add to that the androgynous beauty of his youth, and well, it can't be easy growing old. The press constantly writes about his lips—which are not what they once were. No one's are. Still, I always felt that Mick never acknowledges or relishes what he does best—which is sing the blues. He wanted, and still might want, pop hits. He wanted, and still might want, to compete with current bands. For someone who wound up sounding as good as the men he started out imitating in 1962, I find it sad.

Keith could talk—and has—for hours about music, about the blues. Despite the fact that Mick soaked up all of this as a young man too, he is flippant, offhand. He never wanted to appear as though he thought rock and roll was any kind of art form. He made jokes. He once told me that rock and roll lyrics "weren't exactly flowing Renaissance poetry." Another time, I asked him about the music the band made, and he replied that it wasn't really music. To him, he said, it sounded like a "racket." Sometime in the 1970s he said, "I started playing blues when I was eighteen, or before, really. It's very mature music compared to 'Venus in Blue Jeans,' [which was] the hit [when] I started. I never wanted to be a rock and roll star or a pop star. I was never into teenage lyrics. We were doing blues written by forty . . . fifty . . . sixty-year-old men. 'You Got to Move' was written by a seventy-year-old man. I wanted to be a blues singer."

One of the more memorable times I spent with the Stones was in 1978 at the Toronto Four Seasons Hotel. Margaret Trudeau, the wife of the then Prime Minister of Canada, wandered in and out of the band's rooms wearing only a terrycloth bathrobe. The rumors were that she was involved with Ron Wood. Or Mick Jagger. Or both. I came back to New York, wrote a piece about Mme. Trudeau and the Rolling Stones for the *New York Post*. All hell broke loose. I had to hide from the Canadian press. I fled to the Ritz-Carlton in Boston and registered under the name of the blonde, B-movie actress Beverly Michaels. Another time, in 1984, I went to Mick's townhouse on the

Upper West Side to do an interview. Jerry Hall, who had been living with Mick for seven years and was the mother of their newborn daughter Elizabeth, pulled me into the vestibule. She wanted me to ask Mick: since they'd been living together for seven years and had a child, wasn't it just like being married? And if so, why didn't they get married? I said I'd try to get that in. During our talk, I asked Mick if he always needed to be attached to somebody. That English thing of having the little woman at home, waiting, cooking. "Oh, give me a break," he said. "Really, this propaganda about women that's been done against me. I can't bear it. I can cook perfectly well myself and I don't need to go home, I can go out and eat somewhere around the corner, probably better than I can eat at home."

We talked about sex. He admitted that he probably deserved his reputation as a roué. But he said he wasn't concerned about AIDS. Even with random sex on the road, he didn't think it was a problem if he was just getting blow jobs. He said that sex was a motivating factor in his relationships, but it didn't rule his life. It was, he said, in balance. "If you're being fucked to death in the morning, then there's no way you can go picking up girls at midnight, right? Being in tune with somebody that way is great. It makes everything else go along so beautifully." I asked what he was like when he didn't have a lot of sex in his life. "Nervous, vicious, mean, narcissistic, homosexual," he said. Homosexual? "That was a joke," he said. "Don't take everything I say seriously just because I'm trying to make the interview more interesting." When pressed, he said, "Basically it's been girls all the way." Then he talked about how he knew a lot of gay people and how, at one time in his life, it had been nice to be attractive to men, that he liked the attention. That it had been new, something he hadn't considered before, and, he emphasized, this was during "that androgynous era, in the 1960s."

I asked him why English men, sooner or later, at some point, have a propensity to wind up in drag. "English men don't need much convincing to dress up as women," Mick admitted. "If you get bored at the weekend and you've got friends over and you want to dress as women and go down to the pub, it doesn't take more than just asking. With English guys, it's in the blood." We discussed marriage. He wasn't keen on marriage. "It's like signing a 365-page contract," he said, "without knowing what's in it." (A few years after he said this, Mick and Jerry, who would eventually have four children together, got married in some mumbo-jumbo ceremony on the top of a mountain in Bali. Most people assumed it wasn't really legal.)

We talked about age. Mick was forty-one at the time, and while he said he didn't know anyone who wouldn't be more comfortable being twenty-one, there wasn't much to be done about it. When he turned forty, he said, Pete Townshend hadn't helped much when he wrote some "garbage" (Mick's term) in the London *Times*. "I found it rather strange," Mick said. "As far as I could see, it was all about him and his problems getting older. He has more problems with it than I do."

In 1991, Mick was in Los Angeles, making his third solo album (*Wandering Spirit*) with producer Rick Rubin. Rick was also working with a blues band called the Red Devils. They performed at a club on La Brea and 6th Street called King King. Members of ZZ Top, the Black Crowes and the Red Hot Chili Peppers would stop by and jam. There were a lot of great-looking girls in the club and Mick occasionally went to check out the scene. He'd get onstage and sing with the band. At some point, Rick produced an entire album of Mick singing blues with the Red Devils. It was done live at Ocean Way Studios. While it's been heavily bootlegged, it was never officially released. For me, it was then, and still is now, the best solo album Mick has ever done.

Keith Richards and I talked all throughout the 1980s and the 1990s. Largely because of my friendship with his manager Jane Rose, we've stayed in touch to this day. After he stopped using heroin, and long before his extraordinary 2010 memoir *Life*, Keith's interviews were candid, honest and forthcoming. No frills. Like he told me in 1975—no flab. We would meet at his apartment on East 4th Street between Broadway and Lafayette. Or in various hotels. Or at his house in Westport, Connecticut. Or where the Stones rehearsed for tours—like Long View Farm, in Massachusetts. It was there that Keith recorded the now famous bootleg of him singing Hoagy Carmichael songs and playing piano. In 1981, after John Lennon's murder, I asked Keith if he was ever afraid of crazed fans. In typical Keith fashion, he said, "There's always nutters around. I don't think this is a high point for nutters; they've just had a lucky year. I mean the Pope . . . Reagan . . . On the average, they're lousy shots. Which gives you some hope." We talked about his "rebel" image. "With the Stones it all gets put under a magnifying glass," he said. "And it gets concentrated until it comes down to . . . HIM. The *green one*, over there. He's going too far. So I got lumbered with it all. I do time for these guys. Well, by an incredible stroke of luck, I haven't yet." He talked about how he got bored with heroin. "It gets to a point where all you're doing is getting to where you feel normal. You don't get high. Dope is full time. You want to talk about seduction, it's unbelievable. But don't let anybody fool you—it ain't that hard to kick dope. I'd rather kick dope than stop smoking cigarettes."

In 1988, Keith and I talked about age, the Stones, and the blues. He talked about Muddy Waters, who died in 1983. "With Muddy," Keith said, "there was a gig booked. And one day, people had to have their tickets refunded because the guy kicked the bucket right before the gig. To me, that's the way to go. That, to me, is commitment. If you're going to do it, do it all the way. You retire only if your functions fail." And, as always, we talked about Ian Stewart. "Stu was so down to earth," Keith said. "Bullshit is bullshit and it stopped with Stu. We always had a piano on the stage for him. It was his choice whether to play it or not. He may have had *Golf Digest* on the stand and have a read-through during the show, but he was the glue for all the madness. Stu was always there. He was the rock. The greatest compliment he would ever give you was 'not bad.' He was the anchor for us. He was the conscience of the Rolling Stones." I asked Keith if he was amazed that the band's career had lasted as long as it had, and that they made so much money. He replied: "Yes, I'm amazed. And I'm still waiting for the money."

In 1989, the Stones left Bill Graham and employed a new promoter for the band's "Steel Wheels" tour. Bill Graham's life was producing concerts. Getting the Stones had been a big coup. He was certain he'd get the 1989 tour. He went to Mick again and again, and made concessions unheard of at that time. Instead, Mick chose the Canadian promoter Michael Cohl, who presumably offered more money. It broke Bill Graham's heart. He referred to the Stones as "whores." He never recovered from the rejection. By the time the Stones did their "Bridges to Babylon" tour in 1998, I had seen them in concert for twenty-nine years. I had been backstage at their concerts for twenty-three years. I had seen them rehearse in airplane hangars and school gyms. I saw them in small clubs (Toronto's El Mocambo, New Haven's Toad's) and stadiums. I saw Mick and Keith jam at friends' apartments and in hotel rooms. I especially saw some great shows at Madison Square Garden. But the one on January 14, 1998, was different. The VIP tickets, at $300 each, were sky-high for the time. The backstage area for friends was a small hallway. Much of the rest of the backstage was roped off for "corporate suites"—which basically were cubicles separated by curtains. For $500 a ticket, people could have a beer, some potato chips and a fast meet-and-greet with Ronnie Wood. I thought about how, in 1975, years before corporate sponsorship and the new Stones' promoters, Bill Graham had set up hot dog carts and egg cream stands backstage at the New York shows. By 1998, it was all about business. Ghosts were everywhere. Ian Stewart, especially. The songs were great, the band still played great. But none of it seemed to matter anymore. With my memories, I left midway through the show.

I once talked to Bono about my writing this book. He suggested that I start in 1969 when I first saw the Stones at Madison Square Garden and end with that 1998 show. I told him there was still more to the story. In 1999, I was getting bored because so much music was getting so bad. Then, I discovered Jon Brion at his regular Friday night one-man show at the Largo in Hollywood. Jon can play "Purple Rain" on a ukulele in the style of Les Paul. Or something from the Beach Boys' *Pet Sounds* on electric guitar and make it sound like the Velvet Underground. Through extemporaneous sampling and layering of drums, bass, piano and guitar, Jon creates little symphonies all by himself. Onstage, right in front of your eyes. Countless Friday nights when I was in California, no matter where I was or what else I was doing—at a press junket in Santa Barbara to watch Matchbox 20, or at the bedside of a sick friend at Cedars-Sinai hospital—I would make it my business to race back to the Largo to see Jon Brion's magic act. Not unlike the way one goes to Lourdes. He has never disappointed me. His talent reaffirms my faith. It makes me remember why I got into this racket in the first place.

In 1999, when I started writing for *Vanity Fair*, I began to oversee photo shoots for the magazine's music issue portfolios. I assisted Annie Leibovitz with her *American Music* book. I went back to the South. This time, I was prepared. In 2002, Annie and I went to Memphis where she shot a Stax Records reunion photo in front of the orig-

inal Stax studios at 926 East McLemore Avenue. We stayed at the
Peabody Hotel where, twice a day, ducks line up in the lobby and
walk into a pond. The night before the Stax shoot, we had a dinner in
a private room at the Peabody. Isaac Hayes, Booker T. Jones, Steve
Cropper, Duck Dunn, Carla Thomas, David Porter, William Bell,
Eddie Floyd, Mavis and Yvonne Staples, Stax executive Deanie
Parker and the label's co-founder Al Bell all reminisced for hours. I
was furious at myself for not bringing a video camera.

In 2006, I went back to Nashville. I visited the great country
singer George Jones at his estate—where musical notes decorate his
front gates. He had a hair salon in his house. He was obsessive about
mowing his lawn. He had an entire cupboard stocked with green
Eclipse gum. He told me tales about how, when he was so drunk that
they took away the keys to his cars and trucks, he drove a tractor
into town to a bar. I set up a photo with the singer/violinist Alison
Krauss and the legendary bluegrass banjo player Ralph Stanley.
Ralph Stanley sang "O Death" in the movie *O Brother, Where Art
Thou?* He is old-time Appalachian mountain music personified. Hear-
ing his voice is like walking through the valley of the shadow of death.
Mark Seliger photographed Alison and Ralph in the back of the
Hatch Show Print poster shop with the old printing presses. I can
still smell the inks. In 2003 I went to Willie Nelson's seventieth birthday concert at Nashville's Ryman Auditorium, where I introduced
Norah Jones to Keith Richards. That same year in Memphis, I got
Emmylou Harris, Dwight Yoakam, Lyle Lovett and Rosanne Cash
together for a photo at Sun Studios in Memphis. Johnny Cash had
died three and a half years earlier. It was the first time Rosanne had
gone back to the studio where her father began his career. When she
got out of the car in the parking lot, she started to cry. I told her how
all this music had been passed on. Full circle. Then I went inside to
the studio to make sure that the photos of her father, Elvis Presley,

Jerry Lee Lewis and Carl Perkins were all still on the wall. For some reason, the picture of Bono had been taken down. And that same summer, I organized a photo in San Antonio with T Bone Burnett, Stephen Bruton, Joe Ely, Jimmie Dale Gilmore, Waylon Jennings' wife Jessi Colter and other Texas musicians in front of the Alamo— where Ken Regan had photographed the Rolling Stones in 1975.

In 2003, I was apprehensive about hearing the country-rock singer Lucinda Williams' newest album in her presence. She had recorded it in a big house in Silverlake, Los Angeles. The house looked like a Moorish palace. It had wall-to-wall Persian carpets. Two years later, Jon Brion moved in and recorded and lived there for a few years. But on that day, with just Lucinda and me and the engineer, I was reminded how there are very few things as uncomfortable as listening to new music in a studio with the musician right there . . . *hovering*. But Lucinda—wacky, brilliant, sad, poetic, hopeful, lustful, fun— knew she had done something special. "I felt," she said, "that I needed to do something important." From a lesser talent, this would have been an embarrassing boast. From Lucinda, especially during the Bush administration and after September 11th, it was a fact. *World Without Tears* had songs that captured the best of the Stones, Hank Williams, Patsy Cline and Muddy Waters. Jazz and blues and country and folk and rock and roll. It was "Americana" before the Grammys turned that word into a category. Highway 61 revisited.

In 2007, Robert Plant and Alison Krauss recorded an album together with producer T Bone Burnett. Robert was an Englishman who had, from the very beginning, been in love with American music. The Honeydrippers, his side group after Led Zeppelin disbanded, was influenced by R&B and Elvis Presley. It was music of the American South. The fact that Robert and Alison's *Raising Sand* won the 2009

Album of the Year Grammy was a miracle. When he was a teenager, Robert's very first band was called the Band of Joy. They had played black music, like the songs of Otis Clay. Almost forty years after I first saw Led Zeppelin perform in Jacksonville, Florida, I watched Robert perform with his new Band of Joy. They played Led Zeppelin songs, but they didn't sound the way they had with Led Zeppelin. Robert slowed "Rock and Roll" down to a shuffle. He turned "Black Dog" into a sensual, dark, swampy groove. In the 1970s, Robert was a young man inspired by old men. Now, in the 21st century, he is an older man going back to his roots. He smiled at his band. I got the feeling that despite the many millions he's been offered to reunite Zeppelin, he might prefer to be able to just smile at his band. Maybe. We'll see. He seems at peace with himself and the music he loves. He's been to that mountaintop. He's known tragedy and the blues. And no matter what the idiots thought about Led Zeppelin being a cheesy heavy metal band, their music was always also about banjos, fiddles, blues, boogie-woogie, and the shuffle. Music from the Smoky Mountains. Howlin' Wolf and Muddy Waters and Chicago. The Mississippi Delta. Highway 61 revisited.

In 2012, I asked Gary Clark Jr., the twenty-eight-year-old guitarist from Austin, Texas, why more young black musicians didn't play the blues. He said that, for many of them, it sounded like oppression, pre–Civil Rights. But, he added, "It's the foundation, it's where we come from." Gary grew up in Austin and played onstage at Antone's when he was a teenager. He met many of the same men I did. He played with a lot of them. Despite the fact that he had grown up listening to Motown and was a Michael Jackson fanatic, Gary was hit hard by the blues. Especially Jimi Hendrix (to whom he's been compared) and Stevie Ray Vaughan. He talked to me about the blues. "In Memphis," he said, "a woman put it in perspective for me. She said that Jimmy Reed sang 'Big Boss Man.' And, as a black man, he sang something he couldn't say in the workplace. Guys like that were ballsy enough so that now, we can all say whatever the fuck we want to say. How can you deny that? How can you abandon it?"

In 2012, Led Zeppelin received the Kennedy Center Honors along with David Letterman, Buddy Guy and others. Kid Rock and Lenny Kravitz performed Zeppelin songs. President Obama nodded his head in time to "Stairway to Heaven" (not an easy feat until the song goes into the fast part). Heart's Ann Wilson sang it backed by a choir whose members all dressed in John Bonham *Clockwork Orange* boilersuits and bowler hats. Robert Plant, watching from the honorees box, wiped a tear from his eye. I've no idea what he was thinking. What I was thinking was what Lillian Roxon had said to me years earlier about the perversion of culture. And how Mick Jagger had quoted Jean-Paul Sartre when the Rolling Stones were inducted into the Rock and Roll Hall of Fame: "First you shock them, then they put you in a museum."

In that same year, the Stones performed a few concerts to celebrate their 50th anniversary. Lady Gaga was a special guest at the show in Newark's Prudential Center. She did "Gimme Shelter" as a duet with Mick. She came onstage all wild, high energy and belted out the song. She nailed it, and then proceeded to twirl around on the stage—you couldn't take your eyes off her. Then, later on in the Stones set, she went out into the audience, stood in front of the stage and, as a fan, danced through the rest of their show. And I remembered how, in 1978, when Patti Smith opened the show for the Stones at Atlanta's Fox Theatre, after she and her band performed their set, she went into the crowd, stood in front of the stage, and danced and punched the air with her fists during the rest of the Stones' performance. The

Rolling Stones. Patti Smith. Lady Gaga . . . For me, it was like bringing it all back home.

Professor Longhair died in 1980. Bill Graham died in 1991. Tom Dowd died in 2002. Ahmet Ertegun died in 2006. His death was a result of a stroke after he fell backstage at a Rolling Stones concert at New York's Beacon Theatre. Jim Dickinson died in 2009. (I haven't been able to delete him from my address book.) His music lives on in Dickinson's sons, Luther and Cody, who front the blues, punk, rock band the North Mississippi Allstars. Stephen Bruton died of cancer at T Bone Burnett's house in Los Angeles on May 9, 2009. They were in the middle of recording the music for *Crazy Heart*. T Bone emailed me to say that when Bruton drew his last breath, a meditation bell rang in the house. Maybe it did, maybe it didn't. T Bone's father was a minister or something and he believes in this stuff. I can still hear Bruton's voice, with that unmistakable "Darlin'," on the phone. (And I haven't been able to take Bruton out of my address book either.) Pinetop Perkins died in March 2011 at the age of ninety-seven. Duck Dunn died while on tour in Japan in May 2012 at age seventy. Hubert Sumlin died in December 2011. Mick Jagger and Keith Richards paid for his funeral.

In February 2012, I saw Jon Brion at Capitol Records' recording studios in Hollywood. He was restoring Frank Sinatra's great 1950s Capitol recordings (*Only the Lonely, Come Fly with Me*) back to the original masters. Those master recordings had been lying around in the basement of Capitol's studios. Jon was taking off all the "gunk" that had "polished," "improved" and digitized the original songs. When Jon played me the vocal track for "What's New," fifty years after Sinatra had recorded the song, you could hear Sinatra breathe.

He was literally in the room with you. It was thrilling. They're so great when they're great. Jon was restoring songs with such lyrics as "What's new, how is the world treating you," and "One for my baby, and one more for the road." And once again, it reminded me why I got into all of this in the first place. Ghosts everywhere. Passing it on. Let the good times roll. One more for the road. Full circle. The music remains. Some things last forever.

ACKNOWLEDGMENTS

Most of all to Richard, without whom I would not have had a life in rock and roll.

To my sister Deane Zimmerman—whose invaluable assistance has always been essential to my work.

At *Vanity Fair*: Graydon Carter, Aimee Bell, Punch Hutton, Chris Garrett and Amanda Meigher. My agent Suzanne Gluck and Caroline Donofrio and Eve Attermann. To Geoff Kloske, Laura Perciasepe, Casey Blue James, Linda Rosenberg, Rob Sternitzky, Claire Sullivan, Jynne Martin, Claire McGinnis, Glory Plata and everyone at Riverhead Books.

And to Karen Mulligan at Leibovitz Studio and all the photographers who so generously gave me photos for this book: Annie Leibovitz, Bob Gruen, Leee Black Childers, Christopher Simon Sykes, Andrew Kent, Jonathan Becker, Michael Putland, Mick Rock, Jane Rose, Sarah Czeladnicki, Kevin Mazur, Benjamin Tietge, Paul Rosenberg and Gabe Tesoriero.

INDEX